P9-DBY-356

San Francisco

Barry Parr
Photography by Michael Yamashita
and Kerrick James

COMPASS AMERICAN GUIDES
An Imprint of Fodor's Travel Publications, Inc.

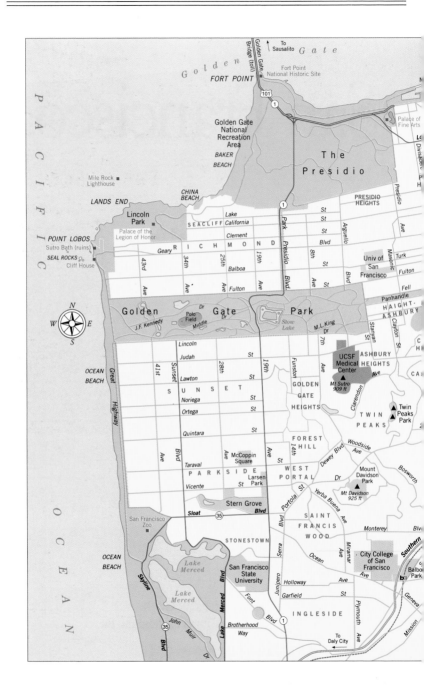

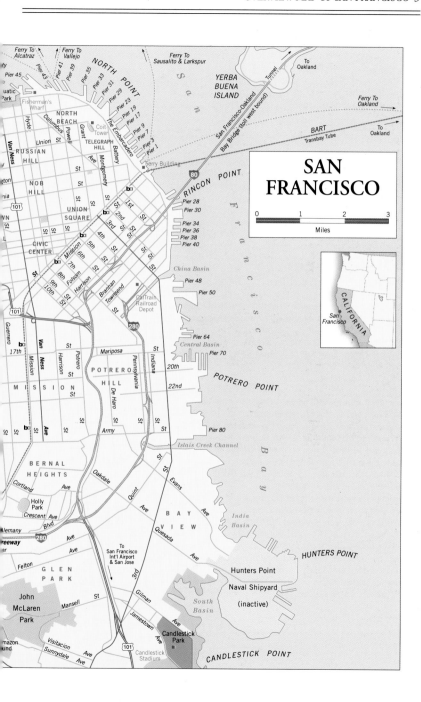

SAN FRANCISCO

0   1   2   3

Miles

CALIFORNIA

San Francisco

San Francisco
Fifth Edition

Copyright © 1996, 1999 Fodor's Travel Publications, Inc.
Maps Copyright © 1996, 1999 Fodor's Travel Publications, Inc.

ISBN 0-679-00229-4

Editors: Deke Castleman, Julia Dillon, Michael Oliver
Managing Editor: Kit Duane
Contributing Conceptual Editor: Kit Duane

Designers: Christopher Burt, David Hurst
Photo Editor: Christopher Burt
Map Design: Mark Stroud, Moon Street Cartography
Cover Design: Siobhan O'Hare

Compass American Guides, 5332 College Ave., Suite 201, Oakland, CA 94618
Production House: Twin Age Ltd., Hong Kong   Manufactured in China
10 9 8 7 6 5 4 3 2 1

ACKNOWLEDGMENTS
Thanks are due to my fifth edition editors, **Michael Oliver** and **Julia Dillon,** for their insider's advice, perseverance, and first-hand contributions to the book, and especially to Julia for her splendidly insightful and entertaining "RESTAURANTS" chapter. Kudos also to **Chris Burt** for his skillful design. I am also grateful to Managing Editor **Kit Duane** for her encouragements over the years. I salute **Mike Yamashita** and **Kerrick James,** photographers par excellence, and **Deke Castleman,** whose articulate, friendly editorial guidance brought the first edition to light. Thanks to **Mark Stroud** for his outstanding city and Bay Area maps. Thanks to **John Doerper** for his expertise on the Wine Country, and to **Debi Dunn** for last minute indexing.

Unless otherwise stated, all photography is by Michael Yamashita. The photographs on pp. 5, 15, 75 are used courtesy of Wells Fargo Bank; p. 27 courtesy of California State Library; pp. 16, 24, 39, 43 by permission of the Oakland Museum; pp. 31, 36, 41, 44, 49, 64, 79, 180 courtesy of the San Francisco Library; p.182 aerial photography by Galen Rowell; p. 229 courtesy of Buena Vista Carneros Estate. "A Supermarket in California" by Allen Ginsberg from *Allen Ginsberg Collected Poems 1947-1980,* © 1984 by Allen Ginsberg is reprinted by permission of Harper & Row, Publishers, Inc. "Taking the Plunge" from *Tales of the City* © 1978 by Armistead Maupin reprinted by permission of HarperCollins, Inc. The satellite image of San Francisco and other parts of the world can be purchased from Spaceshots, Inc., 33950 Barnby Rd., Acton, CA 93510; (800) 272-2779.

*To my parents, Harold and Loraine,
who introduced me to my subject.*

C O N T E N T S

Literary Extracts

Maps

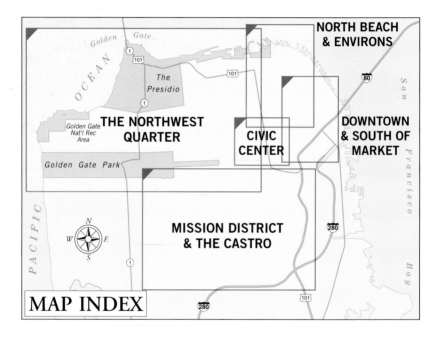

P R E F A C E

GUIDEBOOKS EMPHASIZE WHAT INTERESTS THEIR WRITERS. So it should be asked here, what interests the writer of this guide?

In brief, most everything. The morning's first cappuccino, and the evening's last espresso. Hash browns in a noisy diner. Fog horns, lamenting, from Clement Street at night. The engine room of the liberty ship *Jeremiah O'Brien*, pounding under a full head of steam. Bagging a cheap Bierce or Sterling in a used-book store, and cracking it open on the N-Judah, a hundred-some-odd rattling feet beneath Buena Vista Park. Taking the kids to visit the crocs at the Academy of Sciences, or coaxing them down the murky steps of the rock tomb at the Rosicrucian Egyptian Museum. Cézanne, in silence, at the de Young. An aria hauntingly floating upon the glittering air of the War Memorial Opera House; or better yet, over the fast-disappearing tortellini at Ratto's. The oily reek of the Cable Car Barn, the whir of the cable pulleys, the frantic clang of bells. Starched tablecloths and blunt waiters at an old city grill.

Christmas shopping at Union Square. The salty tang on the air at the Hyde Street Pier. The warm lights of Sausalito, seen from the deck of the homeward ferry. The view from Diamond Heights. The ivy-covered stones and musty caves of the Buena Vista wine cellars. The softness of the path beneath enormous redwoods. A German beer at Schroeder's at noon, and at five, an Anchor Steam at Vesuvio's. . . .

I could go on and on. In fact, I do.

Certainly if I had to organize these and all my other interests in order of preference, the book would run differently. Instead, I list them geographically, as befits a guidebook, starting with San Francisco, and proceeding on to day trips around the Bay Area. In the "RESTAURANTS," "HOTELS & INNS," AND "PRACTICALITIES" chapters you will find some names and addresses of a recommended hotels, restaurants, museums, and tour companies; they are by no means the only good ones. And since I cannot know or even like everything, in "RECOMMENDED READING" I've suggested a few of the many wonderful books which cover ground that I have lightly tread.

O V E R V I E W

D O W N T O W N

San Francisco's high-rise **Financial District** meets the bay along the curving **Embarcadero**, stretching from **Jackson Square** to **Market Street**. **South of Market**, or SOMA, embraces a rich mixture of old warehouses, high-tech new buildings, and trendy art spaces. **Union Square** hums by day with shoppers and by night with theater-goers. Beyond lies **Civic Center**, where government offices—as well as the main library and the magnificent halls of ballet, symphony, and opera companies—gather in a stately cluster around City Hall.

N A B O B S , S O J O U R N E R S , B O H E M I A N S

Nob Hill, once the domain of the rich and powerful, is today an elite retreat of stately hotels. **Chinatown** clings from its eastern slopes, while **Russian Hill** rises on its north. Between Russian and **Telegraph hills**, the longtime Italian (and onetime Beatnik) enclave of **North Beach** remains a lively quarter of cafes and nightlife. Rolling north, North Beach meets the bay at **Fisherman's Wharf**, where tourists are the major catch.

C U L T I V A T E D Q U A R T E R

The northwest quarter offers culture and lovely patches of green. Fort Mason, the Exploratorium, and the Palace of Fine Arts frame the **Marina District**, with picturesque **Union Street** on its south. Standing guard is the **Presidio**, the woodsy old army headquarters. South across aristocratic Presidio Heights stretches elegant upper **Fillmore Street**, followed by **Japantown**. The residential

Richmond District, hedged in on its north by **Lincoln Park**, on its south by **Golden Gate Park**, and on its west by **Ocean Beach**. Haight Street still waters in the lee of the **Panhandle**.

THE CITY'S SOUTHERN EXPOSURE

San Francisco's southern half, cut off by the lofty ridge of **Twin Peaks**, contains the quiet **Sunset District**, as well as the **Mission District**, where the City's largest Latino population mixes with a growing community of the young, hip, and artistically inclined, creating a vibrant neighborhood fused with martini bars and authentic taquerias. Clus-

tered around Twin Peaks are the attractive **Castro**, the nation's largest gay neighborhood, and the well-kept Victorians of almost suburban **Noe Valley**. Farther south, **Bernal Heights** and **Potrero Hill** enjoy their incognito status as neighborly residential havens seldom bothered by outsiders.

EXCURSIONS

Among San Francisco's many rare endowments, there's none more wonderful than the ease with which you can leave the town. **Marin County** captivates locals and tourists alike with charming towns like **Sausalito** and alluring parklands including **Point Reyes** and the **Muir Woods.** The beautiful hills and valleys of **Napa** and **Sonoma**

Counties are world famous as the **Wine Country,** and also shelter many historical and lit-

erary associations. **Oakland** is known for its refurbished old business district and the waterfront's **Jack London Square.** Brainy and eccentric **Berkeley** centers around the beautiful campus of the **University of California**, where visitors come to see museums, architecture, and antics of student life. **The Peninsula** stretches south from San Francisco to **San Jose,** known as the capital of thriving **Silicon Valley**, including **Palo Alto's Stanford University.**

(Photos on page 12 and top of page 13 by Kerrick James; photos in center and at bottom of page 13 by Michael Yamashita.)

I N T R O D U C T I O N

LIKE MANY GREAT CITIES, San Francisco was built on a harbor. And like many hardscrabble, tin-pot, boom-and-bust towns scattered through the Wild West, she was also slapped down in a rush on barren hills; worse yet, on hills stranded at the tip of a long, foggy peninsula. To these two accidents of history San Francisco owes both her prosperity and her character.

It's hard to conceive of a worse place to build a *serious* city. Maybe not quite as ridiculous as Venice, sinking in the sea, or Timbuktu, stranded by a roving river in the sandy wastes. But those are has-beens, museum pieces forsaken by the type of supercharged entrepreneurs who built them. San Francisco, for better or worse, still plays the role of a dynamic, world-class city.

Still, as thoughtful San Franciscans sometimes admit, maybe the comparison to Venice is not all that far off. The wharfs and factories have long declined, and tourism has become San Francisco's biggest growth industry. That's a hard lump to take for a city that was once the undisputed Queen of the West.

From her Gold Rush birth till the rise of other regional capitals at the turn of the century, San Francisco set the standards of American civilization west of the Mississippi. Culturally and economically, she stood at the center of a vast sphere of influence reaching east to the Rockies, north to Alaska, and south and west to however far American ambitions might be carried by its traders and soldiers of fortune.

From Tombstone to the Klondike, when frontier capitalists sought to sink a mine or corner a market, they bankrolled it in San Francisco. Along the Yukon, when miners craved news of the outside world, they'd part with gold for a Frisco paper. When the Modocs went to war and almost won, it was San Francisco who received the summons for help, and later, the beaten warriors themselves, ferried in chains to Alcatraz. From San Francisco sailed the fleets that seized the Philippines, and likewise, rolled the whiskey and oysters that kept times flush in Virginia City. And in return, whole mountains of silver ore and gold from a thousand godforsaken sagebrush towns were mined, crushed, refined, and shipped, as a matter of course, to San Francisco.

Good or bad, those times have passed. Much of what she was, she is no longer. But to her credit, San Francisco has weathered the loss of stature gracefully. Even now her citizens lay plans to recapture a starring role in the coming Pacific Rim century.

Say what you will about the wealth and influence of upstart Los Angeles (and most Northern Californians can contrive a few choice epithets), San Francisco remains a city of extraordinary presence. Small she may be, but she can part a path through throngs of larger cities with the cast of her eye alone. In her time, she has drunk champagne from a slipper and gone barefoot, dined on both the gristle and the tenderloin, embraced the noblest ideals of humankind, and packed more red-eyed mornings, tragedy, laughter, and waywardness than many a town three and four times her age.

"There are just three big cities in the United States that are *story* cities," observed the novelist Frank Norris. "New York, of course, New Orleans, and best of the lot, San Francisco."

And what great stories they are. Just *look* at the company she's kept—bohemians, frontiersmen, merchants, poets, prostitutes, big spenders, bridge builders, lovers, lunatics, bankers, sailors, bums, rapscallions. . . . Ask any one of them, "What is San Francisco like?" and each would describe a place unlike any other.

A tent "city" sprang up on Telegraph Hill during the gold rush.

San Francisco sporting goods, ca. 1850.

To the ancient Ohlones, she was a cold, foggy shore on the fringe of paradise. To the conquistadores, grinding northward with cross and sword, she was the dire end of banishment, a wilderness of salvageable souls.

To enterprising Yankees, San Francisco will always be the instant city, miraculously begat on barren hills by hordes from every nation: the city of tents and mud, of gold and Comstock silver, alternately burning and rising, each time more stately, to the Grand Finale of 1906 when, from utter destruction, she triumphed phoenix-like from the ashes. This is the city of nabobs in gilded mansions, of cable cars and grand hotels, of gamblers and dance hall girls and the big, bad Barbary Coast; of Mark Twain swapping jokes at the Exchange Saloon, of six-shooters and sawdust-covered floors; of Clark Gable grinning, cigar in teeth, and Jeanette MacDonald belting out her song as the city burns around her.

And then there is the real city of rusty plumbing and moldy closets: the working stiff, the unions, the firetrap slums, the shipyards, the great strikes and greater civil engineering projects, the steel bridges, the WPA murals in Coit Tower. This is the city of the Mooney trial, greasy-spoon lunch counters, crowded steam vents, and Salvation Army bands playing street corners South of Market.

For every mother's son and daughter, San Francisco is a gathering of immigrants, each with their separate festivals and foods, and each sampling freely from their neighbors—Chinatown, Russian Richmond, Little Italy, Hunters Point, Little Osaka, and the Mexican, German, Irish, and Samoan settlements of the sprawling Mission District. It's a feast of exotic smells and flavors, of cappuccino in small cafes, sourdough French bread, local wine, Dungeness crab, fortune cookies, chop suey, pasta, cioppino, and Joe's Special. Where else can you dine on Ukranian *golubtzy* to the sound of foghorns, or pick the remnants of Mongolian lamb from your teeth to the accompaniment of an Oktoberfest accordion band?

To the sailor Frisco was a fabled port of call, a town of honky-tonks, tattoo parlors, topless joints, Anchor Steam beer, and monumental Saturday night drunks; a city of blurred Monday mornings, slowly clearing; of sea gulls, white caps, and uniforms, a crisp flag whipping in a clean wind.

Then there's Sam Spade's turf. Hard-boiled, tender at the core. Fedora pulled low, cigarette on lip, dame on elbow. Al Capone doing hard time on The Rock. Crack dealers menacing the Projects. She can be one tough babe.

Yet, always over the next hill lies romantic San Francisco, that "cool, grey City of Love," where couples haunt the stairways, gazing out over a blue bay, flecked with white, gracefully trimmed with gossamer bridges. . . .

Then it's 6 A.M. and the bridges are jammed with commuters bound for Wall Street West—corporate headquarters, bankers' clubs, bustling clerks, martini lunches, rising steel towers, migraine headaches. Duck left, and you're in the West Coast bastion of progressive idealism: the city of John Muir, the Sierra Club, the Gay Rights Movement, Free Speech, holistic health, and raised consciousness; but also the radical chic, dead-end divisive politics and the cults and movements that continue to repel a fascinated Middle America. The United Nations was born in San Francisco; so were Jonestown and the Symbionese Liberation Army.

Nor let us forget the pipe-dream of Bohemia, where every generation finds and loses a new Latin Quarter. Gone are the artists and their cage birds from the shacks of Telegraph Hill; gone the poets from Papa Coppa's; faded the beatniks, with their wine and jazz; and gone, too, the flower children from a street called Love. Only their stories live on . . . .

More than an accumulation of wood, steel, glass, and brick, San Francisco is a collection of people and their stories. Some are new. Some have been told and embellished for generations. Some are ugly. Some are stranger than fiction. Let the historians dicker which is which; to the traveler who seeks to know San Francisco, they are all of interest.

TAKING THE PLUNGE

*M*ary Ann Singleton was twenty-five years old when she saw San Francisco for the first time.

She came to the city alone for an eight-day vacation. On the fifth night, she drank three Irish coffees at the Buena Vista, realized that her Mood Ring was blue, and decided to phone her mother in Cleveland.

"Hi, Mom. It's me."

"Oh, darling. Your daddy and I were just talking about you. There was this crazy man on 'McMillan and Wife' who was strangling all these secretaries, and I just couldn't help thinking . . . "

"Mom . . . "

"I know. Just crazy ol' Mom, worrying herself sick over nothing. But you never can tell about those things. Look at that poor Patty Hearst, locked up in that closet with all those awful . . . "

"Mom . . . long distance."

"Oh . . . yes. You must be having a grand time."

"God . . . you wouldn't believe it! The people here are so friendly I feel like I've . . . "

"Have you been to the Top of the Mark like I told you?"

"Not yet."

"Well, don't you dare miss that! You know, your daddy took me there when he got back from the South Pacific. I remember he slipped the bandleader five dollars, so we could dance to 'Moonlight Serenade,' and I spilled Tom Collins all over his beautiful white Navy . . . "

"Mom, I want you to do me a favor."

"Of course, darling. Just listen to me. Oh . . . before I forget it, I ran into Mr. Lassiter yesterday at the Ridgemont Mall, and he said the office is just falling apart with you gone. They don't get many good secretaries at Lassiter Fertilizers."

"Mom, that's sort of why I called."

"Yes, darling?"

"I want you to call Mr. Lassiter and tell him I won't be in on Monday morning."

"Oh . . . Mary Ann, I'm not sure you should ask for an extension on your vacation."

"It's not an extension, Mom."

"Well, then why . . . ?"

"I'm not coming home, Mom."

Silence. Then, dimly in the distance, a television voice began to tell Mary Ann's father about the temporary relief of hemorrhoids. Finally her mother spoke: "Don't be silly, darling."

—Armistead Maupin, *Tales of the City*, 1978

SAN FRANCISCO'S STORY

SAN FRANCISCO SITS WITH REASONABLE STABILITY on the southern shore of the Golden Gate, surrounded on three sides by seawater. To the west is the Pacific Ocean, perennially chilled by strong Alaskan currents, even on the hottest days, and torn by rough seas murderous to swimmers, and all too often inhospitable to ships. To the east is San Francisco Bay, deep, protected, and so surpassing a harbor that it has been called by many the finest in the world. The two are joined by the Golden Gate, a narrow passage three miles long and a mile wide, which cuts San Francisco off from the northern part of the state.

The famous hills of San Francisco and the Bay Area are part of the Coast Ranges, which run north and south along almost the entire California coast. Their formidable barrier shields the inland valleys from the fogs and winds that plague San Francisco, making a summer hothouse of the interior. East of the Coast Ranges sprawls the fertile Central Valley, the nation's largest fruit and vegetable garden, and east of that, the longest block of granite in the world, the Sierra Nevada mountains. The rivers of the Sierra Nevada, cherished now for their precious water as they once were for their gold, pour down into the Central Valley, gathering into the Sacramento and San Joaquin Rivers. Flowing from the north and south, respectively, these two rivers join in the delta east of Carquinez Straits, where they enter San Francisco Bay and are carried off by strong currents through the Golden Gate. In millennia past, these rivers gouged out the Gate and emptied into the sea some distance beyond. When the oceans rose at the end of the last Ice Age, the canyon and the valley behind were flooded, creating the inland bay of San Francisco.

Of the forces that shaped San Francisco, and which shape her still, the one most likely to concern residents and visitors alike is the process of tectonic movement, better known as earthquakes. California's longest and most famous earthquake fault, the San Andreas, runs 650 miles up the coast of California, slipping into the sea just south of San Francisco, and emerging on land again to the north, at Point Reyes. The plate to the west of the San Andreas moves north at an average speed of two inches per year. When pressure builds at a sticking point, and then suddenly breaks loose, the surrounding earth slips and shakes. Earthquakes are an unavoidable feature of the San Francisco Bay Area. The famous quake of 1906 was by no means the first—nor will the powerful shaker of 1989 be the last.

PETALUMA

VALLEJO

San Pablo Bay

Grizzly Bay

Sacramento

Honker Bay

River

POINT SAN PEDRO

CONCORD

BRIONES HILLS

HAYWARD

SAN PABLO RIDGE

MOUNT DIABLO

MT. TAMALPAIS

ANGEL ISLAND

BERKELEY

ALCATRAZ ISLAND

YERBA BUENA ISLAND

LAS TRAMPAS RIDGE

POINT BONITA

OAKLAND

San

POINT LOBOS

SAN FRANCISCO

LIVERMORE

SAN

Pacific

Seal Cove

San Gregorio Fault

San Francisco earthquake epicenter, 1906

CANDLESTICK POINT

Francisco

SUNOL RIDGE

Calaveras Fault

POINT SAN PEDRO

HAYWARD

HAYWARD FAULT

ANDREAS

COYOTE POINT

Bay

Ocean

MONTARA MOUNTAIN

FREMONT

SANTA

PALO ALTO

N

W   E

S

CRUZ

SAN JOSE

San Andreas Fault

BAY AREA & NATURAL FEATURES

BUTANO

MOUNTAINS

RIDGE

FAULT

Major Fault

Concealed or Inferred Fault

0   5   10

Copyright: Spaceshots, Inc. Miles

■ THE FIRST INHABITANTS

Unlike the desolate, windswept, and inhospitable site of San Francisco itself, the Bay Area counties to the south, east, and north have always shown a natural hospitality to residents. When people first began crossing the Bering Straits from Asia some 20,000–36,000 years ago, the Bay Area was brimming with all the requirements of life. The gentle climate and rich patchwork of woodland, marsh, oak savannah, and upland habitats nurtured an abundance of seabirds, shellfish, ducks, antelope, deer, bear, elk, otter, fox, and rabbit, as well as edible grasses, roots, and acorns. The region also supported a human population of about 10,000 people, who built some 30 or 40 permanent villages around the bay and south to Big Sur. The San Francisco Bay Area was the most densely populated region on the continent north of Mexico, but the site of San Francisco itself attracted few residents.

Based on language groupings, anthropologists identify the native people north of the Golden Gate as the Coast Miwok, while the dominant group throughout the rest of the Bay Area is known by the Spanish names of Ohlone, or Costanoan. In fact, each Ohlone sub-tribe considered itself independent and unique, separated from its neighbors by dialect and customs, despite regular trade and intermarriage. They shared a common dependence on shellfish, as is attested by the 450 gigantic piles of cast-off shells still found around the bay, most spectacularly at Coyote Hills in southern Alameda County. During summer they migrated inland to hunt game and collect acorns to make their mush and bread. Several thousand years of this stable cycle produced a gentle, musical, unwarlike culture that did not keep records of its own past. For an Ohlone to discuss the dead was taboo. Merely making mention of a dead relative in the Ohlone culture was an impropriety equal to cursing one in Western or Asian cultures. Perhaps that is why, after thousands of years on the shores of the bay, their annihilation passed so quietly.

Legends of California flittered about the taverns and libraries of Europe for years before anyone actually came for a look. Recent discoveries of ancient coins and stone anchors suggest that Chinese ships possibly visited the California coast centuries before Columbus blundered into the Caribbean. The first *documented* visit by a foreigner to Northern California, however, was made by the Portuguese explorer, João Cabrilho, who sailed up the coast in 1542, somehow missing the Golden Gate. Thirty-seven years later, in 1579, the English privateer Sir Francis Drake, while on an extended mission to harass the Spanish galleons and seize their treasures, made a landing somewhere in the Bay Area. Drake apparently also missed the narrow entrance to the Golden Gate in the fog. His chronicler's description of their anchorage leads most historians to place it at what is now called Drakes Bay, below Point Reyes. Pausing several weeks to repair his ships, Drake claimed the land for Queen Elizabeth I of England and christened it Nova Albion, inscribing his claim on a brass plate. The plate—or a convincing forgery—was found in 1933, and is now on display at the University of California in Berkeley.

■ THE HISPANICS

Another two hundred years passed before a European saw San Francisco Bay. While searching for Monterey Bay, glowingly described almost two centuries earlier by explorer Sebastían Vizcaíno, a Spanish scouting party under the command of Gaspar de Portolá stumbled on San Francisco Bay in 1769, having overshot their true mark. Realizing that *this* couldn't possibly be Monterey Bay, the soldierly Portolá stuck to his orders, and retraced his steps south.

The task of colonizing this amazing new discovery was assigned to a determined soldier, Juan Bautista de Anza. With his lieutenant, Jose Moraga, a Franciscan priest named Francisco Palóu, and a party of 34 pioneer families, Anza set out on foot from Sonora, Mexico. After a grueling desert march, they arrived at the tip of the peninsula on June 27, 1776 (seven days before another landmark date on the opposite side of the continent). There they took possession for Spain by founding a fortress, the Presidio, on a strategic hill overlooking the Golden Gate, and a church a mile south on a small lake that they named in honor of Our Lady of Sorrows (Nuestra Señora de los Dolores). The adobe church that Father Palóu built on the site, the first of five missions around the bay, was dedicated to Saint Francis of Assisi. In time, the lake's name stuck as the popular name for Mission Dolores, while the great bay itself acquired the Mission's official name, San Francisco.

The Ohlones greeted the newcomers with amazement. Many believed them to be gods—a reason, perhaps, why they succumbed so readily to the new order. The Spanish in California were decidedly more interested in the native peoples *as subjects* than were the English settlers on the Atlantic shore. Their stated purpose was to convert the natives to Christianity, to save their souls while teaching them enough farming, husbandry, and industry to create a self-perpetuating rural society in California. The plan was disastrous. For people accustomed to the subtler pace of seasonal migrations, mission life was hellish. The natives lived in barracks, segregated by sex, and did forced labor. Many ran away, only to be caught, returned, and punished by soldiers. New diseases decimated them. The death rate quickly surpassed the birth rate. Then, in 1821, Mexico broke away from Spain, and the new government secularized the missions. Order, harsh as it was, broke down. The missions decayed. Hopelessly lost from their old ways of life, the Ohlones starved in their homeland. Some drifted off to work the ranches, others to roam in homeless bands that were hunted down and killed. As a people, the Ohlone never recovered. Five thousand Indians, over half the population of the Bay Area before the Spanish arrived, lie buried in unmarked graves at Mission Dolores, Our Lady of Sorrows.

In the wake of sword and cross, Spanish (and later Mexican) civilian families, like Noé, Bernal, Moraga, and Vallejo, settled on vast government land grants, where they built cattle ranches and ruled as benevolent feudal lords. Like the Ohlones before them, the new *Californios* discovered that life in bounteous California could be very sweet indeed. Their ranches produced all that they needed, including an annual cash "crop" of hides, which they sold to passing ships for a good profit. Among the most ambitious of the rancho chieftains was a Swiss, Augustus Sutter, who built a fort to secure his vast empire near the spot where the American River empties into the Sacramento River—today the site of California's state capital, Sacramento.

Ironically, the hide trade destroyed the ranchers' isolation by bringing foreign ships to San Francisco in slowly increasing numbers. The Western world was in an expansive mood. The Pacific was opening up, and San Francisco Bay made a splendid anchorage for a Pacific empire. Mexico lacked the power to enforce her claim. As early as 1812, the Russians established Fort Ross, ostensibly as a hunting station, 60 miles north of San Francisco. French and English ships were investigating. When the Yankee sailor-turned-writer Richard Henry Dana described his 1835 visit to the bay in *Two Years Before the Mast*, Americans pricked up their ears. Expansionists among them were particularly intrigued to learn that a small, mostly Yankee settlement was already established above a cove on the eastern side of the San Francisco peninsula.

■ THE YANKEES

American and English ships had long preferred Yerba Buena Cove to the traditional Spanish anchorage off the Presidio, because it was better sheltered. In the year of Dana's visit, an Anglo sailor named William Richardson built a house there, laying out a street and a village plaza. Being married to the Presidio *commandante's* daughter, Richardson settled with official blessing. Others followed, and the settlement became known as Yerba Buena.

With classic entrepreneurial spirit, Yerba Buena found a need and filled it, in this case, with a ship's chandler and a couple of grog shops. But it was enough. On the verge of the cataclysmic 1840s, the three sprigs on which San Francisco would bloom had sprouted. Each was separated by an hour's walk from the others. Two—the Mission Dolores and the Presidio—were fast declining, but the third, the wretched, flea-bitten, sand-blown, largely Yankee village of Yerba Buena, was preparing to take up the torch. Richardson's street, Calle de la Fundación (Foundation Street), would one day become Grant Avenue, and the dusty village plaza would become Portsmouth Plaza.

Spanish armor.

The American presence in California grew in the 1840s as increasing numbers of immigrants cut south from the Oregon Trail. The Mexican governor complained uselessly about the "hoards of Yankee emigrants whose progress we cannot arrest." America was expanding. "Manifest Destiny!" was the cry justifying westward migration, settlement, and war. In 1846, the United States annexed Texas and invaded Mexico. U.S. Senator Daniel Webster's dexterous tongue was claiming that San Francisco Bay alone was worth 10 Texases.

The climax came that same year. A party of bombastic Yankees in Sonoma,

California, prodded on by a meddlesome American soldier of fortune named Captain John C. Frémont, raised a flag with a picture of a bear on it, and declared independence from Mexico. The California Republic lasted less than a month. On July 9, 1846, a party of American marines and sailors from the warship *Portsmouth*, under command of Captain John Montgomery, seized the plaza at Yerba Buena and ran the Stars and Stripes up a pole. The Presidio, staffed by 12 Mexican soldiers and a sergeant, surrendered peacefully. Yerba Buena was now American territory.

Big changes came quickly to Yerba Buena. Most propitiously, the citizens changed the town's name to San Francisco. Boosters argued that by taking the name of the famous bay, their town would grow famous by association and, more to the point, attract shipping away from any other bayside ports. It was a shrewd move of enormous consequences. In keeping with their grand hopes, San Francisco's first elected administrator hired an Irish sailor, Jasper O'Farrell, to draw up a street plan for the town.

Even more ambitious plans were being laid by an enterprising newcomer named Sam Brannan, who had arrived at the head of a party of Mormons shortly after the American seizure. Some have called Brannan San Francisco's founding

SAILING WITH DANA

*W*e sailed down this magnificent bay with a light wind, the tide, which was running out, carrying us at the rate of four or five knots. It was a fine day; the first of entire sunshine we had had for more than a month. We passed directly under the high cliff on which the presidio is built, and stood into the middle of the bay, from whence we could see small bays making up into the interior, large and beautifully wooded islands, and the mouths of several small rivers. If California ever becomes a prosperous country, this bay will be the center of its prosperity. The abundance of wood and water; the extreme fertility of its shores; the excellence of its climate, which is as near to being perfect as any in the world; and its facilities for navigation, affording the best anchoring grounds in the whole western coast of America,—all fit it for a place of great importance.

—Richard Henry Dana, *Two Years Before the Mast,* 1840

father. Others dismiss him as an opportunist or even a charlatan. Still, by hook or crook, Brannan managed to push to the head of nearly every scheme of improvement in San Francisco over the next booming decade. Brannan quickly broke with the Salt Lake church, and became San Francisco's leading booster. He delivered San Francisco's first English sermon, performed its first non-Catholic marriage, founded its first newspaper *(The California Star),* helped establish the first school, and built stores both in San Francisco and at Sutter's Fort. Yet Sam Brannan's greatest coup came in 1848, after Sutter's foreman, James Marshall, discovered gold in the American River. Fearful of the awful turmoil that the discovery would bring to his rancho, Sutter sought advice from Brannan, begging his confidence. Brannan offered solace. By most accounts, he then quickly bought up waterfront lots and placed orders to stock his stores in Sacramento and San Francisco with food, dry goods, and digging tools. The next week found him in San Francisco with a bottle of the glittering metal, shouting "Gold! Gold from the American River!"

As a lesson in history and shrewd business practices, let it not be forgotten that of the thousands of gold seekers who rushed into California in the ensuing madness, a few struck it rich. But it was Sam Brannan who became San Francisco's first millionaire.

■ THE GOLD RUSH

The California Gold Rush is arguably the most extraordinary event to ever befall an American city in peacetime. At the beginning of 1848, the year that gold was discovered, San Francisco was a backwater of some 800 souls. Within a few months, its population was approaching 25,000, and its postal service handling an estimated million letters a year. By 1852, despite having been practically burnt to the ground on six occasions, San Francisco was the fourth largest entrepôt in the United States. By 1860, 14 years after Montgomery had seized the sleepy village, it was a metropolis of 56,000, poised to underwrite a large portion of Union expenses in the Civil War.

In time, California's rich land and climate undoubtedly would have attracted floods of immigrants, but the Gold Rush telescoped a half century of growth into half a year. Within weeks, the news that had electrified California and Mexico was spreading like a shipboard plague to the Eastern seaboard, the Midwest, South America, Asia, Europe, and Australia. Within months, about 90,000 men (and a very few women) struck out for California. (Another 150,000 would arrive before the rush ended in 1852.) Thousands of Americans commenced walking west, and thousands more set sail around Cape Horn or to the Isthmus of Panama. Packed ships sailed from Central and South America, the Sandwich Islands (Hawaii), China, and every seaport of Europe. The lucky ones who arrived in 1848 got first crack at the gold, but the bulk who arrived in 1849 earned the eternal sobriquet of *forty-niners.*

Most of those who came by ship landed in San Francisco, the first convenient anchorage within the Golden Gate. Other rival settlements on San Francisco Bay, particularly Benicia, were closer to the mines, but most of the argonauts were ignorant of California geography, and San Francisco *was* the famous name. On landing, many asked the way to the Mother Lode in the Sierra Nevada as though it were just up the street. Finding that a long overland journey still awaited them, they stopped to buy supplies and make plans. A tent city sprang up to house and serve them. As crews deserted to join the rush, abandoned ships were winched ashore (or the shore built out to them) for use as storehouses and hotels. Demand for nearly everything ran rampant, and supplies were perpetually being hoarded or

Miners in 1852 wash the gold from their diggings in a "long tom."

liquidated by speculators. Prices for basic commodities (food, cots, picks, shovels) rocketed to heights that won't be seen again, if we're lucky, until well into the 21st century—yet they sold briskly enough in 1849.

Overnight, San Francisco became the most cosmopolitan city on Earth. Although Americans comprised about half the population from 1847 to 1860, the other half was a mixture of British subjects, with the Irish in the lead, and considerable minorities of Chinese, Hispanics, continental Europeans, and Hawaiians. Most of the Hispanics came from Mexico and Chile, while Germany, France, Switzerland, Poland, Sweden, Belgium, and Italy supplied most of the Continentals. In 1860, 10 percent of San Francisco was non-white, mostly Chinese.

The ratio between the sexes was downright alarming. In 1847, men outnumbered women two to one. Things worsened drastically by 1849, when the ratio jumped to ten to one. The relative lack of women remained a serious problem in San Francisco throughout most of the century, no doubt adding fire to the Barbary Coast, the city's notorious red-light district.

San Francisco's was a youthful population, liberally sprinkled with professionals and educated gentlemen. Most had come with every intention of returning home just as soon as they made their millions. For the majority, that day never came. Surface gold was picked clean by 1849, and the deeper placers, painstakingly washed through pans and cradles, wore thin by 1852. Gold mining was becoming a corporate enterprise, better suited to companies that could raise the capital to bore tunnels or invest in expensive hydraulic mining equipment. The independent forty-niner was an anachronism. A handful went home rich. Many more departed poor. Others fanned out through the West in search of another bonanza. Solvent or broke, thousands more made their way to San Francisco.

California gold played fickle with the forty-niners, but it had not eluded San Francisco. In 1853, some tents still crowded the hillsides, but a substantial city of wood and brick had taken root. Fires roared through the city regularly. Heinrich Schliemann, the German archaeologist, was roused from his Portsmouth Square Hotel bed by the huge fire of May 4, 1851, which burned a quarter of the city. He fled up Telegraph Hill in time to catch a "frightful but sublime view" of "the roaring of the storm, the cracking of the gunpowder, the cracking of the falling stonewalls, the cries of the people and the wonderful spectacle of an immense city burning. . . ." San Francisco rebuilt, only to burn again on November 9, 1852.

San Francisco rebuilt again. Aside from a permanent population well exceeding

Benicia's old state capitol recalls its fleeting year of glory (1853–54).

30,000 people, the city now supported a lending library, scores of warehouses, theaters, eateries, hotels, brothels, a dozen newspapers, a handful of churches, and hundreds of saloons and gambling halls. New piers and landfill pushed out where Yerba Buena Cove once was, burying the old harbor along with the ships anchored therein. Forty square blocks of downtown were built on the landfill. Stockton Street, on the hill above, was the fashionable residential avenue. A new residential quarter reached south of Market to soon-to-be-fashionable Rincon Hill. Hispanic and Mediterranean settlers were already transforming Telegraph Hill and North Beach into a "Latin quarter." The Chinese had dispersed throughout the city, but their main settlement was forming along Sacramento Street. Another village of Chinese fishermen stood at the foot of Rincon Hill, in the shadow of today's Bay Bridge. Pacific Street, along the base of Telegraph Hill, was taking in some rough Australian characters, who called themselves the Sydney Ducks; in time, "Sydneytown" would reach full bloom as the notorious Barbary Coast.

A city full of frisky young gents can get a bit wild. Duels were fought in the crowded streets. Gangs of criminals robbed, extorted, and terrorized, sometimes setting fires and looting. The Chilean settlement on Telegraph Hill was a frequent target of hooligans like the Hounds, a gang of New Yorkers and Australians. The law was slow and the citizens impatient. In 1849, and again in 1851, Sam Brannan harangued the city's established community into taking justice into their own hands. The first incident ended with exile for six Hounds, but the mob settled for nothing less than lynching the second time around.

Vigilantism struck again in May 1856, after the righteous editor of the *Evening Bulletin*, James King of William, was gunned down by a shady city councilman who resented the *Bulletin*'s charges of corruption. Thousands of citizens rallied around a new Committee of Vigilance, seizing the councilman, James Casey, and lynching him and a cohort, a gambler named Charles Cora. Taking up quarters in a sand-bagged building on Sacramento Street, nicknamed Fort Gunnybags, the committee set about striking terror in the criminal populace with torchlight parades and more lynchings. It finally disbanded on July 29, leaving its supporters and condemners both claiming victory, and the criminal element temporarily cowed.

Manic times breed eccentric characters, and San Francisco has bred more than a few from its earliest days. There was James Lick, the fabulous millionaire who was so tight that he wore cast-off clothes, until he repented toward the end of his life and gave his fortune away. Then there was William Walker, the adventurer who tried to make himself dictator of Nicaragua, only to die before a Honduran firing squad. And there was "Honest" Harry Meiggs, the beloved city booster who funded large and generous civic improvement schemes with borrowed cash, and skipped town hours before the bubble burst. The most fantastic eccentric of all, however, was Emperor Norton.

Joshua A. Norton came to San Francisco from London in 1849. He became a merchant, reinvested his profits in land, and prospered. In 1854, he set plans to corner the rice market, pouring all his resources into the scheme. Unfortunately for him, a rice ship sailed through the Golden Gate while he still held his hoard, and prices plummeted. Norton went bankrupt and disappeared. Then one day, several months later, he reappeared on Montgomery Street in military costume with epaulets, plumed hat, and a cane. Stopping by the offices of the *San Francisco Bulletin*, he announced that he was henceforth to be known as Norton I, Emperor of the United States and Protector of Mexico.

Norton I, Emperor of the United States and Protector of Mexico.

Short, slight, bearded, with clear, fierce eyes and a proud mien, Emperor Norton set about seriously to rule his empire. San Francisco, tongue in cheek, decided to play along. A printer agreed to print the Emperor's currency, and merchants agreed to honor it. The Emperor dined gratis wherever he pleased, and restaurateurs vied for the publicity of his patronage. It was said that no theater opened a performance between 1855 and 1880 without reserving free first-night seats for the Emperor and his faithful dogs, Lazarus and Bummer. Another seat was kept for him in the Sacramento legislature, which he addressed in earnest on occasion. When his uniform became ragged, he appeared before the Board of Supervisors, who amended the city charter so that he would receive an allowance for as long as he lived. In short, the city kept up its end of the madman's charade for almost 30 years, and he in turn never wore out his welcome. In fact, he took some pains to govern conscientiously. His directive to erect a tree for children at Christmas on Union Square is honored to this day. It was said that he attended both Christian and Jewish services to encourage religious harmony, and that he once diffused an anti-Chinese riot by standing at the front and reciting the Lord's Prayer till the combatants put down their fists and departed in shame. When he died in 1880, thousands from every quarter of the city came to bury him with all the pomp and dignity befitting his rank.

■ BOOM TIMES, AND BUST

As the 1850s drew to an end, the spontaneous energy that animated Gold Rush San Francisco lost torque. The economy slowed, men drifted home or took up wage-paying jobs, and society began to stabilize. Californians worried over the recession, but also began to explore other golden opportunities that were awaiting them in farming, industry, and government corruption. By the late 1850s, San Francisco had weathered its first depression and was settling into a pattern of civic and commercial growth typical of most other American cities. Little did anyone expect that San Francisco was in for another big boom.

In 1859, some California drifters stumbled on a fabulous vein of silver in the desert mountains east of the Sierra Nevada. A new rush was on. Rough-and-tumble Virginia City sprang preposterously up on the steep, dry mountainside of Mount Davidson in Washoe, soon to be the new state of Nevada. Unlike the California Gold Rush of a decade earlier, the Comstock Lode, as it came to be known, was a game unsuited to stalwart independents. Capital, heavy equipment, engineers, and organized manpower were needed to run the expensive operation of extracting, crushing, and refining the ore. Experienced San Francisco mining companies responded with a speed and know-how that drove individual prospectors, literally, into the ground. San Francisco had a good return on investment. The Comstock Lode proved to be the world's richest silver deposit. The better part of two decades was needed to exhaust its bounty.

As Virginia City grew into a factory town, where shifts worked round the clock in grim conditions, San Francisco grew fabulously rich. In short time, a new breed of millionaire, the "Bonanza Kings," was staking out gilded mansions on Nob Hill and showering patronage on the plenteous new diversions that mushroomed up to serve them. But San Francisco's benefits did not stop at Nob Hill and luxurious French restaurants. Comstock silver stimulated general prosperity, creating jobs and optimism for the city at large. William C. Ralston, an early Comstock developer and partner in the Bank of California, lent his fortune and stature to many civic projects, including factories, mills, streets, theaters, office buildings, Golden Gate Park, and the largest, most princely hotel of its day, the Palace (see page 70). His contributions and boosterism inspired some to hail him as "the man who built San Francisco."

These colorful times were fortunately well described to us by a host of San Francisco's writers. Bret Harte was among the first to receive national recognition for his heart-tugging stories of the Gold Rush. His cloying sentimentality, which proved popular in the East (and West), was counteracted by the misanthropic genius, Ambrose Bierce, whose "Devil's Dictionary" is a classic of American cynicism. They were backed by a host of lesser lights: South-Seas enthusiast Charles Stoddard and the eccentric frontier poet, Joaquin Miller, as well as the doyen of California poets and scribblers, Ina Coolbrith, loved by many, beloved by all. Most famous of all, and perhaps most characteristic of San Francisco despite the fact that he lived there for less than three years, was Mark Twain. His rambling, humorous, satirical voice *was* the voice of San Francisco's better half—tolerant and curious, appreciative of the finer things, debunking pomposity, comfortably American. Robert Louis Stevenson and Rudyard Kipling passed through town and left their marks, as did Oscar Wilde, in the 1880s. A new generation—George Sterling, Frank Norris, Gertrude Atherton, and Jack London—would rise before the century ended.

The 1860s in San Francisco was an era of robust new confidence. Californians rode out the Civil War in the Union camp with little sacrifice of life and, incidentally,

The extravagant tastes of Victorian San Francisco are reflected in the city's opulent architecture. James Lick imported the Conservatory of Flowers (left), now in Golden Gate Park, for his private garden. The "Painted Ladies" on Alamo Square (top) are oft-cited (and photographed) examples of Victorian architecture, which is known for its fanciful ornamentation. (photos by Kerrick James)

profits intact. Now they were ready to take on the world. They were betting heavily on a new transcontinental railway that was pushing across the Sierra Nevada toward the East, financed by a Congress anxious to tie California (with its gold) and Nevada (with its silver) closer to the Union. Californians saw their isolation from the rest of the country as a barrier to development. It took a month to send a letter east by Panama steamer, and 20 to 24 days by Butterfield Stage. The Pony Express had done it in nine days to Saint Joseph, Missouri, but that enterprise went bankrupt after only 18 months, in 1861. The completion of the first transcontinental telegraph line improved communications, but Californians were betting that the railroad would bring a big boon to the state's economy.

The Central Pacific Railway was the pet project of an engineer named Theodore Judah, who personally surveyed the difficult route across the precipitous Sierra Nevada mountains. He sold his idea to four Sacramento businessmen, who found the government incentive of free land and cheap loans quite irresistible. The Big Four, as they came to be known, pushed the railroad into reality, joining up with the westward-bound Union Pacific at Promontory Point, Utah, in 1869. For their troubles, they reaped vast fortunes and created the most powerful political machine in California, the Southern Pacific Railway. They all built palaces on Nob Hill, where their names—Leland Stanford, Charles Crocker, Collis Huntington, and Mark Hopkins—are today enshrined in some of the finest hotels in San Francisco.

San Franciscans celebrated the transcontinental railroad's completion with characteristic abandon, ignoring the dire predictions of a remarkable economist, Henry George, who

Nob Hill mansions embodi their masters' wealth, powe and ostentatiousness.

wrote in a San Francisco magazine that the railroad would enrich few and impoverish many. He claimed that completion of the line would flood California with cheap manufactured goods from the eastern states, ruining California's fledgling industrial base, while the ranks of the unemployed would swell with terminated railroad workers from all over the west. He was right.

Like everyone else, William Ralston had banked heavily on the transcontinental railway. But when the boom turned to bust, Ralston was caught overextended to the tune of five million dollars. With characteristic attention to smooth business form, he closed the doors of his bank and tendered his formal resignation. That afternoon, he drowned in San Francisco Bay.

The working classes chose another course. The unemployed rose in anger against the rich railroad men and, most tragically, against the thousands of Chinese workers who had been released from the railroad, and on whom they blamed the loss of American jobs. The depression of the 1870s heralded probably the bleakest era in San Francisco's history.

■ THE CHINESE

The largest ethnic group in the city today, and one of the most influential since the beginning of the Gold Rush, the Chinese played an enormously important part in the opening of the West, California in particular. The first Chinese arrived in San Francisco in 1848, and by the following year there were about 300. They were welcomed with curiosity. Their merchants contributed to the material comfort of the rustic city, and American forty-niners readily learned to enjoy Chinese food and festivals.

The era of good feeling lasted only as long as easy gold. When the placers wore thin, laws were passed to restrict foreign competition, and sometimes enforced with violence. Even when forced to work only abandoned claims, most Chinese miners succeeded through persistent toil and lower expectations—after all, an ounce of gold went a lot further in China, where most intended to return, than it did in America. This determination to return to China encouraged few Cantonese miners to learn English or to assimilate, which reinforced their segregation.

Chinese laborers helped to build the dikes along the Sacramento River, and to plant orchards and vineyards in the fertile California valleys. They pioneered California's fisheries, and were instrumental in developing textile manufacturing, leather-working, cigar-making, and other industries. They were highly valued in construction; in fact, San Francisco's first stone structure, the Parrott Building, was quarried in China and assembled by Chinese builders (who, incidentally, staged San Francisco's first labor strike). Their most celebrated job, however, was with the transcontinental railway, when 10,000 Chinese joined other teams in laying the tracks across the formidable Sierra Nevada range. The Chinese proved strong and brave rail men, who tackled dangerous jobs with fortitude, and set records for laying track. When the job was done and the workers released from contract, thousands drifted to San Francisco, raising the ranks of the unemployed.

The depression of the 1870s hit San Francisco hard. California factories found competition from the east coast too much to bear. Bankruptcies put hundreds out of work, sowing militancy among the unemployed. Many tycoons bolstered their profits by hiring Chinese workers at lower wages—which still exceeded what they could earn in China. These practices spurned bitter resentment against the industrialists, but the Chinese were an easier target. With encouragement from sand-lot fire-eaters, hooligans bullied them. Riotous mobs stormed Chinatown, both in San Francisco and other Western towns, destroying property, and all too often committing murder. Labor organizers used the power of the vote to push politicians to

Though it has moved more than once and now occupies a modern building, the Kong Chow Temple is said by some to be the oldest Chinese temple in the United States.

pass laws, like the Exclusion Act, to harass the Chinese, and ultimately to end Chinese immigration. The Chinese could not vote; the efforts of their organizations to fight these laws in court came to naught.

To understand what happened next, it helps to understand how Chinatown was organized.

Chinatown was, and in some respects still is, a village within a city. Partly in response to outside prejudice, but also out of inclination to live in a familiar society, Chinese emigrants during the nineteenth century built Chinatowns wherever they settled. There were many throughout the American West, but San Francisco's was the largest. In violent times its population swelled with refugees.

Most Chinese who came to America in the 19th century joined a *tong*, or social organization, based on their place of origin. A cross between a labor guild and an insurance company, tongs negotiated contracts for members, and provided protection and support in return for dues. Rivalry between different tongs, carried over from regional rivalries on the Chinese mainland, sometimes resulted in violence.

To control tong rivalry, Chinese merchants formed a federation of representatives of six of the largest tongs, called The Six Companies. (Membership later expanded to seven, but the name remained the same.) With occasional involvement by the Consul General of China, who had an office in San Francisco, the Six Companies managed Chinatown's public affairs, including its official relations with the outside community.

Until toppled in 1911, the Manchu government forced all Chinese males to wear queues.

The Six Companies was a paternalistic organization. It took care of such matters as arbitrating disputes, issuing exit certificates to persons who could prove they had paid their debts, caring for the sick, and dispensing charity. The Six Companies' leadership also protested, unsuccessfully, against importing prostitutes from China. Unfortunately, their purpose was completely misunderstood by the non-Chinese public, who confused them with the fighting tongs, and charged them with violence and duplicity. Ironically, had the public backed the Six Companies, they probably could have prevented the era of Chinatown lawlessness called the tong wars.

The failure of the Six Companies to halt the tong wars was a direct result of anti-Chinese legislation—the Geary Act of 1892, which declared that all Chinese had to carry identity papers or face deportation. The Six Companies opposed the law by advising Chinese not to comply, while levying a small sum from members to hire lawyers to fight it in court. Although many of the best lawyers of the day insisted that the act was unconstitutional, it passed and was enforced. When the first Chinese were arrested for not carrying proper documentation, the Six Companies suffered a monumental loss of prestige. Underworld leaders moved fast to take advantage of the vacuum, strengthening individual tongs at the expense of the federation. Rival interests of different tongs quickly crossed, and rivalry quickly turned to violence.

The tongs fought over control of gambling and prostitution—diversions quite popular in the bachelor societies fossilized by the Exclusion Act. Extortion grew rampant, and the gangsters enforced their dictates with professional gunmen, known to police and later Hollywood films as highbinders, or hachetmen. The law-abiding majority of Chinatown, caught between an unsympathetic American public and lethal terrorism from within, suffered tremendously.

The tong wars were a reign of terror, and yet one that most non-Chinese followed only as a curiosity in the morning newspapers. It's only fair to note, however, that many non-Chinese rose to their defense. Many policemen genuinely served to protect the community, despite language barriers and widespread, often justified, mistrust of police. Working with English-speaking (and extremely brave, considering the risks) merchants, dedicated officers managed to bring some of the criminals to justice, but others were freed by corrupt lawyers and courts, returning to Chinatown swearing vengeance on their betrayers. Religious groups like the Methodists and the Presbyterians joined the fray.

Probably the most flamboyant crusader against the tong-controlled prostitution trade was a woman of splendidly ferocious character by the name of Donaldina

*Children were
a rare sight in
Chinatown
until relatively
recent years.*

Cameron. The spearhead of a Presbyterian mission force to rescue Chinese prostitutes, she swooped into her work with gargantuan energy. She was assisted in this
war by a band of equally courageous (and even less well-known) agents and associates from Chinatown, who lived willingly under constant, deadly threat—for
though gangsters were hesitant to harm a white woman (and to suffer the full
force of U.S. law tumbling down on their heads), they worried considerably less
about assassinating a fellow Chinese. It was said that Donaldina Cameron knew
every rooftop and passageway of Chinatown, and was a veritable devil at hunting
down hidden bagnios, which she physically stormed with the backup of her iron-
hearted comrades and a police contingent. Even more importantly, she followed
up on arrests with court battles. As her reputation grew, escaping prostitutes
sought her refuge, often with the help of merchants or young lovers, who took
grave risks, and sometimes paid with their lives. To this day, this extraordinary
woman is still remembered as Lo Ma (Old Mother) in Chinatown.

Donaldina Cameron helped drive the tongs into retreat, but two other phenomena really struck the killing blows. One was the 1906 earthquake, which initiated a complete rebuilding of Chinatown and the reestablishment of the Six Companies' prestige. The other, and most important, cause was the Americanization of
the Chinese, which ended the hold that the tongs had over the community.

■ THE EARTHQUAKE AND FIRE

The years before 1906—especially the era of Mayor Eugene Schmitz and his grafting king-maker, Abe Ruef—were the most perniciously corrupt that the city ever knew. The Gilded Age, as it was known, pampered millionaires on Nob Hill while the labor movement boiled under pressure in the tenements south of Market. The middle classes built rows of wooden Victorians on hills far removed from the strife of Chinatown and the Barbary Coast, while confident downtown businesses expanded ever upward in daring new "skyscrapers." The port, bolstered by new business in the Philippines following the 1898 Spanish-American War, was booming. Ferries steamed between the new Ferry Building and the growing suburbs of Oakland and Marin County. Cable cars and streetcars linked distant neighborhoods of the city, pushing its boundaries to the Western Addition, the Mission District, and beyond. Theaters played to lively houses, and the higher-class red-light district, the Tenderloin, waxed complacent under semi-official protection. In Golden Gate Park, the citizenry gathered in their Sunday best to stroll, picnic, and race fast coaches. San Francisco was *the* metropolis of the Pacific, the largest, finest, most powerful American city west of Chicago.

On the morning of April 18, 1906, San Francisco's 400,000 citizens were jolted awake by a quake now estimated at 8.25 on the Richter Scale. Chimneys crashed through roofs, gas and water mains broke all over town, and fissures opened in landfill streets. Surveying damage in the better residential districts, San Franciscans were relieved to see that the city had been spared calamity. Except for the flimsy tenements south of Market Street, the wooden Victorian neighborhoods had withstood the quake with only minor damage.

Downtown, however, received a worse shock. City Hall crumbled into rubble, a victim of the scams and shortcuts taken by scoundrelly politicians and their contractors. The Central Emergency Hospital also fell, burying doctors, nurses, and patients. Considering the severity of the quake, loss of life was small, yet devastating, in that one of the victims was Fire Chief Dennis Sullivan. More than any man in the city, Sullivan might have checked the disaster that followed.

Fifty-two fires broke out that morning. The fire department fought desperately, but with water mains broken and the fire chief dying, the flames spread unchecked. Racing through the tinderbox tenements south of Market, firestorms engulfed the Palace Hotel, torched the skyscrapers, leaped over Market, and roared into the Financial District.

The lofty esteem that old-time San Franciscans held for their fire fighters is eloquently illustrated in this splendid helmet of bygone days. San Francisco, which always has been and still is predominantly a city of wood, burned to the ground on more than one occasion, despite the often heroic deeds of the fire department. Separate fire companies used to compete for the glory of being the first on the scene of a blaze, and San Franciscans followed the exploits of their neighborhood companies in much the same way as modern citizens support their local sport teams.

The fire of 1906 burned so hot that it melted metal, fused dishes (left), and according to one story, actually incinerated a collection of diamonds stored in a South of Market safe.

TWAIN MEETS HIS FIRST EARTHQUAKE

A month afterward I enjoyed my first earthquake. It was one which was long called the "great" earthquake, and is doubtless so distinguished till this day. It was just after noon, on a bright October day. I was coming down Third Street. The only objects in motion anywhere in sight in that thickly built and populous quarter, were a man in a buggy behind me, and a street car wending slowly up the cross street. Otherwise, all was solitude and a Sabbath stillness. As I turned the corner, around a frame house, there was a great rattle and jar, and it occurred to me that here was an item!—no doubt a fight in that house. Before I could turn and seek the door, there came a really terrific shock; the ground seemed to roll under me in waves, interrupted by a violent joggling up and down, and there was a heavy grinding noise as of brick houses rubbing together . . .

The "curiosities" of the earthquake were simply endless. Gentlemen and ladies who were sick, or were taking a siesta, or had dissipated till a late hour and were making up lost sleep, thronged into the public streets in all sorts of queer apparel, and some without any at all. One woman who had been washing a naked child, ran down the street holding it by the ankles as if it were a dressed turkey. Prominent citizens who were supposed to keep the Sabbath strictly, rushed out of saloons in their shirt-sleeves, with billiard cues in their hands. Dozens of men with necks swathed in napkins, rushed from barber-shops, lathered to the eyes or with one cheek clean shaved and the other still bearing a hairy stubble. . . . A lady sitting in her rocking and quaking parlor, saw the wall part at the ceiling, open and shut twice, like a mouth, and then drop the end of a brick on the floor like a tooth. She was a woman easily disgusted with foolishness, and she arose and went out of there. One lady who was coming down stairs was astonished to see a bronze Hercules lean forward on its pedestal as if to strike her with its club. They both reached the bottom of the flight at the same time—the woman insensible from the fright. . . .

—Mark Twain, description of the 1865 earthquake, from *Roughing It,* 1872

The fire of 1906 destroyed far more buildings than the earthquake.

As thousands of refugees streamed to makeshift shelters in the parks and Presidio, others escaped by ferry to Oakland and Marin County. The army took over law and order in the city, with orders to kill looters on sight. Seven, in fact, were shot, one accidentally. Army dynamiters blasted through old neighborhoods in a clumsy attempt to clear firebreaks. By night, Oaklanders stared in horror at the burning city across the bay.

The flames burned for four days, destroying the downtown districts, Chinatown, North Beach, Russian Hill, Telegraph Hill, Nob Hill, and parts of the Mission District. It was finally contained at wide Van Ness by dynamiting the mansions along the eastern curb. The docks, protected by seawater sprayed by fireboats, survived, as did tiny pockets along the crests of Russian and Telegraph hills, and in the Barbary Coast. The Old Mint likewise survived to assume the role of the city's bank in the days ahead.

In all, 674 persons were listed as killed or missing. Three quarters of the city's residences and businesses burned, including almost the entire city center. More than half the city's population were homeless, with property loss estimated at $350 million. Nonetheless, San Franciscans remained remarkably upbeat. Survivors reported an almost holiday atmosphere in some tent cities. Relief funds poured in from around the country and many foreign countries. Japan sent the largest donation (a favor that San Francisco returned in the 1923 Tokyo quake).

Reconstruction started almost immediately. While government officials debated the merits of rebuilding on a newer, Paris-inspired street plan, merchants and homeowners went to work. Gutted buildings, like the Fairmont Hotel and the Merchants' Exchange, were quickly restored. Chinatown rose on its old site. South of Market districts started building vital new factories and warehouses. One after another, new theaters opened. Electric streetcars were installed, replacing cable car lines.

The citizens also took the opportunity to procure themselves a new government. Abe Ruef pleaded guilty to extortion, and was sentenced to 14 years in San Quentin Prison. Ex-Mayor Schmitz himself was awarded five years in exchange for 27 counts of graft and bribery; on appeal, however, his conviction was overturned. In 1912, with the city back on its feet, San Francisco found a mayor after its own heart in "Sunny Jim" Rolph. Mayor Rolph presided over construction of a brand new Civic Center and world's fair, the Panama Pacific International Exposition of 1915. Officially a celebration of the opening of the Panama Canal, the fair was San Francisco's boast to the world that it had recovered from 1906 with flying colors.

■ GROWTH OF THE MODERN CITY

After its amazing recovery from the devastation of 1906 and its hugely successful party in 1915, San Francisco began to win acclaim as "the city that knows how." Few cities have ever deserved the "can-do" reputation more than San Francisco during the first half of the 20th century. Girding itself with a new sea wall, it bored tunnels through its hills to run its new electric streetcars. New streets terraced up its steep hills, and whole tracts rose in the sandy wastes of the Richmond and Sunset districts. Stimulating the growth of new towns and farms in California, its banks led San Francisco to international stature as a financial center. In 1934 the city, entirely with local funding, dammed the canyon of Hetch Hetchy, 150 miles east in the Sierra Nevada, and linked it by aqueduct to the new reservoirs on the Peninsula. The following year, it commenced the first scheduled air service to the Orient, Pan Am's *China Clipper.*

Most amazingly, in the midst of the Great Depression, it confidently set out to build three of the biggest public works projects ever undertaken. The largest bridge in the world, the Oakland Bay Bridge, opened in 1936, followed five months later by the formidable link across the Golden Gate, then the planet's longest span. In 1939, the city completed construction of the largest man-made island in the world, Treasure Island, which was appropriated (before being turned over to the Navy) for a new world's fair, the Golden Gate International Exposition.

When labor and capital were not working together to conquer San Francisco's natural barriers, they were often wrestling with the social barriers between them. Labor's demands for better pay and an eight-hour work day were justified, but its methods and influence were sometimes pernicious. The Workingman's Party, during the bitter years of the late 19th century, was a leading instigator of anti-Chinese protest. The Union Labor Party had put Schmitz in office. Still, they were no worse than the robber barons of the Gilded Age, who damned the public while raking in millions.

Labor unrest continued into the new century. San Francisco restaurant workers, teamsters, and machinists went on strike in 1901, and railway workers followed in 1906. Laundry workers sought eight-hour days in 1907, and streetcar drivers walked off soon after. Tensions reached a climax on July 22, 1916, when Mayor Rolph organized a Preparedness Day Parade in anticipation of American entry into World War I. Many unionists blasted involvement in the war as a working-class burden and a diversion from domestic problems. In short, threats were made, and when a pipe bomb exploded along the parade route, killing 10 and injuring others, the unions were blamed. Two union militants, Tom Mooney and Warren Billings, were arrested, charged, and convicted—without sufficient evidence. For the next two decades they languished in prison, international symbols of labor's struggle, until the pair were released (and Mooney pardoned) in 1939.

The largest strike action in American history was the San Francisco longshoremen's walkout of May 1930. When strikebreakers tried to force the lines, two people were killed and scores injured in the ensuing riots. The union fought back with a call for a general strike, which closed down the city for four days, inspiring solidarity among other Bay Area communities. It ended with the longshoremen winning their demands.

The Great Depression ended early in San Francisco, thanks in part to the injection of jobs and money by the bridge construction projects. World War II brought even greater growth—embittered, of course, by bloody losses in Europe and the Pacific—as local shipyards cranked up to battle speed. One and a half million troops embarked for the Pacific theater from San Francisco, and the city watched anxiously as the Army built bunkers and batteries in anticipation of a Japanese invasion. Fortunately they were never needed. The big guns were obsolete before the war ended.

The war brought compounded tragedy to San Francisco's citizens of Japanese ancestry. Like other mainland issei, nisei, and sansei (first, second, and third generations of Japanese Americans), the San Francisco community was evacuated wholesale and imprisoned in camps. Despite the humiliation of their incarceration, more than 33,000 Japanese Americans (about a third of the total number detained) volunteered for military service. California's contingent, the 100th Battalion, had so many casualties in Europe that it was known as the Purple Heart Battalion. Joined with the Japanese-American 442nd Regiment from Hawaii, they fought through seven major campaigns, sustaining withering losses, and finished the war as the most heavily decorated regiment in American history. General "Vinegar Joe" Stilwell, who slogged through some of the bitterest fighting of World War II, bristled with feisty indignation when he spoke of the Japanese-American persecution and sacrifice: "They bought an awful hunk of America with their blood . . . you're damn right those nisei boys have a place in the American heart, now and forever. We cannot allow a single injustice to be done to the nisei without defeating the purpose for which we fought."

A vaulting triumph of human ingenuity: the Golden Gate Bridge.

■ NEW DIRECTIONS

The war brought great changes to San Francisco. Thousands of African Americans from the South, arriving to work in the shipyards during World War II, settled in Hunters Point and the Western Addition. The city's work force more than doubled as thousands of workers manned (and womanned) the wartime industries. Household economies and social patterns altered permanently as more women became breadwinners. The influx of new residents continued after the war ended. Suburban communities took the brunt of this new growth, unprecedented since the Gold Rush, as prosperous groups like the Italians (who were the dominant ethnic group in San Francisco for much of this century) and Irish started moving out in larger numbers.

The decades following the war also saw increased immigration from Asia and Latin America. A new atmosphere of tolerance had emerged from the war, fostered by American prosperity. Reformed immigration laws and overseas unrest, including the Chinese revolution of 1949, and the Korean and Vietnam wars, boosted the numbers of Asian immigrants. Many prospered. Chinese Americans replaced Italian Americans as San Francisco's largest ethnic group in the 1980s. Ironically, as burgeoning numbers of Chinese immigrants increasingly replace the American-born and European populations in many parts of North Beach, the Richmond, the Sunset, and other districts throughout the city, San Franciscans in greater numbers (including Asian Americans) are, more than a century after the anti-Chinese Geary Act, again expressing exasperation with Chinese immigration.

When the war ended and the yards closed or scaled down operations, many African Americans were unable to find work in the civil sector. Hunters Point and the Western Addition sank into localized depressions, deteriorating into slums. Though San Franciscans had learned to embrace Chinatown as a cultural (and tourist-industry) asset, they condemned these new inner-city ghettos as an embarrassing blight. During the 1950s and 1960s, clumsy government renovation efforts destroyed whole sectors of Victorian housing. Many of the poorly managed and inadequately policed government projects that replaced them would slide into drug-driven violence during the 1970s and 1980s, problems that have grown to epidemic proportions in the 1990s. San Franciscans were shaken to realize that their city was not immune from what they considered Eastern "rust belt" urban problems.

Today, the Golden Gate Bridge is admired both as an awesome accomplishment, as well as an elegant addendum to the Bay Area's natural beauty. (Kerrick James)

Looking at it from the outside, however, San Francisco of the 1950s and 1960s seemed to offer an urbane, unspoiled, and exciting alternative to the problem-plagued cities of the American Northeast. The beatniks and hippies were only the most visible heralds of San Francisco's growing reputation as a haven from the established mores and constraints of Middle America. San Francisco's tolerance of alternative thinking appealed to the American gay community and other groups whose views on health, conservation, the arts, society, religion, and politics ran counter to the established grain. This mix of new ideas and people brought new dynamism to city life. Middle America, however, called it madness.

Changes do not come without turmoil. Since the 1960s, cults, fads, and weird events have spawned on San Francisco's Bay like caddis flies. One of the strangest episodes was the February 1974 kidnapping of Patty Hearst, a wealthy local newspaper publisher's daughter, by a radical group called the Symbionese Liberation Army (SLA). Patty soon announced that she had joined up with her abductors for the revolution, leading the FBI on a violent trail of robbery and fiery death to her capture in San Francisco more than a year later. An even more bizarre episode transpired in November 1978, when a transplanted San Francisco group called the People's Temple, led by Jim Jones, committed mass suicide in the jungles of Guyana. That same month, an ex-city supervisor named Dan White, whose request for reinstatement had been rejected by Mayor George Moscone, assassinated the mayor and gay supervisor Harvey Milk, right in City Hall.

The decade of the '80s saw a rise in special-interest groups and single-issue politicians with no knack or desire for compromise, rendering the city's government incapable of clear consensus. Large-scale public works projects, like Yerba Buena Gardens and plans for the city's new ballpark, bogged down for years in political debate. As demonstrations, litigation, and ceaseless dickering continue to clog the city's arteries, thoughtful San Franciscans wondered if "the city that knows how" had lost its know-how.

The view from the end of the 20th century seems to bolster that notion. San Francisco's economy is more dependent on tourism than ever. At the heart of the matter is the fact that San Franciscans value style more than substance—a perfectly understandable attitude among people of urbane tastes, for indeed, it is beguiling to partake of a sophisticated city's many pleasures. But no great city can afford to confuse high style with dynamism, pastiche with vigor. Although San

Francisco yet remains dynamic in many ways—not least in its booming multimedia businesses, museums, arts, restaurants, parks, and entertainment venues—its citizens increasingly do not control the resources, factories, and financial institutions that built the city and maintained the infrastructure that generated the luxuries and cultural institutions that we take for granted. For a buck-fifty less than $5, we can indulge ourselves with pampered lattes in a thousand different store-front windows, but an honest cup of java poured from a thermos is as rare a sight as a longshoreman, bridge-builder, industrialist, or factory worker.

Today the port is virtually dead to commercial shipping. Most industries have moved out. Even large corporations, complaining of high rents and anti-business attitudes in San Francisco, are retreating to the suburbs or merging with out of state corporations. The AIDS epidemic drains millions of dollars from the local economy, and smothers thousands with a haunting fear. In the 1990s, the federal government slammed the Bay Area with the largest block of military base closures in the country, including San Francisco's Presidio and Treasure Island.

Still, the resources and spirit of creative entrepreneurship that built San Francisco have not retreated very far in every case. Nearby Silicon Valley is the world's center of the high-technology and biomedical fields. Oakland's neighboring port, while not exactly booming, is busy. Universities and research institutes around the Bay Area still turn out among the best educated and most creative citizens to be found anywhere. The fields and vineyards of the Central Valley and Wine Country still rank among the preeminent agricultural regions in the United States. All of Northern California still looks to San Francisco as its cultural and retail hub, and all benefit in turn by its worldwide reputation as the urbane complement to the natural wonders of the region's towering redwoods, spectacular coastline, and enchanting Sierra Nevada mountains. Taken altogether, San Francisco sits at the heart of what is arguably the world's most desirable place to live or to visit.

D O W N T O W N

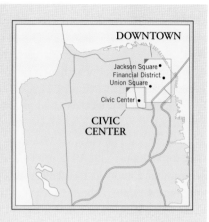

DOWNTOWN

Jackson Square •
Financial District •
Union Square •

Civic Center •

CIVIC
CENTER

SAN FRANCISCANS DIVIDE THEIR CITY INTO TWO ESTATES: the residential neighborhoods, and Downtown. The two, according to common perception, are locked in eternal conflict. To local politicians, downtown interests serve big business, conservatives, and suburbanite commuters, while the neighborhoods represent liberal politics, the socially and environmentally conscious, and minority views. There's a good deal of truth in this, as there is in most grossly oversimplified generalizations.

Downtown is San Francisco's interface with the rest of the world. Every working day, some 225,000 people from the 'burbs (suburbs, exurbs) jam the bridges, trains, MUNI, BART, ferries, streets, and sidewalks—not to mention parking lots—in a herculean effort to staff the offices and drive the wheels of international commerce. And needless to say, every evening finds them strangling the highways and skyways in a frantic rush to go home again. Fortunately for San Francisco, they don't take the keys with them. The lights of the grand hotels, shops, fine restaurants, and bars continue to blaze long after the offices close down for the night, catering in part to the thousands of San Franciscans who also *live* downtown.

In a city renowned for spectacular entrances, there's none more exhilarating than the high road from Oakland across the Bay Bridge, when, rising from the water, San Francisco bursts into view, an urbane, stunning, civilized vision of hills and towers.

Downtown San Francisco and the Financial District were built to a compact, walkable scale. All the key touchstones—banks, brokers, exchanges, law offices,

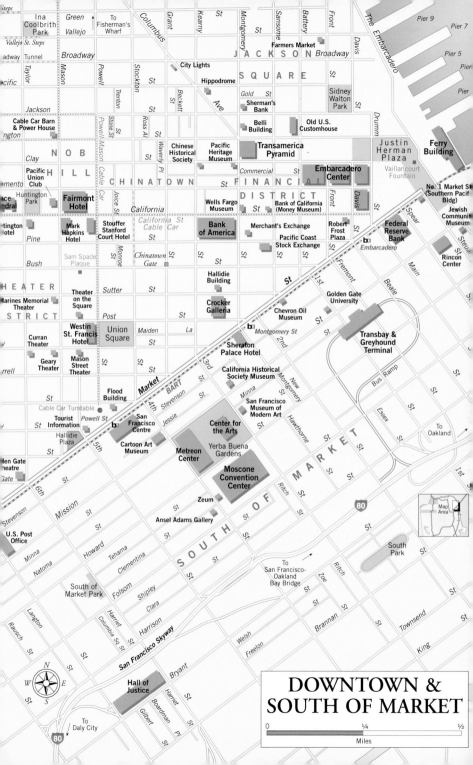

DOWNTOWN & SOUTH OF MARKET

0   ¼   ½
Miles

clubs, shopping areas, theaters, toney watering holes—are within ready walking distance from one another, and mercifully free of the city's infamously steep hills. The Financial District rose on land filled in where Yerba Buena Cove once lapped at the feet of Rincon, Telegraph, Nob, and Russian Hills. Hundreds of Gold Rush ships abandoned here in 1849 still lie at anchor today, beneath the streets and foundations of America's Wall Street West.

■ UNION SQUARE AND THE SHOPPING DISTRICT

Powell slams into Market at **Hallidie Plaza**, crossroads of the city. The lion's share of San Francisco's hotels are located nearby, as are many prominent theaters, restaurants, art galleries, shops, and department stores. The cable cars prelude their clanging journey to Nob Hill, Chinatown, and Fisherman's Wharf with a clumsy, yet charming, pirouette on the Powell Street turntable. Here, the trajectories of callow executives from nearby office buildings collide with the paths of sheepish tourists, a small army of panhandlers, suburbanites with shopping bags, and park-bench prophets ruminating on the world's end. Meanwhile, information and maps can be gathered at the main **Convention and Visitors Bureau** office, downstairs near the Powell Street BART station; *415-391-2000.*

San Francisco's downtown retail shopping district is the second largest in the country in terms of sales, and it whips number one, New York's Fifth Avenue, for compactness and convenience. The district is well served by buses and the Powell Street station of BART and MUNI, and has more than 5,500 parking spaces for those shortsighted shoppers who insist on driving. And believe me, you might have to wait to get one of those spaces.

◆ UNION SQUARE

Union Square, at the heart of the shopping district, was named for the pro-Union rallies held here during the Civil War, when there was a controversy whether California (and its gold) would throw in its lot with the North or South. Largely by the oratory of San Francisco preacher Thomas Starr King, the city went firmly pro-Union; and as San Francisco went, so went the state. Union Square is now the grassy roof of the world's first underground multilevel parking garage. A statue commemorating Dewey's victory at Manila during the Spanish-American War gathers pigeons at center stage. Flower stands at the square's busy corners splash color through the streets, while local color of the human variety gathers in and around the square.

◆ Shopping District Highlights

Westin Saint Francis

This landmark hotel on the west side of Union Square was gutted in the 1906 fire, but was promptly rebuilt to its present glory. You can stroll through the elegant arcade, or rocket to the top of the new tower annex in spectacular, outside glass elevators. It was here that President Gerald Ford made his lucky escape from an assassin's bullet in 1975. *335 Powell St.; 415-397-7000.*

Macy's

Occupying two city blocks, the New York-based institution is now the largest department store in the city. The Yuletide madrigals and cheerful lighting displays during the holidays will put you in mind of a fine old Washington Irving Christmas, too. *Main entrance at Stockton and O'Farrell Sts.; 415-397-3333.*

Nieman Marcus

This fashionable emporium occupies the old site of the City of Paris, a San Francisco retail landmark born in the 1890s. The current building retains the old stained-glass dome, now arching over the entrance. The Rotunda Restaurant, on an upper level of the open vestibule, is a suave perch for taking afternoon tea and watching the crowds. *150 Stockton St.; 415-362-3900.*

San Francisco Centre

More than 100 shops occupy this "vertical mall," but the main tenant is the Nordstrom department store. The building boasts the country's first semi-spiral escalators, which wind mantra-like up the eight-story central well to a dome that opens to the sky on fine days. There's usually someone tickling the ivories on the sixth floor, close to the atrium. *Corner of Market and Fifth Sts.*

At San Francisco Centre, shoppers descend from Nordstrom on semi-spiral escalators.

Rare Book Shops

Union Square is ground zero for the rare book trade in San Francisco, where you might find anything from illuminated medieval texts to a signed first edition of John Muir. Among the many preeminent dealers are John Scopazzi *(130 Maiden Lane; 415-362-5708)*, specializing in rare maps as well as books; Argonaut Books *(786 Sutter St.; 415-474-9067)* focusing on California titles and Western Americana; and The Bookstall *(570 Sutter St.; 415-362-6353)* and Emmett Harrington *(Third floor, 251 Post St.; 415-646-0060)*, both offering a more general stock. The greatest treasure box of old books sits at 49 Geary, where you'll find no fewer than five antiquarian dealers.

Maiden Lane

Now a rather refined pedestrian thoroughfare leading east from Union Square, Maiden Lane has a risque past. She was once none other than notorious Morton Street, yet another of San Francisco's red-light districts. Frank Lloyd Wright designed the **Circle Gallery Building**, a smaller version, but an obvious prototype, of his famed spiral interior in the Guggenheim Museum in New York. It now houses three galleries with awesome collections of folk art, tribal art, and jewelry from around the world: **Folk Art International, Xanadu Tribal Arts,** and **Boretti Amber and Designs.** *140 Maiden Lane; 415-392-9999.*

Gump's

This lavish San Francisco institution has an Old-World feel that matches the rarity of its wares. Much of what they sell you will not find anywhere else, for Gump's specializes in one-of-a-kind treasures. Their jade collection is renowned the world-round. Their furniture and decorations are works of art, and their works of art are, well, exceedingly expensive. Sally Stanford, San Francisco's favorite madame (and a woman of discriminating tastes), once referred to Gump's as "the Metropolitan Museum with cash registers. . . ." *135 Post St.; 415-982-1616.*

Crocker Galleria

An attractive arcade of gardens and shops under a barrel-vaulted roof, flooding the place with natural light, the elegant Galleria was inspired by the Vittorio Emmanuelle of Milan, Italy. Its rooftop gardens are an inviting place to catch some sun and relaxation. *Bounded by Post, Montgomery, Sutter, and Kearny Sts.*

Hallidie Building

Framed at the northern end of the Galleria, the Hallidie Building is reputed to be the world's first glass-curtain-walled building. (If glass-curtain walling fails to induce shivers up and down your spine, try thinking of it as the original glass-walled skyscraper.) When architect Willis Polk completed it in 1918, he was way ahead of his time. Polk, who left his mark throughout San Francisco, was a man devoted to perfection, and indifferent to the petty interests of ordinary mortals. Once, when a New York corporate potentate seeking his services tried to praise his designs, the architect replied, "I would feel complimented if I thought you knew anything about art." *130 Sutter St.; 415-362-7397.*

(right) A street musician plies his trade on Maiden Lane (Kerrick James).

■ SOUTH OF MARKET

No part of San Francisco has changed so much and so fast as the area south of Market Street. Wealthy people began to flock to the up-and-coming residential enclave of Rincon Hill in the 1850s, but they just as rapidly left it when the new cable cars turned Nob Hill into the city's mansion district. As the rich took flight, middle-class, and later working-class, people moved in. The district became known as South o' the Slot, in reference to the cable car lines (which have slots for the cables) that ran up Market Street. In the 1906 fire, the blocks of cheap wooden houses burned so fast and hot that iron melted. The district was rebuilt with factories, warehouses, train yards, and businesses serving the port at China Basin. For the next 70 years, select streets of South of Market, particularly Howard, were known as Skid Row.

◆ SOUTH OF MARKET INTO "SOMA"

Today, most of the factories, train yards, and warehouses have closed or moved away. The sailors, and many of the hotels that catered to them, have followed the port out of town. Even the drunks and other sad down-and-outers have mostly moved up to Fifth Street and beyond. In deference to New York's SoHo (South of Houston) district, South of Market is known as "SoMa." Like SoHo, SoMa's gentrifying vanguard were the painters, photographers, sculptors, and multimedia artists who moved into the low-rent warehouses and abandoned factories, converting them into studios. On their heels came factory retail outlets for designer clothes, with lunch-time cafes in their train, and nightspots catering to a mostly young and city-savvy crowd.

Meanwhile, rising land values north of Market were pushing the Financial District steadily south of Market along an expanding frontier line of offices and restaurants. The opening of the Moscone Convention Center, Yerba Buena Gardens, hotels, restaurants, and suave residential developments are attracting ever larger numbers of middle-class residents and visitors to SoMa. Along the shore as far south as the China Basin wharves, even the old harbor has been gussied up into docks for private pleasure craft. Like the sailors and pensioners before them, the struggling artists and factory outlets are in retreat—though many still hold their own in the nether regions south of Folsom and west of Fifth.

Also holding their own are some of the nightclubs opened here in the '80s, especially those farther south along Harrison and Folsom, which have become established dance and music venues. Meanwhile, new (or newly named) hotspots seem to pop up every week. Leave your car parked on Folsom and Seventh on a Saturday night, and you'll come back to a windshield littered with flashy postcard notices for one-night-a-week clubs like "New Wave City" or "Trannyshack."

◆ SOUTH PARK

South Park, on the other hand, is a quirky remnant of the area's brief fling as San Francisco's pedigreed residential district. Built in 1856 on a plan inspired by London's Berkeley Square, the oval park was fenced and surrounded by mansions, whose owners kept the keys to the gate. With the invention of cable cars, the rich departed South Park for Nob Hill, abandoning it to poorer families, factories, warehouses, and sailor hotels. It bottomed out as a skid row when construction of the Bay Bridge leveled Rincon Hill for a western anchorage. South Park remained depressed until recently, when artists, designers, and small software- and Web-related companies discovered that its abandoned warehouses made great studios. Now, a wealthier class is once again returning. The sidewalk tables of the South Park Cafe add a touch of class to the oval. Jack London was born in 1876 around the corner from South Park, at 615 Third Street. The house burned in the fire of 1906, but the approximate site is marked by a plaque.

South Park is a quirky remnant of the area's brief fling as the city's pedigreed residential district. Today you'll find cafes, boutiques, and Internet-related firms. (Kerrick James)

◆ SoMa Highlights

Yerba Buena Gardens and Environs

The symbolic heart of new SoMa is Yerba Buena Gardens, a committee-designed green where artist and patron, convention-eer and tourist all meet on common turf. Decades passed from its first proposal till its opening in autumn of 1993, and many more years will pass before all the full contingent of promised gardens, playgrounds, hotels, and museums see light of day.

Center for the Arts at Yerba Buena

Anchoring one corner of the square, the Center for the Arts comprises galleries for the visual arts, a sculpture court with changing exhibits and statues, and a 755-seat theater. Balancing the sum are an ice-skating rink and a beautiful old working carousel. **The Esplanade Gardens** and dining terraces are very pleasant oases in the midst of a metropolis; in summer, noontime concerts and dance performances draw crowds of office workers on their lunch break. A rushing waterfall partially conceals the **Martin Luther King Jr. Memorial**, comprised of panels translated into several languages, advocating peace and tolerance.

Moscone Center

The vanguard of SoMa's development was Moscone Center, San Francisco's prime convention complex. Named for San Francisco's assassinated mayor, George Moscone, the exhibit hall is an engineering curiosity well worth contemplating, if you happen to be there anyway. The arched roof supports are designed like a series of great, taut hunting bows, with the ends strung together by cables running under the floor. By tightening the cables, structural engineer T. Y. Lin was able to spring enough upward thrust to counter the enormous weight of the ground-level gardens on the roof, without employing a single interior column. The result is a vast, open hall, one of the largest underground spaces in the world. *Entire block of Howard between Third, Fourth, and Folsom Streets.*

S.F. Museum of Modern Art

Across the street from Yerba Buena Gardens stands the dazzling home of the San Francisco Museum of Modern Art, with five floors of galleries designed around a spectacular skylight, vast collections of paintings and works on paper, sculpture, architectural drawings, furniture and graphic design, photography, video, film, and other time-based media, the museum also boasts works by Georgia O'Keeffe, Andy Warhol, Imogen Cunningham, Paul Klee, Willem de Kooning, and others, including Diego Rivera's *The Flower Carrier,* Jackson Pollock's *Guardians of the Secret,* Picasso's *Women of Algiers,* and *Woman with a Hat,* by Matisse. All the major schools and artists of the 20th century are represented, with substantial holdings of German Expressionism, Fauvism, and American Abstract Expressionism; numerous pieces by Mexican and California artists round out the exhibits.

The biggest attraction, however, is the building itself; Swiss architect Mario Botta's classically receding hallways, dramatic spaces, and curiously placed picture

Natural light floods the atrium and catwalk inside the Museum of Modern Art. (Kerrick James)

windows are very much enhanced themselves by the works of art that they are meant to enhance. A 125-foot skylight, gingerly crossed on the top floor by a dramatic footbridge, scoops in most of the light for the museum's five sprawling stories. There's a decent cafe, and the bookshop is one of the West's largest retailers of art books, posters, cards, catalogs, artistic toys, and T-shirts. *151 Third St.; 415-357-4000.*

Sony Metreon

This four-story, high-tech entertainment complex is basically a shopping mall full of brand-name technology stores and well-endowed with cinemas—15 standard screens and one 600-seat IMAX theater. What sets this mall apart from others are the several "interactive attractions," a unique array of amusements that you can lay your mitts on, or even step into. For instance, there's a walk-in re-creation of Maurice Sendak's *Where the Wild Things Are,* and another based on David Macaulay's book *The Way Things Work.* The biggest hit among older kids and adults is the Airtight Garage, a high-tech video arcade. Among the games is the Virtual Bowling alley, where you can heave a bowling ball down one of San Francisco's steepest streets without causing any havoc or damage. *Third St. between Mission and Howard; 415-537-3400.*

Ansel Adams Center

On the western side of Yerba Buena Gardens, the Ansel Adams Center hosts five galleries devoted to the art of photography, as well as a research library, bookstore, photography classes, and other programs. One gallery is permanently set aside for the work of San Francisco native Ansel Adams, whose

black-and-white landscapes of Yosemite and the American West are among the world's most widely recognized photographs. *250 Fourth St.; 415-495-7000.*

Cartoon Art Museum

This quirky museum devotes itself to the preservation and study of a vigorous American art form, the cartoon. On top of its rotating displays, this small archive maintains a gift shop and permanent library of comic books, editorial cartoons, comic strips, animation, advertising, greeting card art, and more. *814 Mission St.; 415-227-8666.*

California Historical Society

This venerable organization culls its changing exhibits from its large archival collection of manuscripts, photographs, books, prints, paintings, maps, and other documents from California's colorful past. *678 Mission St.; 415-357-1848.*

Pacific Bell Museum

Occupying a room off the ornate lobby of the 1925 Pacific Tel and Tel headquarters building, this small museum displays an assorted selection of telephone equipment and trinkets, some dating to the 1870s. *140 New Montgomery; 415-542-0182.*

Zeum

At this high-tech, hands-on museum for the digital generation, kids and teens can use computers to learn how to do animation, video production, and Internet broadcasting. Parents watching attentively over their childrens' shoulders might also learn a thing or two. Younger kids will have a blast at the

adjacent carousel, while old-timers may enjoy a pang of nostalgia when they recognize it as the magical old merry-go-round from the long-defunct Playland at Ocean Beach. *221 Fourth St.; 415-777-2800.*

Jewish Community Museum

This excellent museum mounts rotating exhibits on Jewish history and culture. Past exhibits have dealt with such diverse themes as Jewish ghetto life in 15th-century Italy, the plight of Ethiopian Jews in Israel, and political art inspired by the trial and 1953 execution of Julius and Ethel Rosenberg. *121 Steuart St.; 415-543-8880.*

SS Jeremiah O'Brien

Just a short stroll south of the Bay Bridge is the *SS Jeremiah O'Brien,* the last Liberty Ship still in regular operation. It carried grain, arms, and cargo in both the Atlantic and the Pacific during World War II, and it was present at the D-Day invasion. Visitors always have free run of the ship, but try to see it when the steam's up and crew's aboard, when you can climb to the chart room for a chat with the captain, or crank around the gun turrets under orders of the gunnery mate. You'll skirt pounding pistons and scalding pipes, as you descend to the stifling engine room, a spectacle of well-crafted and cared-for machinery. Squeeze down the narrow screw shaft passage to the ship's stern. The crew fires up the engines on the third weekend of every month, except December. *Pier 32, at the foot of Brannan St.; 415-441-3101.*

(previous pages) Yerba Buena Gardens is a peaceful oasis amid the hustle of downtown. (Kerrick James)

■ THE MARKET STREET CORRIDOR

Market Street is San Francisco's main transport corridor, where BART and MUNI rush commuters in and out through tubes and tunnels, while buses, taxis, cars, bikes, and pedestrians vie for space above. When Jasper O'Farrell laid out the street plan in 1847, he envisioned Market as a grand thoroughfare cutting in a wide diagonal from the bay to the foot of Twin Peaks. But O'Farrell failed to foresee the havoc his plan would wreak on modern traffic. North of Market, he laid out small, human-scale city blocks in a grid aligned on a north-south axis. South of Market, he planned a much larger grid, better suited for vehicular traffic than pedestrians, and running roughly on a northwest-southeast axis. In consequence, every street intersecting Market hits at an awkward angle, and worse, the streets north of Market never meet the ones from the south, except by luck or some fancy driving. Instead of becoming a focal point for the Financial District, Market Street became the barrier to its southward expansion for the next 140 years. The barrier was breached on a large scale only in the 1970s, thanks to building-height restrictions and spiraling real-estate prices north of Market.

Palace Hotel

Opposite the strategic intersection where Montgomery spills into Market, William Ralston built the Palace Hotel in 1873. With well over 700 rooms, it was the largest and most celebrated hostelry in the world at the time. Ralston had big plans for his small city, and furnished the hotel with little regard for reason or expense. Champagne and oysters were standard fare, and traveling royalty made it their home away from home. From the Crystal Roof Garden on the top floor, resident millionaires gazed down upon the carriages arriving in the Grand Court, seven stories below. Oscar Wilde and Rudyard Kipling lodged at the Palace in the 1880s, and opera sensation Enrico Caruso got the snub of his career here on an April morning in 1906, when he was rudely awakened by a falling ceiling. The Palace burned in the fire that followed, and the heartily offended virtuoso left town swearing never to return.

A new Palace rose on the foundations of the old. Make a point to visit it, if only for a peek at the elegant **Garden Court**, inspired by the earlier Grand Court and one of the most grandiose dining rooms in the city. The famous Maxfield Parrish painting of the Pied Piper of Hamelin in **Maxfield's Restaurant** evokes strong memories of long-forgotten bedtime stories.

Rand McNally Bookstore

A block east of the Palace Hotel, the excellent Rand McNally travel bookstore offers an enormous selection of maps, atlases, and books, as well as a vast selection of travel accessories. *Corner of Second and Market Sts.; 415-777-3131.*

American Indian Contemporary Arts

American Indian Contemporary Arts exhibits crafts and art of the many native cultures of the United States. Hand-made Navajo blankets and jewelry, books, art, traditional clothing, taped music, and various other cultural treasures are sold in the gallery shop. *23 Grant St., Sixth floor; 415-989-7003.*

Chevron Oil Museum

At the Chevron Oil Museum in the Standard Oil Building, you can try your hand at discovering oil reserves by computer. *555 Market; 415-894-7700.*

Federal Reserve Bank

Anyone uninitiated in the workings of the Financial District will want to stop by for an explanation at the Federal Reserve Bank, where they may study an interpretive display and film explaining its role as the "bankers' bank." *100 Market; 415-974-2000.*

Rincon Center

Rincon Center incorporates a 1940 post office annex. The murals on the annex walls stirred bitter controversy when painted after World War II by Anton Refregier, a Russian immigrant, because they showed the dirt under San Francisco's nails. A case in point is his rendition of Vigilante Days, depicting the assassination of James King of William by James Casey, while a menacing Vigilante Committee marches in the background and a man gets lynched. Other panels illustrate the anti-Chinese rabble-rousing, the transcontinental railway, the Mooney case, the 1906 earthquake, and an imaginary convocation of writers associated with San Francisco, including Mark Twain, Bret Harte, Jack London, Robert Louis Stevenson, and Ambrose Bierce. Through the modest annex door, the center bursts into a soaring atrium surrounded by little bistros and soothed by the patter of a rain column falling 85 feet from the lofty skylight. *Encompasses the entire block bounded by Mission, Howard, Steuart, and Spear Sts.*

Number One Market Street

The Southern Pacific railroad was the successor of the Central Pacific, builder of the first transcontinental railway, linking California to the East. The railroad also opened enormous tracts of California to farming and settlement, while acquiring vast landholdings and influence. By the latter third of the 19th century, railroad corporations had become the most powerful private institutions in the state. Frank Norris fiercely attacked their monopolistic rape of a Central Valley farming community in his novel *The Octopus.* In Number One Market Street, architects Michael Paynor and Associates incorporated the 1917 Southern Pacific Building into their 1978 structure, which features a huge mosaic clock, an indoor plaza, and a cheerful fountain that curtains off a plaza restaurant.

(left) Old San Francisco's dash and opulence were mirrored in the original Palace Hotel.

■ ALONG THE EMBARCADERO

Market Street terminates its long run through the city just short of the Embarcadero, a wide road built atop a sea wall stretching six miles from China Basin in the south to Fisherman's Wharf in the north. Up and down the Embarcadero's length spreads further testimony to the past glories of San Francisco's port. The docks and wharves along Embarcadero once roared and clanged with people and ships at work. Freighters, schooners, steamers, passenger liners, merchant ships, ferries, junks, square riggers, fishing boats, destroyers, and whaling barks have all, in their respective times, crowded these docks, where longshoremen and sailors labored hard and raised hell in the nearby saloons, chophouses, and flophouses. Virtually all are gone now, lost to the "mainland" ports of Oakland and Long Beach. Palm trees now march down the new Embarcadero, which is lined on the waterfront by a broad promenade, Herb Caen Way, named for the beloved *Chronicle* columnist. Joggers, cyclists, skateboarders, and lunching worker bees from nearby highrises now make brisk use of the open spaces and stirring views.

◆ EMBARCADERO HIGHLIGHTS

Ferry Building

On the bay at the foot of Market Street stands the Ferry Building, built in 1898 and for many years serving as the gateway to the city. Completed in 1903, it survived the 1906 holocaust through heroic effort of fireboat crews, and went on to become the second busiest transport terminal in the world, after London's Charing Cross Railway Station. Up to 50 million passengers every year crossed the gangways of 170 daily ferries binding San Francisco to the American "mainland." All that ended with the opening of the Bay Bridge in 1937. Today, the Ferry Building is a shadow of its former preeminence. Its once-beckoning wings have been converted to offices. On the pier, a lifelike statue of Mahatma Gandhi, symbol of peaceful resistance and founder of the Indian state, is frozen in vigorous stride.

Ferries

As the names implies, the Ferry Building is indeed the place to catch a boat out of the city. Ferries depart for **Oakland's Jack London Square** *(see page 241)*, a 20-minute sail that slides under the Bay Bridge and past Yerba Buena and Treasure Islands; **Sausalito** *(see page 218)*, a charming waterfront town; and **Larkspur Landing** in Marin County, by way of a route used primarily by commuters that offers a lovely ride right up the middle of the bay past Angel Island and the swaybacked Richmond–San Rafael Bridge. All three destinations are enjoyable in their own right, though the journey across the bay— the bracing salt air and stirring views of bridges, hills, and sail boats—is a joy unto itself. *For information on the Oakland ferry, call 415-705-5555; for Sausalito and Larkspur Landing, call 415-923-2000.*

(right) Skaters and strollers jam the Embarcadero on a sunny day. (Kerrick James)

Pier Seven and Adjacent Wharves

Pier Seven remains the city's longest wharf, a public promenade bedecked with genteel benches and lampposts, utilitarian fish-gutting sinks, and stirring views of bridge, bay, hill, and tower. From the Ferry Building south to beyond the Bay Bridge, the wharves have been razed, affording spectacular views of bridge and harbor that no doubt compensate for the high cost of living in the fancy new housing developments that fan out south of the bridge.

Farmer's Market

Overflowing with locally grown organic produce that ranges from the everyday to the exotic, this long-running outdoor marketplace is held from 8 A.M. to 1 P.M. on Saturday, and afternoons on Tuesday, in a parking lot at the corner where Green Street meets the Embarcadero.

Justin Herman Plaza

The Financial District meets the Ferry Building at Justin Herman Plaza, where banks of steps and al fresco tables gather a bustling lunchtime crowd of brown-baggers in business suits. In winter, an outdoor ice-skating rink attracts participants and spectators alike.

Vaillancourt Fountain

The plaza's focal point is the Vaillancourt Fountain, a colossal work of public art that provokes strong passions of love and hate. Those who love it find it dynamic and hugely inviting on hot days. At least one wag, who presumably weighs in on the denigrators' side, has likened it to something left by a gargantuan dog with square bowels. Its designer, Mr. Vaillancourt, gave San Francisco another display of his talents in 1987, when a musician from the rock group U2 vented his artistic expression with spray paint across the fountain. Hearing of the vandalism, Vaillancourt caught a flight from Montreal to San Francisco in time to repay the group in kind across their concert stage.

Embarcadero Center

Behind and above Justin Herman Plaza sprawls Embarcadero Center, an urbane oasis consisting of four high-rise buildings—Embarcadero One through Four—linked together by landscaped walkways, bridges, patios, and courtyards. The 41st floor of Embarcadero One is open to the public as an observation platform, the **Skydeck,** boasting the highest view from a downtown building that can be had without buying a drink or getting a job, though you do have to shell out $7 for a ticket; *415-772-0555.*

Of Embarcadero Center's many fine shops, restaurants, and hotels catering to a largely corporate clientele, the showpiece is the **Hyatt Regency Hotel**, with its spectacular atrium, dripping with vines from the open-sided corridors lofting 17 stories above. The nucleus of the atrium is a four-story sculptured ball by Charles Perry, set amid a rippling creek and lush trees. Glass elevators glide silently up and down the walls and through the ceiling to the **Equinox,** a revolving cocktail lounge suspended in the midst of glittering towers; *415-788-1234.*

■ FINANCIAL DISTRICT

Just outside the Hyatt's front door, where California intersects Market, the California Street cable car begins its run from **Robert Frost Plaza** to Van Ness Avenue. Frost, the beloved New England poet, was in fact a native son of San Francisco. Though he moved away while still a boy, Frost never forgot the city of his childhood, and wrote fondly:

> *Such was life in the Golden Gate:*
> *Gold dusted all we drank and ate,*
> *And I was one of the children told,*
> *We all must eat our peck of gold.*

Those who bypass the cable car in favor of walking can explore the heart of the Financial District. Reminders of San Francisco's days as queen of the Wild West can still be found amid the far more overwhelming symbols of the booming present. Along flag-bedecked California Street, the best monuments of postmodern architecture blend sky-scraping power with touches of humanity. The round tower at **101 California**, designed by Philip Johnson and John Burgee, sports an Italianate plaza with flower-filled urns and a greenhouse lobby. **California Center**, standing at 222 Sansome, is a massive building straddling handsome shopping arcades and houses the spectacular **Mandarin Oriental Hotel** in its crown—twin towers linked by sensational glass "skybridges," guaranteed to knock the toupee off anyone suffering from vertigo.

Financial District activity is most concentrated at the intersection of Montgomery and California. Raked by honking horns and pounding jackhammers, the district's flavor shows up best during business hours, when frantic bike messengers in tribal regalia ride breakneck through the bustling streets, and the bistros and restaurants buzz with big-money deals. With all due respect to Wyatt Earp and Bat Masterson, it was the banking establishment of San Francisco who *really* won the West. Behind these mild-mannered facades whir the financial dynamos that powered the growth of mines, farms, towns, factories, and transport arteries, driving the frontier farther and farther east, till it finally died of exhaustion in the barren wilds of the Rocky Mountains. Unfortunately for San Francisco's once-vaunted reputation as a powerhouse financial center, the last two years of the 1990s saw the mighty Bank of America bought and moved out of state, while the Pacific Stock Exchange announced plans to close its trading floor, a victim of Internet trading.

◆ FINANCIAL DISTRICT HIGHLIGHTS

Museum of the Money of the American West

The Bank of California, oldest banking corporation in the state, built its 1908 headquarters on California Street, and is now the Union Bank of California. This was the bank of William Ralston, who bankrolled one of the Comstock's greatest bonanzas. The tidy little collection features gold nuggets, minting paraphernalia, and mementos of the Comstock. Most intriguing are the pistols used in the notorious duel between California Chief Justice David S. Terry and U.S. Senator David Broderick. Judge Terry was a Southerner and supporter of slavery, Senator Broderick an ardent Union man. Neither got along politically or personally, and their bandied insults finally resulted in a challenge and acceptance. They met at Lake Merced on the morning of September 15, 1859, with Judge Terry supplying the pistols. On the toss of a coin, he also won first choice. Such details might have stayed mere footnotes of history had not the gun presented to Senator Broderick misfired. Judge Terry immediately returned fire, and plugged Broderick in the chest. Broderick died a martyr, Terry was hissed as a villain, and pro-Union sympathies soared in California. Take a close look at those pistols; 13 decades ago, there were many who'd have envied you the chance. *Basement, 400 California St.; 415-765-0400.*

Pacific Heritage Museum

The original U.S. Subtreasury Building was erected in 1875 on the site of San Francisco's first U.S. Mint, which operated there from 1854 to 1874. The sturdy walls and basement coin vaults of the old Subtreasury have now been magnanimously incorporated into the modern Bank of Canton tower, and transformed into this elegant museum, a skylit venue for changing exhibits of Asian art. *608 Commercial St.; 415-399-1124.*

Pacific Coast Stock Exchange

The country's largest stock exchange outside New York is the Pacific Coast Stock Exchange. Visitors may enter only by special arrangement, but you can usually catch a glimpse of the oft-frantic trading action through the open front door. *Corner of Pine and Sansome Sts.; 415-393-4198.*

Bank of America Building

This massive, 52-story skyscraper was built in 1969 for what was then the largest bank in the world. In 1998 Bank of America was bought by a North Carolina bank, and the headquarters headed out of town. The building still supports a sizable workday population, and after 3 P.M., when the top-floor Bankers Club transforms into the Carnelian Room, it offers some of the best views of the city open to the general public; *52nd floor; 415-433-7500.* On the plaza below, the large, hard, fist-like sculpture of black marble is known by Financial District clerks as *The Banker's Heart*. (Its real name is *Transcendence*, by Masayuki Nagari.) *555 California St.*

Wells Fargo History Room

Wells Fargo, a name that still calls up images of cracking whips and rattling coaches, keeps the vision alive in this museum where an original Wells Fargo stagecoach, maps, weapons, and displays of Western paraphernalia crowd the two floors. Among the most interesting items are samples of Emperor Norton's currency and memorabilia of one Charles E. Bolton, alias Charles Boles, alias Black Bart. Bart was a dapper little guy who, in the 1870s and '80s, made his living by highway robbery. His fame rests not only on his 28 stage holdups, but on the leaves of doggerel that he occasionally left behind with the pilfered strong boxes, signed "Black Bart, Po8."

I rob the rich to feed the poor,
Which hardly is a sin;
A widow ne'er knocked at my door
But what I let her in.

So blame me not for what I've done,
I don't deserve your curses,
And if for any cause I'm hung,
Let it be for my verses.

Unfortunately for Bart and po8try lovers, he carelessly dropped a handkerchief at a robbery. Special Detective Harry N. Morse traced it to a San Francisco laundry, and was waiting there when Charles Bolton came to call. Engaging him in conversation about mining ventures, the detective invited Bolton back to his offices at Wells Fargo and Company, where he promptly arrested him. After serving four years of a seven-year sentence, he was paroled for good behavior, and was never heard from—as bandit or bard—again. *420 Montgomery; 415-369-2619.*

◆ TRANSAMERICA PYRAMID AND THE "MONKEY BLOCK"

The most distinctive landmark of San Francisco's skyline, the Transamerica Pyramid, rises at the end of Leidesdorff. At 853 feet, it is the tallest building in the city. On a warm day, to sit in the shade of the redwood grove growing on its eastern side is a delicious pleasure. When the fog blows in, parting at the needle like a silent, pale river round a monolithic rock, it's an almost Zen-like experience.

The Pony Express once stopped across the street, at Montgomery and Merchant, where a plaque marks the end of the 1,966-mile run from St. Joseph, Missouri. Yet it is the Pyramid's site itself that is most haunted by history, and most mourned by those who love San Francisco. The Montgomery Block, affectionately known as the Monkey Block by many generations of citizens, once stood here. Built in 1853 by the soon-to-be Civil War general, Henry Halleck, it was for decades the largest, sturdiest building west of the Mississippi, accommodating law offices, newspapers, and bars that contributed enormously to the culture and history of the city. Here it was that James Casey gunned down James King of William in 1855, activating the Second Vigilance Committee, which hanged Casey for his crime. It was here also that Mark Twain met the original Tom Sawyer, who owned a Turkish bath in the basement, and where he downed Pisco Punches in the Exchange Saloon while admiring the painting of Samson and Delilah above the bar (as did most male patrons, noted Twain). Twain kept rooms here, as did Ambrose Bierce, George Sterling, Frank Norris, Charlie Stoddard, Joaquin Miller, Gelett Burgess, and other writers. Dr. Sun Yat-sen also settled in for a spell to write the English version of the Chinese constitution while on world tour in quest of funds for the revolution. And at the turn of the century, Pappa Coppa's restaurant on this site was San Francisco's most frequented rendezvous of bohemian writers, poets, and artists, who decorated the walls with their works. Thus, through peace, revolution, rollicking nights, decadence, and stolidity, the Monkey Block nursed—in classic San Francisco style—as egalitarian an array of characters as ever graced a city. It survived the earthquake and, even more remarkably, the fire of 1906, but it could not survive the wrecker's ball, and fell for a parking lot in 1959.

(right) The Financial District and the 853-foot-tall Transamerica Pyramid, the city's tallest building, rise before the hills of San Francisco. (Kerrick James)

■ JACKSON SQUARE

On to the Barbary Coast, nowadays more properly called the **Jackson Square Historical District,** which is found across Washington Street north of the Pyramid. Once infamous as the most perverted hellhole on Earth, San Francisco's Barbary Coast in its heyday set standards of wickedness and depravity that would have made Shanghai blush. At least that's the legend; whatever it was *really* like—and no doubt it was a mean and dirty place—it couldn't *possibly* compare with the legend.

Spawned in the Gold Rush to cater to the lusts of a huge city of males drained of hope and with no passage home, the Barbary Coast coaxed the worst of mankind to do their worst, and the best to do no better. The Coast's main thoroughfare was Pacific Street, known to aficionados as "Terrific Pacific," a string of saloons, gambling dens, raunchy dance halls, and other attractions stretching some half a dozen blocks west from the waterfront. Choice sections of the Coast acquired their own sobriquets: Murderer's Corner, Battle Row, Devil's Acre, Dead Man's Alley. Brutality, prostitution, murder, drunkenness, and bestiality were commonplace. Vicious men lurched through torchlit streets, meeting casual death in grog shops with names like the Morgue, the Goat and Compass, Bull Run, and Devil's Kitchen. Human beings were reduced to the lowest forms in performances of the grossest degradation. Hundreds of prostitutes worked the "cowyards" in narrow cribs stacked up to four stories high, or performed on stages with horses, pigs, and grizzly bears. One pathetic creature known as Oofty Goofty built a reputation by selling the privilege of beating him with a baseball bat across the backside, until the fighter John L. Sullivan crippled him with a pool cue for 50 cents. Another gent by the name of Dirty Tom McAlear made his living (and severely taxed his clients' imaginations) by eating anything that was plopped down before him, for pennies. Here also was sanctuary for the brutal gangs of hoodlums (a word said to have been coined in the Barbary Coast) who terrorized Chinatown. (Another Barbary Coast coinage was the word *shanghaied,* which described what happened to unsuspecting sailors who imbibed spiked drinks, called *Mickey Finns.* Mr. Mickey Finn himself, incidentally, was the Barbary Coast chemist who supplied the drugs.)

The Barbary Coast raged on for over six decades, eventually feeding on its own notoriety by catering to intrepid tourists and local slumming parties. Outraged preachers and newspaper editors called for divine punishment, or at the very least, government action, to clean up the Coast. Not surprisingly, Heaven made the first move. In April of 1906, the day of reckoning came. The earth shook, buildings crumbled; firestorms swept through the city, leaving 500 square blocks of San Francisco incinerated. But curiously, as the smoke and flames cleared, the very heart of the Barbary Coast was seen yet standing amid the coals, miraculously spared. The party wasn't over! Not until 1917 did a government decree even attempt to bring the Coast to heel, and even then a smaller, tamer version called the International Settlement staggered on until mid-century.

◆ BARBARY COAST INTO JACKSON SQUARE

Today, the Barbary Coast is well and truly dead, though fortunately, many of its buildings live on for our edification. It is now a thoroughly gentrified district of old brick structures quaintly renovated to quarter architects, antique sellers, and design studios, some of which cater only to professionals and are not welcoming of casual browsers (unless they be very well-padded, and in any event, possessing of an appointment). Even the old name has been turned out in favor of a peculiarly inappropriate euphemism, Jackson Square. You won't find a square here, but it is very worth your while to wander through the elegant, tree-lined streets, peering through windows and hunting down a few old landmarks.

Old Barbary Coast inmates take a break from the action.

◆ BARBARY COAST HIGHLIGHTS

700 Block of Montogomery

The **Belli Building** and its neighbors on the 700 block of Montgomery, for instance, are curious relics of the 1850s, though sadly weakened in the Loma Prieta quake of 1989. The Belli Building saw action as a rowdy Barbery Coast cabaret, and later in life became home to the law offices of Marvin Belli. At number 728, Bret Harte purportedly wrote "The Luck of Roaring Camp."

A. P. Hotaling's Buildings

Around the corner on Jackson, the brick and cast-iron buildings at 451, 445, and 463 once housed **A. P. Hotaling's offices**, including his wholesale whiskey operation. The latter establishment occupies an esteemed position in the lore of the Barbary Coast, for its survival in the fire of 1906 inspired an immortal ode on cosmic justice:

> *If, as they say, God spanked the town*
> *for being over-frisky,*
> *Why did He burn the churches down*
> *and spare Hotaling's whiskey?*

Hippodrome Theater

Other points of interest include the bawdy Hippodrome Theater. It's now a furniture design company, but still intact is the resplendent foyer in carved bas-relief featuring flitting nudes that were once considered very shocking indeed. *555 Pacific Street.*

Gold Street

Gold Street, an alley that predates the Barbary Coast, appears little changed since the 1850s, though most building interiors have been fortified against earthquakes. Its western end is marked by the **Bank of Lucas, Turner & Company**, 1853, better known today as the bank once managed by William Tecumseh Sherman, who later went on to burn Atlanta in the Civil War.

Stout's Architectural

This bookstore is required browsing for anyone with the faintest interest in architecture and design. The varied stock might surprise you with that hard-to-find title you've been searching for. *804 Montgomery; 415-391-6757.*

■ THEATER DISTRICT

San Francisco's answer to Times Square, albeit a quiet answer, begins with **Lotta's Fountain** at the intersection of Geary, Kearny, and Market. The fountain was presented by the actress Lotta Crabtree, who got her start as a child dancer in California during the Gold Rush. Here San Francisco celebrated its most sentimental Christmas Eve, in 1910, when the Italian coloratura soprano, Luisa Tetrazzini, expressed her passionate gratitude to the city that "discovered" her five years earlier, by singing free to a crowd of thousands that filled the streets.

San Franciscans love and have always loved the theater and its troupers. During the Gold Rush, miners used to lob bags of gold dust on stage when young Lotta Crabtree danced, though rotten vegetables and worse were kept on hand for more critical judgment calls. The forty-niners were not really a brutish lot; in fact, Gold Rush San Franciscans were on average better educated than New Yorkers of their day. They enjoyed poetry, sat through Cantonese opera, and were passionately devoted to Shakespeare and grand opera, even in the most far-flung mining camps. San Francisco's first opera house opened to clamoring audiences as early as 1851. Though woolly and remote from European capitals, from the start it was pulling in stage companies from the grand opera and theater circuits, solely by the extraordinary enthusiasm of its audiences (and gate receipts). European superstars Lola Montez and Lillie Langtry forsook their royal lovers for San Francisco's adulation, and settled for a time in small California towns. As the great 19th-century actress Helena Modjeska, used to say, "If they like you in San Francisco, you're all right."

Aside from Lotta Crabtree and Tetrazzini, San Francisco launched the careers of Adah Menken, Edwin Booth, and native son David Belasco. Ironically, San Francisco cannot claim discovery of her most influential daughter of the footlights, Isadora Duncan. Duncan's fortune and fame as the progenitor of modern dance were first

The facade of the newly refurbished A.C.T. Theater on Geary Street. (Kerrick James)

recognized in New York and the capitals of Europe. Appropriately, Isadora's birthplace is in the heart of San Francisco's theater district. The original building, at 501 Taylor Street, is gone, but a plaque marks the site.

The Bay Area supports a tremendous number and range of theaters and drama companies, so it seems a bit confining to pin the name "Theater District" on one small area. After all, several other nationally celebrated theater companies are in other neighborhood districts and around the Bay Area. Still, if blue-haired theater matrons and jaded cabbies alike agree to call the half-dozen scattered blocks west of Union Square "The Theater District," who am I to argue? Scores of other Bay Area theaters present "Broadway" plays, musicals, and classic drama, but the Theater District offers them professionally produced, with larger budgets than are available to smaller neighborhood companies. Adding to the special theatrical atmosphere are the late-night cafes. For an up-to-date schedule of performances, check the pink "Datebook" section in the Sunday *Chronicle*.

HOT ON THE BLACK BIRD'S TAIL

Spade went to the Geary Theatre, failed to see Cairo in the lobby, and posted himself on the curb in front, facing the theatre. The youth loitered with other loiterers before Marquard's restaurant below.

At ten minutes past eight Joel Cairo appeared, walking up Geary Street with his little mincing bobbing steps. Apparently he did not see Spade until the private detective touched his shoulder. He seemed moderately surprised for a moment, and then said: "Oh, yes, of course you saw the ticket."

"Uh-huh. I've got something I want to show you." Spade drew Cairo back towards the curb a little away from the other waiting theatre-goers. "The kid in the cap down by Marquard's."

Cairo murmured, "I'll see," and looked at his watch. He looked up Geary Street. He looked at the theatre-sign in front of him on which George Arliss was shown costumed as Shylock, and then his dark eyes crawled sidewise in their sockets until they were looking at the kid in the cap, at his cool pale face with curling lashes hiding lowered eyes.

"Who is he?" Spade asked.

Cairo smiled up at Spade. "I do not know him."

—Dashiell Hammett, *The Maltese Falcon*, 1929

◆ THEATER DISTRICT VENUES

Geary Theater (ACT)

Built in 1909, this 1,300-seat theater is a national historic landmark and the flagship venue of San Francisco's mainstream theater. It was badly damaged in the 1989 earthquake, and remained closed for retrofitting and reconstruction until 1996. Opening in a blaze of gilt ornamentation, it resumed its longtime role as the home of the American Conservatory Theater Company (ACT), always dependable for a solid season featuring the works of playwrights such as Shakespeare, Marlowe, O'Neill, and Stoppard, as well as a steady stream of world premieres. *415 Geary Blvd; 415-749-2228.*

The Curran

The other grand dame of San Francisco theaters, this venerable national historic landmark opened in 1922 and is the city's most popular venue for long-running Broadway musicals such as *Les Miserables* and *Phantom of the Opera. 445 Geary; 415-551-2000.*

Golden Gate Theatre

This 2,400-seat theater specializes in traveling musical road shows and revivals, many of them major productions with limited engagements. *One Taylor St.; 415-551-2000.*

Mason Street Theater

This is an intimate theater that books a lot of small and experimental dramatic groups. *340 Mason St.; 415-982-5463.*

The Orpheum

This recently refurbished old theater makes the best of its downbeat location by staging upbeat musicals such as *Showboat* and *Miss Saigon. 1192 Market; 415-551-2000.*

Great American Music Hall

Like the name says, this is a great venue for seeing live music, ranging from blues to jazz fusion. *859 O'Farrell St.; 415-885-0750.*

Lorraine Hansberry Theater

This small space presents works mainly by African American dramatists, featuring up-and-coming playwrights as well as established authors. *620 Sutter St.; 415-474-8800.*

Cable Car Theater

One of the more intimate city theaters hosting a wide variety of productions. *430 Mason St.; 415-434-3832.*

Theater on the Square

Another one of the district's intimate venues, this popular theater is known to engage small productions for extended runs. *450 Post St.; 415-433-9500.*

The Warfield

This ornate Romanesque movie palace was built in 1921, and renovated to its former glory as a venue for live music, mostly rock. *982 Market St.; 415-775-7722.*

Walking north from the Theater District, you'll soon notice the steep rise of Nob Hill. The finer things in life come thick and fast here: hotels, shopping, restaurants, galleries, clubs. The ironically exclusive **Bohemian Club,** on the corner of Taylor and Post, was founded by people who would have laughed uproariously to see it now, a sanctuary for the likes of Henry Kissinger, Gerald Ford, and other powerful establishment figures. The club's early members—George Sterling, Jack London, Ina Coolbrith, Ambrose Bierce, John Muir, and Joaquin Miller— were the *original* bohemians.

But other things change fast too. A short stroll immediately *south* of the Theater District you'll notice a drastic swing in socio-economics as you enter one of the city's tougher neighborhoods.

■ THE TENDERLOIN

Situated between the downtown shopping district and the Civic Center, this high-crime district is easy to stumble into. Its exact boundaries are fuzzy, but it is generally pinned down between Larkin, Mason, and O'Farrell Streets, with a dogleg over Market and down Sixth Street toward Howard.

The Tenderloin is a kind of vigorous skid row and red-light district of porn shops, pimps, streetwalkers, and massage parlor fronts. It attracts runaways and their exploiters, as well as drug dealers, drunks, transvestites, and down-and-outers—not to mention stag businessmen and conventioneers. The Tenderloin has the highest rate of rape in the city, and ought to be avoided by unaccompanied females, even by day. Because of cheap rents, the Tenderloin also has the largest concentration of elderly poor people. Many live a life of fear, barricaded behind locked doors.

But all is not a tale of woe. The Tenderloin is in the midst of change. Within the past decade, Southeast Asian families have been quietly colonizing a large swatch of territory here, especially in the blocks along Ellis Street. Most of them are ethnic Chinese from Vietnam, Laos, and Cambodia, many of whom survived 40 years of warfare and unbelievable hardship to get here, and who do not flinch easily at the mere reputation of mean streets. The Southeast Asian influence may yet transform the Tenderloin from a no-man's land to a thriving family community. Already, the area's markets and restaurants are attracting patrons from other neighborhoods, and even some tourists. Especially inviting are the small neighborhood cafes, mostly of the cheap and hearty Vietnamese type called *phö,* where a huge bowl of spiced beef noodle soup, with a condiment of fresh bean sprouts, lemon, pepper, and mint leaf or fresh cilantro, is the pièce de resistance.

■ CIVIC CENTER

No spectacle of civic architecture in the country is more grand than San Francisco's Civic Center. City Hall's magnificent dome is a symbol of proportion and reason, a triumph of beauty and benevolent power. The proximity of the Tenderloin and its army of transients is another symbol, an ambiguous one that says little for control and order, ideals, or compassion. Where to house them is, of course, a problem with no easy answers, but until a solution is found, visitors should be prepared to deal with a gauntlet of panhandlers.

Civic Center is a supreme example of the Beaux Arts style in America. Beaux Arts was a movement initiated by young American architects who had studied at the French Ecole des Beaux-Arts. Inspired by classical architecture and infused with the City Beautiful movement, the new school of civic planning called for formality in design, with wide boulevards, colonnades, parks, and plazas. Its ideas swept the country at the turn of the 20th century. When enthused San Franciscans asked Chicago architect Daniel Burnham to draft new plans for their city, he retreated to the top of Twin Peaks for two years of study and sketching. Published in 1905, his Burnham Plan called for a Paris-style revamp of San Francisco's streets, making use of the hills as great, park-like pedestals for monuments, with grand boulevards leading off from a magnificent Civic Center.

The 1906 earthquake wiped the slate clean, and seemed a god-given opportunity to institute the Burnham Plan. But San Franciscans were in a hurry to rebuild, and before the bureaucrats could rouse themselves, the city's commercial and residential sections were already rising on the old street grid. Fortunately, government sloth for once paid off at Civic Center, which was rebuilt more slowly on City Beautiful principles. Old City Hall had crumbled in the quake, a victim of government corruption that siphoned off construction funds and used substandard materials. Outraged San Franciscans mandated a new government, and a new Civic Center. One of the first acts of Mayor "Sunny Jim" Rolph when elected in 1911 was to call for bids for a new city hall. The winning design came from the firm of Bakewell & Brown, two local boys who had submitted it with no serious expectation that San Francisco would choose such an extravagant plan.

◆ CIVIC CENTER HIGHLIGHTS

San Francisco City Hall

City Hall's dome, refurbished to a brilliant black and gold in the late 1990s, was modeled after Saint Peter's at the Vatican. It soars three feet higher above its floor than does that of the nation's Capitol. To stand below that ornate dome and flowing staircase inspires awe for the powers of Caesar. Henri Crenier's Renaissance-style sculptures over the Polk Street entrance represent the figures of San Francisco, California's Riches, Commerce, and Navigation. Watching over the Van Ness Avenue entrance are Labor, Industry, Truth, Learning, the Arts, and Wisdom.

United Nations Plaza

Just off Market Street, this plaza commemorates the charter meeting of that august body, which took place in June 1945 at the War Memorial Opera House. On Wednesdays and Sundays, the **Civic Center Market** sets up on the plaza. Rich in color and vitality, this farmers' market bursts with fresh, hard-to-find Southeast Asian vegetables.

San Francisco Main Library

Kitty-corner to the newly refurbished Bill Graham Civic Auditorium, San Francisco's Main Library fronts the plaza. Opened in April 1996, the library emphasizes the high-tech storage of information, some would argue at the expense of *books*. With hundreds of on-line computer terminals to supplement its bookshelves, the technology is so pervasive and the interior design so high-tech, that readers accustomed only to shelf-browsing and card catalogs might find the new building somewhat daunting. With children's facilities, collections of historical documents, and specialty libraries devoted to singular San Francisco neighborhoods and communities, the new Main Library is a resource for researchers and for casual browsers, and all are welcome into its soaring, sunlit spaces. (The old Main Library building on the north side of the plaza will become the new home of the Asian Art Museum in 2001. *100 Larkin St; 415-557-4400.*

The magnificent rotunda of City Hall. (Kerrick James)

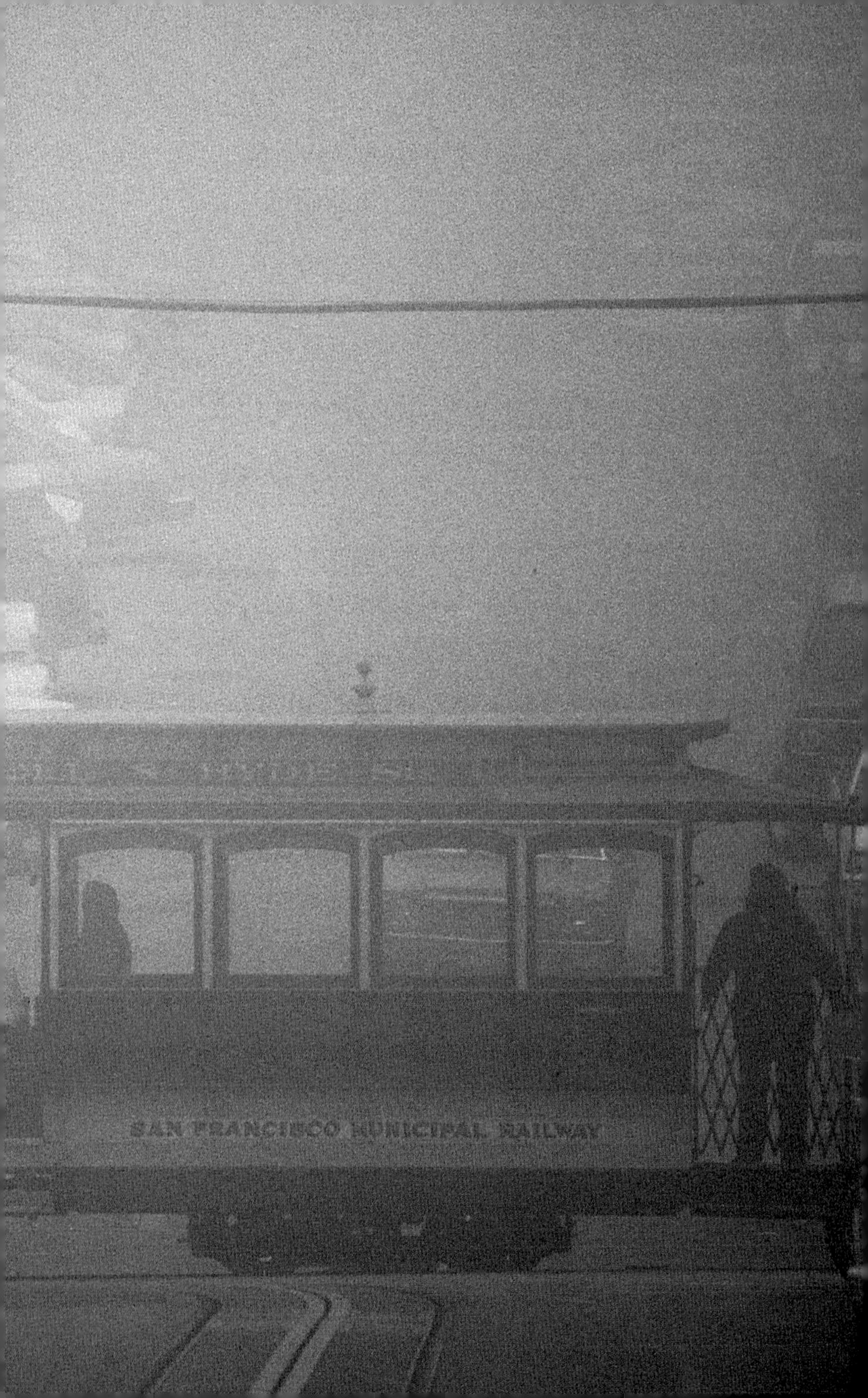
SAN FRANCISCO MUNICIPAL RAILWAY

War Memorial Opera House

The ultimate place to see and be seen in San Francisco is at the opera during its September to December season. Dressed to the nines, San Francisco's glitterati arrive in limousines on opening night, tailed by paparazzi and society editors. Devoted fans of more modest means jam the standing-room-only section when stars come to shake the rafters. The lavish costumes and settings are awe-inspiring; all in all, the San Francisco opera is among the world's most critically acclaimed. *301 Van Ness Ave.; 415-864-3330.*

San Francisco Ballet

One of the nation's oldest dance companies, the San Francisco Ballet also performs in the War Memorial Opera House when the group is not on the road, and presents contemporary as well as classical repertory works. *415-861-5600.*

Louise M. Davies Symphony Hall

The San Francisco Symphony keeps house at Louise M. Davies Hall, built in 1981 on the corner of Van Ness and Grove. The symphony season runs from September through May. Davies Hall is equipped with the largest concert-hall organ in North America, built by the Ruffatti brothers of Padua, Italy. Its 9,235 pipes are played with the help of a sophisticated computer. *201 Van Ness Ave.; 415-431-5400.*

Performing Arts Library and Museum

A mandatory side-trip for aficionados of local theater, opera, dance, and music is the San Francisco Performing Arts Library and Museum, located in the Veteran's Building. A wealth of trappings of the footlit stage—theater posters, playbills, newspaper clippings, and some 4,000 books on the performing arts from the Gold Rush to the present—invest the archives and gallery walls with the smell of greasepaint, the roar of crowds. *401 Van Ness Ave.; 415-255-4800.*

California Culinary Academy

The culinary arts are also well represented in the Civic Center area, thanks in large part to the city's premier training ground for chefs, the California Culinary Academy. In the 16-month course on classical French, Italian, and nouvelle cuisines, the students' training runs the gamut of pastries, wines, appetizers, salads, dressings, canapés, decorative meats, entrees, terrines, garnishes, cut vegetables, soups, and desserts, while learning the economies and etiquette of kitchen and restaurant. Besides operating a retail bakery and small cafe, the academy serves lunch and dinner at set times on weekdays in the Carême Room—a glass-enclosed hall, permitting diners to watch the ongoing work in the kitchens—and in the basement Academy Grill. Service is excellent and prices are extremely reasonable. *625 Polk St.; 415-771-3500.*

(preceding pages) A Hyde Street cable car slices through a morning fog.

NABOBS, SOJOURNERS
& BOHEMIANS

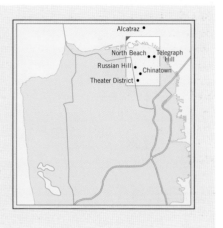

THE LOW HILLS RISING UP BEHIND DOWNTOWN San Francisco are no Rocky Mountains, but they are a formidable barrier nonetheless. The principal civic, financial, and commercial functions of San Francisco cluster on the flat lands around the foot of these hills, where bureaucrats and capitalists (and their esteemed clients) can tread the course of least resistance. But climb any hill out of downtown San Francisco, and you turn your back on the world of big business and big government.

Nob Hill, Telegraph Hill, and Russian Hill, with their attendant communities of North Beach and Chinatown, were among San Francisco's earliest residential areas, nurturing a succession of outcast communities, eccentrics, and escapists, not to mention plenty of just ordinary family folk. Within five minutes' walk of the hard-nosed towers of Montgomery Street, you can buy a Chinese pear or hear Puccini sung on a jukebox. Within 10 minutes, you can watch a game of bocce or pay respects to Kuan Kung, god of war and literature. Within 15, the all-seeing Top of the Mark can be your throne, or if you prefer, a wooden step beneath dangling fuchsias on Telegraph Hill. And all around you, tens of thousands of local residents and passers-by are playing out their lives in neighborhood bistros, schools, markets, churches, temples, restaurants, clubs, newspapers, hospitals, and funeral parlors, while cable cars rattle and clang through the boisterous streets.

Nob Hill (opposite) is famous for its cable cars and its grand historic hotels. At the Fairmont Hotel (top), classic high tea (bottom) is served every day in the lobby. (Kerrick James)

Cynics lament that some of these neighborhoods have become mere symbols of what they used to be. Yes, commercialism has made gross inroads at Fisherman's Wharf. Beatniks and nabobs, for the most part, have moved on, and even the Italians of Little Italy are growing thin on the ground. Yet as long as red wine, jasmine tea, Napier Lane, dim sum, fettuccine, and City Lights Bookstore survive, these most San Franciscan of San Francisco's old neighborhoods will continue to salve the soul and feed the senses.

■ NOB HILL

San Franciscans like to say that the Nob of Nob Hill is a contraction of nabob, meaning a Moghul prince. This etymology is dubious, but it has poetic license. Some of America's favorite nabobs, who ripped their fabulous fortunes from the silver mines and railroad rights-of-way of the American West, built their mansions on the gilded crown of Nob Hill. Hemmed in on the south by Union Square, the Theater District, and the Tenderloin, on the west by busy Polk Gulch, and on the east by teeming Chinatown, Nob Hill stands aloof from the tumultuous city. Today, however, it's not as exclusive as when Robert Louis Stevenson called it "the hill of palaces." But the ghosts of the old Big Four and the Bonanza Kings live on, not only in Nob Hill's place names, but in its rarified air of understated wealth (not that there was anything understated about the hill's colossal Victorian prosperity). Today's fortunes are more restrained, more evenly spread. The palaces have shrunk to town houses, penthouses, and hotel suites. The corps of servants that once bowed to one master and mistress now pamper hordes of splurging tourists.

◆ CABLE CARS AND LELAND STANFORD

The invention of the cable car in 1873 sealed Nob Hill's fate as a suitable aerie for Victorian millionaires. It was said that Leland Stanford built the California Street line for his wife's convenience, laying the tracks right past their door at the corner of Powell and California. Today, you can eyeball those tracks clear down the California Street canyon of the Financial District, past Ralston's and Gianinni's and the Wells Fargo banks, to the imposing Southern Pacific Building on Market Street. Southern Pacific, of course, was the reincarnation of the Central Pacific, the company founded by Stanford and the other Big Four (Hopkins, Crocker, and Huntington) to build the first transcontinental railway. The Big Four reaped obscene fortunes and power from the arrangement. In time, their empire straddled much of the American West, rolling over all who got in its way.

The ultimate triumph of Stanford's life, however, eluded him. He and his wife had a son, Leland Stanford, Jr., whom they doted on. Leland was raised in the lap of Nob Hill, a privileged quarter of chiming clocks and scurrying servants, where rare and wondrous toys for the lad arrived from around the world. The best of everything was lavished upon him, and he grew up showing great talents in several disciplines, particularly archaeology. But sadly, in his sixteenth year, while on European tour, the boy died, plunging his parents into sorrow unallayed by all the money in the world. They returned to San Francisco and channeled their grief into building a memorial to perpetuate his name for the benefit of other sons and daughters of California. That monument is Stanford University.

◆ NOB HILL HIGHLIGHTS

Renaissance Stanford Court Hotel

Like all of Nob Hill's wooden palaces, the great Stanford mansion burned in the 1906 fire. The massive granite wall that once surrounded it still partially encloses the present structure, the Stanford Court Hotel. It is, in the best tradition of nabobbery, one of the finest hotels in the world. Stanford's California Street cable cars still trundle up from the lowlands, pausing briefly outside his vanished front door. The Powell-Mason and Powell-Hyde Street lines cross the California Street line at this same corner. *905 California St.; 415-989-3500.*

Mark Hopkins Inter-Continental Hotel

Mark Hopkins, the Big Four's number two man, built his mansion next door to Stanford's. Today, the Mark Hopkins Hotel rises on the site, capped by the famous view-bar, the **Top of the Mark.** You can see for miles from every window, the celebrated view (though maybe not the venue) that inspired the city's signature song, immortalized by Tony Bennett: "I Left My Heart in San Francisco." *One Nob Hill; 415-392-3434.*

Fairmont Hotel

Another elegant landmark of after-hours San Francisco rises across the street from the Mark Hopkins. Named for Comstock millionaire James Fair, the Fairmont Hotel was built by his daughter, and is a grand survivor of the quake of 1906, though it was gutted in the fire. The Fairmont Crown, reached by a heart-grabbing ride in a glass elevator up the outside of the hotel's modern tower, is San Francisco's loftiest watering hole. The Tonga Room offers dancing by a South Sea lagoon, complete with a tropical thunderstorm. Imagine the Tiki Room at Disneyland with cocktails. *950 Mason St.; 415-772-5000.*

Flood Mansion

Across the street from the Fairmont stands the solid brownstone Flood Mansion. The only Nob Hill mansion to survive the earthquake and fire of 1906, Bonanza King James Flood's one-time residence is now the exclusive Pacific-Union Club. It's called the P-U in local parlance, and don't even bother to knock. *1000 California St.*

◆ GRACE CATHEDRAL

Alone among his partners, Charles Crocker lacks the posthumous honor of having his name grace a Nob Hill hotel. Instead, his old mansion made way for San Francisco's supreme Episcopalian house of God, Grace Cathedral. Gazing at the towers and spire of that high-minded edifice, it is difficult to envision this as the scene of San Francisco's most grotesque example of filthy-rich rascality. There was a time when Charlie Crocker owned most of that block and wanted it all. The elusive corner lot, however, was owned by an undertaker named Nicholas Yung, who declined to sell. In retaliation, Crocker built a 40-foot "spite fence" around Yung's property, boxing in the house on three sides. San Franciscans were outraged, but neither Crocker or Yung would budge. Historian Randolph Delehanty notes that both men died with the stalemate unresolved, leaving their heirs to settle the matter. The Yung estate eventually was sold to the Crocker estate, and all passed quietly to the Episcopal Diocese after the 1906 earthquake rendered the property untenable for worldly use.

No matter how lovely Grace Cathedral looks—and it is a beaut, inspired by Notre Dame in Paris—one does not quite escape the fact that it is made of reinforced concrete. Why that should detract from the *idea* of religious beauty is not hard to understand. The great cathedrals of Europe, built block by block over decades, sometimes centuries, physically embody their builders' inspired, personal devotion. A cathedral erected in compliance with a building code established to protect worshippers from earthquakes and other acts of God just does not epitomize the same fervor of piety. Still, Grace is a lovely cathedral, from the exquisite doors cast from Lorenzo Ghiberti's *Gates of Paradise* at the Cathedral Baptistry in Florence, to the great rose window built in Chartres in 1970 and the Prayer Labyrinth, designed after an original in the Chartres Cathedral. (A line of barefoot "pilgrims," deep in meditation, are usually wending slowly through the maze, a spiritual exercise encouraged by the adjacent Grace Cathedral Labyrinth Project Exhibit.) Most beautiful of all is the flood of music that pours out during the choral evensongs, and when the pipe organ or carillon is played, especially in the Christmas season. Also wonderful, if more secular, are the jazz and contemporary classical concerts which Grace hosts from time to time, and the **Cup of Grace coffee house** out front. *1100 California St.; 415-749-6300.*

◆ HUNTINGTON PARK

Collis P. Huntington, last of the Big Four, once owned the site of Huntington Park, an inviting swatch of green across the street from Grace Cathedral. Huntington bought the land from the widow of Southern Pacific's lawyer, David Colton—which is odd, since the Big Four had accused Colton of embezzlement and sued for a piece of his estate. This lawsuit was the sensation of its age, an unfolding drama of graft and bribery among the rich and famous, which titillated a fascinated public for eight years and scandalized Congress into a flurry of reform laws directed against the robber barons. Today the grand house is gone, and Huntington Park is a quiet, sedate place with a charming little fountain, much beloved by elderly Chinese ladies who do their morning tai chi above the ashes of the Big Four's mansions.

◆ CABLE CAR BARN

Dynamic powerhouse for the nation's only moving national historical monument, this historic brick building is both the garage and central powerhouse for the world's last remaining cable car system. Originally built in 1909, the building hums with power, and is one of the city's most spectacular sights, both sensually and intellectually. Between 1982 and 1984 it was gutted and reinforced against earthquakes, and the interior rebuilt within the original exterior walls.

The cable car was invented by Andrew Hallidie, a British-born mining engineer who specialized in building cable systems used for hauling ore. Hallidie's inspiration, the story goes, came after watching a horse-drawn streetcar slip down one of San Francisco's steep streets, dragging the horses behind. After many experiments, he devised a mechanical system that could pull cars up steep hills and around 90-degree turns. Hallidie successfully tested his first cable car on Clay Street in 1873. Though devilishly complex, it was a work of genius. Before long London, Sydney, and several other American cities had adopted the technology, as well as several other companies within San Francisco, providing a field day for Hallidie's patent attorneys. But as bus, streetcar, and automobile rendered them obsolete, cable cars eventually disappeared from every city, except their sentimental birthplace. Despite their expense and questionable safety record, they are arguably the best-loved symbol of San Francisco.

Operating a cable car is a work of art. They carry no engines. The kinetic energy is all in the continuous loop of steel cable, pulled through a slot in the street at a constant speed of 9.5 miles per hour by engines anchored to the floor of the powerhouse. The system's three cables (one for each cable car line) are steered through their circuitous routes—around 90 degree corners and up and down steep hills—by a series of subterranean sheaves (pulleys). To drive the car forward, the cable car gripman yanks the grip lever, forcing the grip into the slot to seize (or *grip*) the cable; to stop he lets go, and applies the brakes. The gripman's finesse shows up best at corners and where two lines cross, when he has to release the grip before it binds or smashes against the sheaves. After coasting free of the impediment, the gripman then reapplies the grip, and the cable car continues its journey. The brakeman receives his workout on the descent of the city's steep hills, a real test of nerve and machine, particularly on the Hyde Street grade of Russian Hill.

From the mezzanine floor of the Cable Car Barn, you can look down on the humming engines, which drive the 14-foot sheaves that wind the cables. Be sure to walk downstairs to the Sheave Room for a peek under the street, where 8-foot sheaves steer the moving cables in and out of the powerhouse on their subterranean loops through the city. The small museum preserves an early cable car and some well-annotated specimens of the grip and braking mechanisms. You can buy souvenirs and books explaining the operation in much greater detail from the mezzanine shop. The museum is free, and is open daily. *Corner of Washington and Mason Sts.; 415-474-1887.*

The Cable Car Barn hums as its powerful sheaves steer the cables.

■ CHINATOWN

Chinatown is a clash of five senses, a crush of humanity, a blur of ambrosial steams and flavors, a cacophony of clattering pots and market cries, the grim whir of sewing machines behind windowless walls, an odor of dried fungus.

Rudyard Kipling called it "a ward of the city of Canton," setting a theme for later tour guides, who prefer to compare Chinatown to Hong Kong. Which is nonsense. In fact, it's a little like comparing Grover's Corners to the City of London.

Chinatown is a distinctively American hybrid of a Cantonese market town—*Cantonese* inasmuch as most of its residents are ethnically Cantonese, and *American* inasmuch as fortune cookies, Chinese New Year parades, dragon-wrapped lampposts, Miss Chinatown contests, Chinatown tourist kitsch, chop suey restaurants, and much more, are distinctively American phenomena. And that's just scratching the surface.

◆ CHINATOWN HISTORY

Chinatown's founders were mainly from two classes. City merchants, mostly from Guangzhou (Canton City), were few in number, but they rose to prominence in the community by virtue of their wealth, polish, and ability to speak English. The vast majority of early Chinese immigrants, however, were rural males, laborers largely from Toishan County, whose local dialect is unintelligible to people from Guangzhou. Most of these were sojourners, that is, men who intended to return to China after making their fortune—as indeed many did, bringing back new ideas that hastened the downfall of the Qing Dynasty. Few learned English, which contributed to their isolation in America. They banded together in clubs, or tongs, based on their surname or county of origin. The word "tong" has a negative connotation in English today, but in Chinese it means only "association." Most tongs, or associations, in Chinatown were and are perfectly benign social clubs. The tong was the principal political and social force of old Chinatown, most benevolently in the form of a confederation of tongs called the Six Companies; but least so in the form of the fighting tongs of the late 19th century.

This peculiarly masculine, working-class society was mummified by the Exclusion Act of 1882. Instead of developing into a family-oriented neighborhood, San Francisco's Chinatown remained for years a stunted frontier settlement in the midst of a city, where flourished all the vices comforting to lonely men—drugs, gambling, prostitution, and the corruption and violence associated with the control of same.

Ironically, the *real* opium dens, slave girls, and highbinders that inspired sinister Hollywood movies about Chinatown were themselves kept in business largely by the American Exclusion laws. (Chinatown's unique character also inspired stereotypes in the *Chinese* cinema: a stock character of Hong Kong movies and anecdotes up until the 1960s was "Uncle from Gold Mountain"—an aging, rich, spendthrift, good-hearted oaf on the lookout for a young wife.)

◆ CHINATOWN TODAY

Today's Chinatown is a whole different world. Since immigration laws were relaxed in the 1960s, the influx of immigrant families from Hong Kong, China, Taiwan, and Southeast Asia has rejuvenated it. Crusty old Toishan bachelors and Cantonese merchants still hold their own, but they are part of a far richer tapestry of lanky peasants, fry cooks, spoiled-brat starlets, sober-sided professionals and shell-shocked refugees, sophisticates and factory workers, aunties with their daily shopping, and, most precious to a once-stagnant community, children.

Most of this new "community" no longer lives in Chinatown. The prosperous, the educated, and the ambitious move on to the suburbs. In fact, most prosperous immigrants from Hong Kong today completely bypass a stay in Chinatown, though they may own a business there. Non-English-speaking poor immigrants from China, and the elderly poor, for the most part, stay behind. Life for them can be hard. Chinatown is the most densely populated neighborhood in the States outside of Harlem. Housing is poor. Sweatshops exploit immigrants ignorant of American labor laws. For those who move away, however, the grimmer realities of Chinatown fade behind a kind of spiritual, or perhaps visceral, symbol. Here, suburbanites can and do regularly repair to eat Chinese food, read Chinese newspapers, shop for Chinese groceries, browse through the Chinese library and bookstores, go to a Chinese movie, and, in short, retouch some aspect of their (or their forebearers') heritage.

Not all of Chinatown's "suburbs" are distant. The nucleus of Chinatown remains the 24-block area bounded by Kearny, Bush, Powell, and Broadway, but the contiguous community now incorporates the less hectic streets of North Beach, Telegraph Hill, Russian Hill, and Nob Hill. Stockton Street is the main Chinese thoroughfare, while Grant is the tourist mecca. The streets in between—Pacific, Jackson, Washington, Clay, Sacramento, and the alleys that connect them—best retain the atmosphere of old Chinatown.

◆ CHINATOWN HIGHLIGHTS

The only way to tour Chinatown is on foot. The streets are too congested for comfortable driving, and finding a parking space is like winning the lottery. Even the parking garage under Portsmouth Square often has a line of cars waiting just to get in the door. You may have better luck parking beneath the Holiday Inn across the street, or under Saint Mary's Square. Consider joining one of the walking tours that go "behind the scenes" in Chinatown. *Contact the San Francisco Convention & Visitors Bureau at 415-974-6900.*

Chinatown Gate

Chinatown, for most visitors, begins at the Chinatown Gate on Grant at Bush. This is an ornate, touristy version of the ceremonial gate that you might find in Chinese villages. Outside the gate, Grant Avenue is one of San Francisco's fancier shopping streets. Within the gate, the two blocks between Bush and California Streets are the tidiest of Chinatown, attracting classier shops selling silks, gems, embroidered linens and blouses, antiques, furniture, and art goods. You can find some nice things, but in regard to the prices, bear in mind that Grant Avenue caters especially to tourists.

Old Saint Mary's Church

The corner of California and Grant is one of the city's most photographed scenes, embracing cable cars, pagoda-roofed buildings, and Old Saint Mary's Church. Looking down through the Financial District, you can see the Bay Bridge above Market Street. The cable car runs up California to the top of Nob Hill, intersecting Grant about mid-slope. Old Saint Mary's was San Francisco's Catholic cathedral from

1853 to 1891. Its famous brick tower bears a clock and the inscription, "Son, Observe the time and fly from evil." Though gutted by flames in 1906, its sturdy foundation (imported from China) and walls (imported from the East Coast) survived. Emperor Norton, while waving at a passing cable car, collapsed and died here in 1880. *Corner of California and Grant; 415-288-2800.*

Saint Mary's Square

A half block down from California, Saint Mary's Square basks quietly among taller buildings. Saint Mary's restful mood is enhanced by Benjiamano Bufano's peaceful statue of Sun Yat-sen, founder of the Republic of China. A native of Guangdong (Canton) Province, but educated in Hawaii and Hong Kong, Sun sought to overthrow the Qing Dynasty. Under sentence of death in his own country, he traveled around the world drumming up money for the revolution. During his stay in San Francisco, he founded a newspaper and wrote the English version of China's constitution in the Montgomery Block, a short stroll down from Saint Mary's Square, though now demolished. He also made many trips to Chi-

The Li Po (top), a Chinatown watering hole for many years, was named for China's most famous poet. Portsmouth Plaza is the living room of many Chinatown elderly (bottom).

nese communities around the state. Through their generous contributions, Californians were thus instrumental in founding the Republic of China.

Sacramento Street, *Tang Yahn Gai*

Sacramento Street, once Chinatown's main stem, is still known by the name that signifies "Chinatown" to overseas Chinese—*Tang Yahn Gai*, literally "Tang People's Street." (The Tang Dynasty is considered the most brilliant era of Chinese history, hence the Cantonese fondness for referring to themselves as Tang people.) Between Waverly and Hang Ah Streets is one of the outstanding children's playgrounds of San Francisco, with a maze of climbing ladders and slides, and plenty of sand. On the block above Stockton, the clinker-brick Donaldina Cameron House *(920 Sacramento)*, named after the Chinatown crusader, replaced the earlier mission that burned in 1906.

Grant between California and Jackson

Chinatown grows more frenetic in the six-block stretch of Grant Avenue between California and Jackson. Here you will find many of the big restaurants and tourist schlock shops, but also others that offer more curious browsing, such as and the **Ten Ren Tea Company** *(949 Grant)*. A uniquely Chinese-American creation, the cave-like **Li Po Bar** *(916 Grant)* is named after China's most famous poet, a wildly romantic warrior and wine-loving courtier, who drowned while drunkenly embracing the reflection of the moon in a river.

The block of Grant between Washington and Clay was the original street of Yan-

kee San Francisco. Back when the waves of Yerba Buena Cove still lapped at what is now Montgomery Street, Grant Avenue (then called *Calle de la Fundación*, or Foundation Street) was laid out by an English sea captain and his Mexican wife. Their village plaza, just down the hill, proved very useful for corralling the horses and livestock of visiting *vaqueros,* as well as the occasional goat. After American Marines raised the flag here in 1846, seizing San Francisco for the Union, they christened it after their ship, the USS *Portsmouth.*

Portsmouth Plaza

Young Portsmouth Square (*Square* changed back to *Plaza* in 1927) was the heart of Gold Rush San Francisco, hosting a motley array of civic assemblages, town meetings, celebrations, duels, and lynchings, as well as the city's first school, bookstore, and newspaper, and the finest hotels of the era. As landfill pushed the waterfront farther east, however, the business district moved with it, and Portsmouth Square lost its luster. Union Square, and later Civic Center, took over the square's public duties. Today, though rather ill-kempt and sprinkled with panhandlers, Portsmouth Plaza serves as an overcrowded backyard for densely packed Chinatown.

When Robert Louis Stevenson lived in San Francisco (1879–80), he liked to sit in Portsmouth Square to watch the tide of humanity roll by. A monument to him stands at the northwest corner of the plaza, near a replica of the *Goddess of Democracy,* the symbol of the Tiananmen Square protests of 1989 in Beijing, when so many students were killed.

Chinese Cultural Center

The Chinese Cultural Center occupies the third floor of the Chinatown Holiday Inn, across the footbridge from Portsmouth Plaza. The lectures, seminars, and exhibitions of works by Chinese-American artists and writers are geared more for community than tourists, but the center does have a small gift shop. *415-986-1822.*

Ma-Tsu Temple

Old Saint Mary's is not the only religious building near here. The Ma-Tsu Temple of the United States of America combines shrines to Buddha and the popular gods Tin Hau (Queen of Heaven), Kuan Kung, Kwun Yum, and an earth god. As in all Chinatown temples, visitors are welcome, though the caretakers seldom speak English, and photography is not permitted. *31 Beckett; 415-986-8818.*

Ross Alley

Ross Alley is the shadiest-looking thoroughfare in Chinatown. Its history lives up to its appearance, but today its most sinister aspect is the whine of hidden sewing machines in the garment factories. Visitors are welcome in the tiny **Golden Gate Fortune Cookie Factory** *(52 Ross)* to see the cookie machine in action.

Waverly Place

Waverly Place, between Washington and Sacramento, is called the "street of painted balconies," for reasons obvious to anyone who looks up. During the tong war era, Waverly was known as the toughest street in Chinatown. Today it's better known for its temples. A long climb takes you to the fourth-floor **Tin Hau Temple** *(123 Waverly),* the most atmospheric of Chinatown's temples, hung with lanterns and smokey

Children are the most vital ingredient of Chinatown's future.

from incense and the fires of burnt offerings. The main altar is dedicated to Tin Hau, Queen of Heaven and protector of seafarers and sojourners, but the temple also has shrines to other gods. The Buddhist Association of America oversees the **Norras Temple** *(109 Waverly)*. From the street, you can often hear saffron-robed monks chanting and striking bells, while the drums of kung fu clubs performing lion dancing resound from elsewhere in the building.

Washington Street and Herbalist Shops

Along the steep lateral lanes of Chinatown—Pacific, Jackson, Washington, Clay, and Sacramento—keep your eyes open for an abundance of herbalist shops, windows cluttered with medicinal and aphrodisiac potions, ginseng roots, fungus, elk horn, and occasional oddities like snake wine. The old-fashioned herbalist shops are most atmospheric, jammed with chests of Chinese roots, bark, and herbs. Many herbalists are scattered throughout Chinatown, but Washington Street seems particularly rich in them.

Stockton Street

Broad Stockton Street is the main market street for Chinatown residents. Its southern end enters Chinatown by way of the Stockton Tunnel, connecting with the Union Square shopping district at the other side of the tunnel. At the Chinatown end of the tunnel, on the corner of Stockton and Clay above the post office, the **Kong Chow Temple** looks out over Chinatown and the Financial District from the top floor. Though the building itself is entirely modern, some say this is the oldest Chinese temple in the country. Its carved, gilded altars and furnishings are venerable and magnificent. The main shrine honors the god Kuan Kung, a fierce yet noble, poetry-reading general during the Three Kingdoms era (A.D. 220–280), who was deified after being captured and executed. Kuan Kung is now the patron god of warriors and literature, much beloved by persons in professions requiring courage and fighting skill, including both police and criminals. *855 Stockton St.; 415-434-2513.*

The appeal of Stockton Street—unlike that of the dingy alleys down the hill—is not historic but immediate. No more crowded street exists in San Francisco than the stretch of Stockton between Sacramento and Broadway on a Saturday afternoon. Pedestrians throng the sidewalks outside markets crammed with fresh fish, bok choy, cabbages, mangos, bitter melon, apples, oranges, roast ducks, pressed ducks, barbecued pork, dry goods, oils, sweets, and shoppers shouting orders to the quick-fingered meat choppers. Curbside, hawkers haggle over live chickens and ducks from the backs of flatbed trucks, while vats of squirming fish and crabs are hoisted down to aproned butchers.

Chinese Historical Society Museum

Bringing it all together is this excellent museum, the only one in the country devoted

(right) A Chinatown apothecary measures herbs for use in a traditional Chinese medicine.
(Kerrick James)

exclusively to Chinese-American history. The Society's collection attempts to trace and preserve a record of the myriad Chinese contributions to the growth of America, and especially California, where Chinese played key roles in agriculture, fishing, mining, industry, and civil engineering, not to mention the arts, science, military, and service industries. Among the historical treasures in the museum's collection are a tiger fork from the Weaverville tong war, old photographs, and Gold Rush paraphernalia. *644 Broadway, Fourth floor; 415-391-1188.*

Beyond Broadway, Chinatown presses along Stockton into traditionally Italian North Beach, clear to Columbus Avenue. Chinatown's largest supplier of books on China is East Wind Books, in the basement of 1435 Stockton Street. Their English-language store is upstairs on the second floor.

◆ EATING IN CHINATOWN

No visit to Chinatown should neglect the stomach. Chinese is the emperor of world cuisines, and Cantonese is China's own undisputed king—though American palates seem to prefer the spicier northern styles of cooking, which explains the proliferation of Hunan, Sichuan, and Mandarin restaurants in the city. Chinatown's new immigrants are also opening restaurants serving Vietnamese food, as well as the Hakka and Chaozhou variations of the Cantonese. Still, Chinatown's main culinary focus remains traditional Cantonese food, with its two outstanding offerings of dim sum and seafood.

Dim sum are light snacks—little dumplings of shrimp, pork, and scores of other fillings, little pastries, and minced meats—served traditionally from passing carts or trays, with tea. Aside from a few organs that might make the uninitiated queasy—a bit of tripe, a duck's foot, a piece of pig's intestine—dim sum is invariably a happy revelation. Dim sum is traditionally served for breakfast or lunch. Most popular to Western tastes are the wrapped shrimp (*ha gow*), wrapped pork with shrimp (*siu mai*), rice pasta stuffed with meat or shrimp (*cheung fun*), and roast pork buns (*char siu bao*). Most dim sum restaurants are noisy affairs where the varieties of dishes are belted out in piercing tenors and sopranos by the passing serving ladies. If you can't get into the rumbustious spirit of these clamoring, packed-out restaurants, where the maitre d's patrol with walkie-talkies and you may have to order by hunt-and-point methods, then stick to the more genteel northern-style restaurants. But if you like great food in a truly hang-loose setting,

Tai chi, an ancient Chinese form of exercise, is performed in controlled slow motion, rigidly disciplined, painstakingly methodical. Some have called it "Chinese shadow boxing," an inadequate description, for the movements only vaguely resemble the more crudely martial Western form of boxing. If performed diligently over one's lifetime, tai chi is said to keep the muscles and cardiovascular system toned and healthy. Every morning brings devotees, many of them elderly, to the open spaces around Chinatown, particularly Portsmouth Plaza, Huntington Park, and Washington Square, where teachers lead them through the graceful moves.

then by all means come prepared for an invigorating experience. Any Hong Kong expatriate will tell you, however, that the best dim sum is found *outside* Chinatown, at huge Hong Kong-style restaurants, such as North Sea Village in Sausalito, the Hong Kong Flower Lounge in Millbrae and the Richmond District, Yank Sing and Harbor Village in the Financial District, and East Ocean in Emeryville.

Seafood dishes are readily available in most Chinatown restaurants. You can get good seafood at the big, fancy restaurants catering to tourists and special Chinese banquets, or you can pay less for a meal just as good in a modest, casual setting catering to locals. Most of the big, expensive restaurants congregate along Grant Avenue. Washington and Jackson Streets are packed with crowded, tiny restaurants, some downstairs, some up. These are not tourist places, and if you don't mind homey cooking and service, they offer some of San Francisco's best dining bargains.

The Chinatown equivalent of the American diner is the noodle and *juk* shop. They keep late hours and serve quick short-order meals like fried noddles or soup noodles, rice plates and *juk* (rice porridge).

Chinatown groceries are usually stocked with fresh bok choy, ginger, and other produce typically used in Chinese cooking. (Kerrick James)

■ NORTH BEACH

The beach has long been buried by landfill, but its potent name still carries meaning beyond mere geographical reference. On a local level, North Beach represents the focus of the ethnic Italians, a place of trattoria, cappuccino, aromatic delicatessens, and music. On a national level, North Beach means *Bohemia*, or more specifically, *beatnik*. Between the Italians and bohemians, North Beach has been christened San Francisco's Latin Quarter. The reputation is increasingly hard to keep up.

North Beach fills the floor of the valley that hangs between Russian and Telegraph Hills. Columbus Street cuts a wide diagonal right down the middle, and is the main road between downtown San Francisco and Fisherman's Wharf. The northern edge of North Beach, which once pushed almost to Fisherman's Wharf (itself a long-time Italian stronghold) is now obliterated by the hotels and gift shops that cover the waterfront. The southern boundary, traditionally, is Broadway.

Broadway was long known as the Marco Polo Zone because it marked where Chinatown ended and Little Italy began. This is no longer the case. Chinatown now pushes far into North Beach, and the predominant ethnic group in North Beach today is Chinese. A lot of old-time Italians bitterly grumble about this, and no doubt the weakening Italian influence is disheartening to those who love the fascinating distinction between these two wonderful neighborhoods. Sad it may be, but an ethnic community cannot be preserved as a museum. Neighborhoods change. Before North Beach was Italian, it was Irish. Before the Irish came, it was Chilean. (The old church of Nuestra Señora de Guadalupe at 908 Broadway still recalls its Hispanic parishioners.) And for that matter, before Fisherman's Wharf was Italian, it was *Chinese.*

Though Italians were early immigrants to San Francisco, the Italian community of North Beach took root relatively late in the 19th century, filling out after the turn of the century during the heyday of immigration from Italy. By 1940, they were the predominant foreign-born group in the city. Their families prospered, their children grew up as Americans, and they moved to the suburbs, selling the family homes and businesses. The heyday of Chinese immigration, on the other hand, came much later in the century, during the 1970s, '80s, and '90s (though, of course, the 1850s and '60s were also boom decades of Chinese immigration). The old boundaries of Chinatown were rendered inadequate. Paralleling the Italians, the Chinese also prospered, supplanting them as the largest foreign-born group in the city. And like the Italians, the Americanized generations have moved out of the old neighborhood center. As a community of first-generation immigrants in the late 20th century,

Little Italy simply cannot match the vitality of Chinatown.

But let us not sing a dirge for Little Italy. North Beach is still a colorful focus of the Italian-American community. The annual Columbus Day Parade in October is the biggest celebration of the year here. Italian teams still gather at the bocce grounds at North Beach Playground. Best of all, the gustatory pleasures are fully celebrated in North Beach. Its many Italian restaurants, coffeehouses, bakeries, pasta makers, gelato stores, and other establishments make it one of the supremely stimulating neighborhoods of San Francisco.

♦ BROADWAY STRIP

The Financial District, Chinatown, Telegraph Hill, Jackson Square, and North Beach all chafe against one another at Broadway, a strip of nightclubs and sleazy porno joints, barkers, and more than a few perfectly decent establishments. Starting with the infamous Barbary Coast, one block south on Pacific, this area has been a major center of the city's nightlife since the Gold Rush. In the 1950s and 1960s, comedy and folk clubs like the Purple Onion and the hungry i (both around the corner from Broadway, now under new ownership) booked such upstarts as the Smothers Brothers, Dick Gregory, Mort Sahl, Barbra Streisand, Bill Cosby, Lenny Bruce, and Phyllis Diller. Then, in 1964, Carol Doda danced topless at the Condor, revolutionizing the Strip, as it was and is still known. Two years later, the Strip went bottomless, starting a new craze. Strip joints opened up and down, and one place even raised a platform on a pole outside, where go-go dancers shimmied and wiggled for passing cars. Some old-timers still wax nostalgic when they contemplate the Strip's bawdiness of yesteryear; today's efforts have so much less pizzazz. Someone's even gone so far as to erect a pretentious bronze plaque on the wall of the Condor, at the corner of Columbus and Broadway, crediting the Strip as the birthplace of the world's first topless and bottomless stage shows. These claims must be viewed with skepticism. Even without accounting for the grosser perversities of the Barbary Coast, one block and a hundred years south, surely the honor of hosting the first topless dance must belong to Babylon or Gomorrah, to name but two possible precedents.

A good spot to watch the passing scene is **Enrico's,** San Francisco's most venerable alfresco hang-out. Once frequented by Beats, the sidewalk seats are made endurable on chilly nights by space-heaters, hot music, and a spicy crowd. *504 Broadway; 415-982-6223.*

(left) Molinari's deli is a paradise for lovers of Italian salami and salads.

◆ CITY LIGHTS AND THE BEATNIKS

San Francisco's most famous bookstore is Lawrence Ferlinghetti's **City Lights Bookstore**. City Lights was the first all-paperback bookstore in the country; but more than that, its odd-shaped, rambling rooms and basement are the literary focus of North Beach. Overflowing with small-press periodicals and literary programs, City Lights is an inspiration to writers and poets and people who get a charge from ideas that run against the grain. *261 Columbus, at the corner of Broadway; 415-362-8193.*

City Lights is forever associated with the watershed event of the Beat Generation. In 1956, Ferlinghetti published *Howl,* Allen Ginsberg's raging eulogy for an alienated generation. Ginsberg had written it in one weekend in San Francisco, and two weeks later read it to a wildly enthusiastic crowd at the Six Gallery in the Marina District. After publication, local police brought obscenity charges against Ginsberg, Ferlinghetti, and City Lights' manager Shigeyoshi Murao. The long court battle was followed by acquittal, with the judge ruling that an author "should be real in treating his subject and be allowed to express his thoughts and ideas in his own words."

Unfortunately for North Beach, the publicity turned unwanted national atten-

Old bohemians still repair to Vesuvio's.

tion on the new Bohemia. The alienated generation that congregated in its coffee-houses and clubs were called the Beat Generation, a phrase coined by Jack Kerouac in his romantic portrayal of a manic subculture, *On the Road.* New York may have spawned them, but North Beach became their most identifiable symbol. With handy, cheap Chinese and Italian food and wine, and an urbane indifference to eccentric manner and dress, North Beach nurtured the beats, and they in turn cultivated its cafe society and folksy clubs. The beats (or *beatniks*, as San Francisco columnist Herb Caen called them) rejected established mores as absurd, and sought fulfillment (or extinction of conventional behavior and thought) in spontaneous self-expression—free-style poetry, prose, music, art, endless talk, and obsessive hungering for new sensations.

The public loved the caricature of the beatnik: ragged and dirty, angry but cool, libertine, digging everything, lost in a haze of cheap wine, pot, and be-bop music. Before long, tour buses were crawling through the streets of North Beach. To make a long story short, as North Beach became a tourist trap, the things that real bohemians thrive on—cheap rent, cheap eats, and cheap drink—disappeared. The beats, for the most part, went straight or moved on—many of them to the Haight-Ashbury.

♦ NORTH BEACH CAFES AND OTHER DIVERSIONS

Though North Beach today is harder on the pocketbook, fortunately it's still good for the soul. It remains a haunt of cafe society, where locals and visitors still cultivate that fine old European habit of frequenting coffeehouses and bistros, listening to music, chatting, or just sitting and watching the other patrons. The best spots are patronized by neighborhood Italians and a few bohemian-like characters, lovers of conversation, scowlers into morning newspapers, thumbers of noses at establishment values, sketch artists, scribblers of poetry and other hacks, not to mention haughty young wannabes who, for want of talent, cultivate attitude. Plunk down your four bits and join the club.

Classic Beat Cafes

Across the alley from City Lights, on Jack Kerouac Street, **Vesuvio Café** (or "Vesuvio's") has been serving bohemians and other folks since 1949. It's a quirky bar, full of curiosities and interesting people. The Welsh poet Dylan Thomas, on his literary tours, relished his visits there. *255 Columbus Ave.; 415-362-3370.* Across Columbus Avenue and down Adler Lane, **Spec's** is another atmospheric watering hole, chock-full of curios and peopled by a crowd that—if nothing more—at least *looks* literary. *12 Adler Lane; 415-421-4112.* Almost next door is **Tosca**, which, with its operatic jukebox and Tuscan murals, is said to be the origin of the North Beach Cappuccino, an Italian-inspired answer to Irish Coffee. *242 Columbus Ave.; 415-391-1244.* For a detailed listing of other beatnik sites, read Don Herron's *The Literary World of San Francisco.*

Upper Grant Establishments

The heart of Beatnikdom used to be upper Grant, between Broadway and Filbert. The bar in the **Saloon** *(1232 Grant Ave.; 415-989-7666),* has been propping elbows since 1861, while the old beat Coffee Gallery is now a Blues joint called the **Lost and Found Saloon** *(1353 Grant Ave.; 415-392-9126).* Most of the other old haunts are gone, but **Caffè Trieste** *(601 Vallejo; 415-392-6739)* still battens down the corner of Vallejo at Grant, where it opened in 1956, making it the oldest coffeehouse on the West Coast. It stays open late. The jukebox plays Italian folk music and opera.

Heart of Little Italy

The four blocks of Columbus between Broadway and Filbert, and their lively side streets, are the busiest of Little Italy. By night, their window-side tables glow with warm light and jovial company. By day, the lunchtime crowds and shoppers fill the sidewalks. Columbus Avenue hosts the city's largest collection of cafes: **Caffè Puccini, Steps of Rome, Café Stella, Caffè Greco,** and **Café Roma,** to name but five,

not to mention the venerable **Mario's Bohemian Cigar Store** (Columbus at Union), purveyor of espresso and good cheer—though its signs now warn "No Smoking!" A forest of cheeses and sausages and other Italian treats at **Molinari's** *(373 Columbus)* enraptures with the smell alone. For another whiff of heaven, tootle round the corner to Vallejo and Stockton, where **Victoria Bakery's** basement ovens turn out breads, cakes, and cookies from several regions of Italy, including festival and wedding treats.

North Beach Museum

Take a short detour to see this small museum, on the upstairs level of a bank. Rotating collections of photographs and artifacts illustrate the changing demographics of North Beach, its social movements and immigrant families—Italian, Chinese, Irish, and others. The museum keeps banker's hours, and is free. *(1435 Stockton St.; 415-626-7070.)* Nearby, Cavalli & Company sells Italian books, magazines, and recordings. *(1441 Stockton St.; 415-776-9087).*

Club Fugazi

Beach Blanket Babylon has been running here for so long now that it has become a San Francisco institution. The cabaret-style show is famous for its outlandish, gigantic hats, outrageous musical parodies of pop-culture icons, and affectionate lampoons of all things San Franciscan. Reservations are needed. *678 Green St.; 415-421-4222.*

(right) Dining al fresco at one of North Beach's abundant cafes. (Kerrick James)

◆ WASHINGTON SQUARE

Washington Square is the heart of North Beach. Here, mostly Chinese and elderly Italians gather on (usually separate) park benches to talk about the Old Country. Backed by the spectacular **Saints Peter and Paul Catholic Church**, the "Italian Cathedral" of San Francisco, the square really does exude a Mediterranean ambience. As the church was being built in 1922, Cecil B. DeMille showed up to film the construction for a scene in *The Ten Commandments*. A good place to soak it all in is Malvina's, an old North Beach cafe now in newer quarters on Stockton at Union. It opens early for the first cup of the day, with pastries and breads at the ready. Kitty-corner is the city's oldest Italian restaurant, Fior D'Italia, in business since 1886.

The old **statue of Ben Franklin** in the middle of the park stands above a time capsule. It expired in 1979, giving up a hoard of 19th-century temperance tracts. (The statue's patron, a crusading teetotaler named Dr. Cogswell, intended this as a water fountain; note the defunct fountain heads around the base.) The capsule was promptly refilled with a poem by Ferlinghetti, a recording of the Hoodoo Rhythm Devils, a pair of Levi's, and a bottle of wine. Next opening: 2079.

Another statue in Washington Square is a sentimental monument to San Francisco's once-beloved firemen, donated by the eccentric Lillie Hitchcock Coit. The scene shows two firefighters with a rescued child. One fireman stands with an outstretched hand, which passers-by contrive to keep filled with all manner of objects, usually beverage containers. Once upon a time, firefighters were the dashing heros to every child of San Francisco, and to none more so than Lillie Coit. As a child trapped in a house afire, she never forgot the thrill of the clanging engines, and the strong, fearless fireman who climbed up to rescue her. Throughout her life, whenever she heard the bells and horses, she would drop any business (even a wedding) and chase after them, cheering them on. She was a wealthy woman, and before her death she donated the money to build Coit Tower on the top of Telegraph Hill, one of San Francisco's most cherished monuments, and easily visible on Telegraph Hill, above. Look closely; legend claims that it was designed to resemble a fire nozzle, but don't believe it.

A quiet statue of a drinking man stands in the small iron-fenced triangle of park at the southwest corner of Washington Square, on the west side of Columbus Avenue. The sculptor was Melvin Cummings, a professor at the precursor of the San Francisco Art Institute on Russian Hill. The model is said to be the same that Rodin used for *Saint John the Baptist* (which you may see in the Palace of Fine Arts).

Saints Peter and Paul Church, the "Italian Cathedral," rises over the rooftops of North Beach.

■ RUSSIAN HILL

Telegraph and Russian Hills both were cultivating reputations as bohemian districts long before North Beach received the call. Of these, Russian Hill was the earlier. Today it is a retreat of the elite, but its stairways and vistas are open to all. It takes its name not from any large Slavic presence, but from the belief that visiting Russian ship crews, down from Sitka to hunt sea otter, used to bury their dead here.

Movie producers love Russian Hill. It has what many believe to be the most classic San Franciscan vistas: stunning backgrounds of white hill and blue bay, with foreground settings of old bay-windowed houses and suddenly plunging streets, just perfect for dramatic car chases.

To reach Russian Hill, you can ride the Powell-Hyde cable car; in fact, you *ought* to ride it at least once in your life. But neither should you miss the chance to walk around Russian Hill, one of the rarer pleasures of the city. A spectacular walking route from North Beach climbs steeply up **Vallejo Street**; so steeply, in fact, that the road gives way to stairs beyond Mason Street. The city falls away as you rise, opening up Hollywood backdrops of bridges, bay, Coit Tower, and the downtown highrises. Puffing up to Ina Coolbrith Park, at Taylor, you can well understand why Russian Hill was long neglected by the worthies of the community, but greatly appreciated by poor souls with fine tastes. Naturally, it became something of a writers' colony.

◆ INA COOLBRITH PARK

Ina Coolbrith—one of San Francisco's most undersung poets and literary inspirations—was the first American child to enter California in a wagon train, crossing over Beckwourth Pass in a saddle shared with the trailblazing mountain man, Jim Beckwourth. After an unhappy marriage to a businessman in the hamlet of Los Angeles, she relocated to San Francisco, where she made her home on Russian Hill, wrote poetry, and helped to edit the *Overland Monthly*. More than one local scribbler was reputed to have fallen in love with her, including Mark Twain, Bret Harte (who reportedly offered to divorce his wife for her), Charlie Stoddard (who threatened suicide if she didn't marry him), and bitter Ambrose Bierce (who ordinarily hated women, at least intellectually). She never did remarry, however, but invited all to join her literary circle at her house on Russian Hill. She corresponded with European and East Coast poets, and became a librarian both for the Bohemian Club and the Oakland Free Library. It was in that latter capacity that she met 12-year-old Jack London, and set him on a course of reading that defined his formal education. In 1919, she became California's first Poet Laureate.

Cross Taylor Street and continue up the Vallejo Street stairs to the southern "summit" of twin-peaked Russian Hill. This small warren of lanes at the top, now quite exclusive, was once home to an eclectic array of creative types, including Bierce, Gelett Burgess, Frank Norris, and Willis Polk, who built his own house at the top of the stairs (1013 Vallejo). Don Herron notes a tradition that Burgess was inspired by the sight of a cow grazing on Russian Hill to pen his best-known rhyme:

> *I never saw a purple cow*
> *I never hope to see one,*
> *But I can tell you anyhow,*
> *I'd rather see than be one.*

Tiny, pretty **Florence Street** leads off to the south, halting at a small staircase where you should stop to admire the downtown view, including a romantic broadside of Grace Cathedral. Step on down to Broadway. This is not the Broadway of big lights and dancing mammaries. *That* Broadway was channeled by tunnel under Russian Hill to Polk Gulch in the early 1950s. *This* Broadway is the *old* route that climbed over the hill. You can see why they built the tunnel: At this point, Broadway slips so suddenly from underfoot that some thoughtful city planner has built a wall across it to stop cars from going over. Ina Coolbrith's last Russian Hill house (her earlier abode burned in 1906) stands at 1067 Broadway.

The second summit of Russian Hill—six blocks farther north on Hyde Street—is the one best known to tourists. If you're walking, you might want to detour by way of romantic **Macondray Lane**, an Arcadian lane that starts at a rickety staircase on Taylor Street. Less quaint, but certainly more fun, is the **Filbert Street hill**, which drops suddenly down from Hyde Street. Actually, to call Filbert a "hill" is like calling Beethoven's Fifth a snappy tune. At 31.5 degrees, it's the steepest driveable grade in San Francisco. Be warned; if you take it Steve McQueen-style, barreling over the brink and screeching into a right turn up Leavenworth, your car's going to need a fresh set of shocks and a new transmission when you get out of the hospital. Take it easy, and you can do it *twice*.

From the corner of Greenwich and Hyde, poetry lovers (if indeed such creatures still exist) should walk up the Greenwich steps past the Alice Marble tennis courts, to the secluded **George Sterling Glade**. This spot was treasured by Sterling, San Francisco's King of Bohemia, Ambrose Bierce's disciple, Jack London's best friend, a founding member of Carmel's artist colony, a poet called the finest of his age by many of his contemporaries, but also an alcoholic, and finally, in 1926, a suicide.

Sterling died in the Bohemian Club, leaving behind some half-burned snatches of poetry that have since become legends in the cult of Sterling, which appeals to literate romantics, occultists, and counterculture figures, as well as to lovers of intensely beautiful language and imagery. In his day, Sterling was known for (among other things) his sense of horror and demonic imagery, a quality no doubt encouraged by the macabre Bierce. Sterling's most famous lines in this vein, inscribed on the wall of the now-demolished Papa Coppa's restaurant on Montgomery Street, read *"The blue-eyed vampire, sated at her feast, Smiles bloodily against the leprous moon."* Strange, sad, and beautiful character, George Sterling; deserves to be better known.

Another literary touchstone stands on the northwest corner of Lombard and Hyde: Mrs. Robert Louis Stevenson's house. The writer died before Willis Polk built it. The crowds of tourists outside are probably not here to admire it, however. They are more interested in flagging down the Hyde Street cable car or snapping pictures in front of San Francisco's two most famous streets: Hyde and Lombard.

QUOTATIONS FROM BITTER BIERCE

Discriminate: v.i. To note the particulars in which one person or thing is, if possible, more objectionable than another.

Happiness: n. An agreeable sensation arising when contemplating another's misery.

History: n. An account, mostly false, of events mostly unimportant, which are brought about by rulers, mostly knaves, and soldiers, mostly fools.

Love: n. A temporary insanity curable by marriage.

November: n. The eleventh twelfth of a weariness.

Piracy: n. Commerce without its folly-swaddles, just as God made it.

Quill: n. An implement of torture yielded by a goose and wielded by . . . an ass.

Rash: adj. Insensible to the value of our advice.

Rear: n. In American military matters, that exposed part of the Army that is closest to Congress.

Riot: n. A popular entertainment given to the military by innocent bystanders.

Saint: n. A dead sinner, revised and edited.

—Ambrose Bierce, "The Devil's Dictionary," 1906

The "crookedest street in the world" becomes a winding parade of pink hydrangea in the spring.
(Kerrick James)

◆ LOMBARD STREET

"The crookedest street in the world" is the block of Lombard between Hyde and Leavenworth. You can walk down, enjoying its views, gardens, red cobblestones, and the little mid-block terrace called Montclair. But hey, you really ought to enjoy it the way God and Karl Malden intended you to, at the wheel of a sedan, grinding fenders on every turn.

Back at the top of the hill, look straight north, down Hyde Street and over the tall masts on the wharfs, toward Alcatraz and beyond. If you had a nickel for every time a photographer shot a cable car with this backdrop, you could probably retire to Russian Hill. The steep stretch of the Hyde Street grade, between Francisco and Bay Streets, registers 21.3 degrees.

◆ SAN FRANCISCO ART INSTITUTE

Most visitors will want to continue down Hyde to Fisherman's Wharf, but if you wish to explore Russian Hill a little further, you will be rewarded for your efforts. Those who strike west on Francisco, around the terrace to Chestnut, will be within whistling distance of one of Russian Hill's nicest surprises. The San Francisco Art Institute, established in 1871, is the oldest art school in the western U.S. It's an eccentric building, very conducive to artistic temperaments. The entrance brings to mind a medieval Italian monastery, with courtyard, cloisters, tiled fountain, and bell tower; the overgrown vacant lot across the street adds to the effect. It's somewhat of a letdown to know it was built of reinforced concrete (in 1926, by the same outfit that did City Hall and Coit Tower—Bakewell and Brown). The fact that it's concrete doesn't seem to bother the ghost who lives in the tower, however.

The small cafeteria in back is one of the few places in residential Russian Hill where you can enjoy a cup of coffee with a view over Fisherman's Wharf.

Saving the best for last, before you leave, visit the **Diego Rivera Gallery**, to the left of the main entrance on Chestnut. One wall is illuminated with a massive fresco painted by Rivera in 1931, entitled *The Making of a Fresco Showing the Building of a City*. Rivera's work, celebrating the power, color, and epic saga of people who toil, had great influence on San Francisco's Depression-era artists, as you can see when you visit the more famous (because more public) murals in Coit Tower on Telegraph Hill. *800 Chestnut St.; 415-771-7020.*

■ TELEGRAPH HILL

Telegraph Hill was named for the semaphore installed at its crest in 1850 to notify downtown merchants of ship arrivals. As anyone who stands on the top today can attest, the hill's sight lines still reach through the harbor and out the Golden Gate.

Telegraph Hill rises from Broadway so abruptly that residents just half a block up Kearny and Montgomery streets look down on Broadway neon and rooftops. The rise on the west side from North Beach is likewise steep, but neither can match the cliffs of the east side, falling sharply away to the old wharf and warehouse district. These cliffs are largely man-made. Quarries blasted away at the hillside, mostly for landfill and sea walls, until 1914. In earlier days, ships' crews quarried the rock for ballast. As they took on goods in other ports, they left the ballast as paving stones. Thus, the east slope of Telegraph Hill today spreads halfway around the world.

The hill has always been a neighborhood of immigrants. During the Gold Rush, Chileans were among the largest groups to settle there. As San Francisco settled down, the Irish moved up in droves, followed by smaller numbers of Italians, Spanish, Mexicans, Portuguese, Scandinavians, Germans, Chinese, and even some Yankees. After the earthquake of 1906, when the Irish departed for the Mission District, the Italians filled the vacuum, making Telegraph a distinctly Italian hill until recent years. Today, the Chinese have probably surpassed the Italians as the major ethnic group, especially on the North Beach side.

Eastern Telegraph Hill's relative remoteness from the rest of the city in the 1890s made it, like Russian Hill of an earlier era, an attractive district for bohemians, artists, and theatrical people. Even the humblest shacks offered spectacular views. Wine and rent were cheap. The Muses flourished. Charles Stoddard, a writer who spent his youth on Telegraph Hill, described this wonderful bohemia in his book *In the Footprints of the Padres:*

> The cottages were indeed nestlike: they were so small, so compact, so cozy, so overrun with vines and flowering foliage. Usually of one story, or of a story-and-a-half at most, they clung to the hillside facing the water, and looked out upon its noble expanse from tiny balconies as delicate and dainty as toys. . . . They loomed above their front yards while their backyards lorded it over their roofs. . . . They were usually approached by ascending or descending stairways, or by airy bridges that spanned little gullies where ran rivulets in the winter season. There were parrots on

perches at the doorways of those cottages, and songbirds in cages that were hidden away in the vines. There were pet poodles there. I think that there were more lap dogs than watch dogs in that early California.

By the 1940s, the artists were gone. The crest and eastern side of Telegraph had become chic—and so it remains today. It was, in many ways, San Francisco's first gentrified neighborhood, and the artists have been on the run ever since.

To drive on Telegraph Hill requires patience. Between Broadway and Bay Street, nine wide blocks to the north, there are no through roads. Parking is horrendous. If you drive to Coit Tower (up Lombard from North Beach), expect to wait. And wait and wait. It's better to walk, though the steep climb from Washington Square is not for sissies. Filbert and Greenwich Streets, densely packed with houses, give way to stairs and greenery at Telegraph Hill Boulevard, which hooks around from Lombard to Pioneer Park and Coit Tower, on the summit. A statue of Columbus, erected in 1957, stands in the middle of the parking circle, gazing off toward the ex-federal penitentiary on Alcatraz.

◆ COIT TOWER

Coit Tower was built with money left by Lillie Hitchcock Coit as a monument to San Francisco's pluck in the face of frequent blazes. The firm of Arthur Brown drew up plans for a cylindrical observation tower on the top of Telegraph Hill. Work started early in 1933; by October of the same year, the tower was finished. Though only 180 feet tall, Coit Tower gets a 284-foot boost from Telegraph Hill. From the top, the Bay Area spreads out gloriously in every direction. There are coin-operated telescopes for closer looks. You can pick out landmark after landmark: Mount Diablo on the eastern horizon, the Claremont Resort and Spa in the Oakland Hills, the Campanile at Berkeley, the Richmond Bridge, Alcatraz, Sausalito and Mount Tamalpais in Marin County, the Golden Gate Bridge, the Presidio, Fisherman's Wharf, wiggly Lombard Street, the rooftops of Nob Hill and Chinatown, Grace Cathedral, Twin Peaks, the downtown towers, the Bay Bridge . . . .

Back in the tower lobby, take a closer look at the murals on the walls. Commissioned during the Great Depression by the Civil Works Administration, the **frescoes** were painted by a team of 25 local artists. The murals present an incredibly vigorous picture of California life during the 1930s, a gallery of characters and scenes embracing crowded city streets, rich agricultural valleys, the mineral-rich mountains, libraries, ranch and farm hands, engineers, machinery, working animals, and a lunch

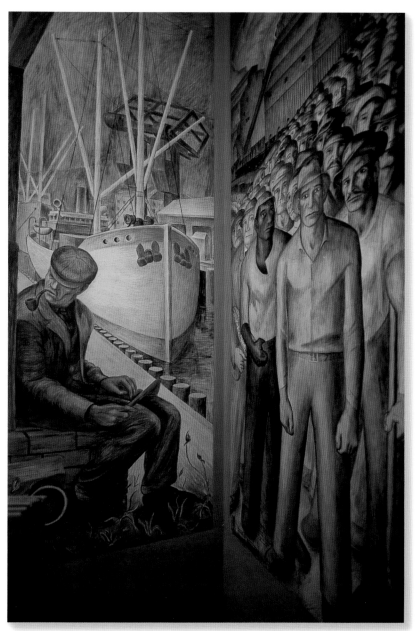

A mural at Coit Tower recalls the drama and vitality of the old waterfront. The nobility of work is the overriding theme of the WPA murals.

From its perch on Telegraph Hill, Coit Tower overlooks "the Rock"—Alcatraz. (Kerrick James)

counter, bank, department store, and press room. For subjects, the artists painted their friends and supervisors, and even Coit Tower's watchman. Their themes celebrate the richness of California's resources and people, the dignity and brotherhood of honest labor (as well as its exploitation), economic injustice, and political anger. The paintings are spiked with signs of militancy—a clenched fist, ominous newspaper headlines, the idle rich gazing at the tattered poor, a robbery in progress in the crowd at the corner of Market and Montgomery—portents of a revolution that many expected and even yearned for in 1934. The controversy over these powerful images delayed their unveiling, and smoldered for years afterward. *For Coit Tower information, call 415-362-0808.*

◆ WALKING TELEGRAPH HILL

If you have time for but one walk in San Francisco, turn your dogs loose on the eastern flank of Telegraph Hill. The steep **Greenwich and Filbert steps** nurture one of the most sylvan cityscapes in the country, most of it unapproachable by automobile. Both stairs start on the east side of Coit Tower: Greenwich Street stairs descend from the parking circle, while the Filbert Street stairs descend just a little farther down the road, where Telegraph Hill Boulevard swerves right. Whether Greenwich or Filbert makes the nicer walk is a moot point. Walk down one and up the other, and you will know the best of both.

Brick-paved Greenwich meanders down through thick foliage to emerge near a cliff on the dead-end of Montgomery Street, where perches a crenelated old wooden restaurant, Julius' Castle. Until they "widened" the street, there used to be a turntable here for automobiles. Glance over the edge before bearing right to the second stretch of Greenwich stairs, marked by a street sign, but otherwise looking like private steps to the side yard of the building. Dropping past old houses and small urban pastures of dog fennel, nasturtium, and fenced garden flowers, the Greenwich stairway lands on Sansome Street, at the eastern foot of Telegraph Hill. Turn south to meet the Filbert steps.

Filbert is the more formally landscaped stairway, a charming companion of roses, fuchsias, lilies, ivy, and other garden flowers and trees. Like Greenwich, the public steps are continuously met by private paths and stairs and picket gates that lead off to houses, coddled in flower pots and foliage, some old, some not. Just above Montgomery, near a romantic, rambling restaurant called The Shadows, there are some small terraces with benches. From here, you can study the handsome Art-Deco apartment house at 1360 Montgomery, on the corner of Filbert.

Take some time to explore **Montgomery Street** before descending to Sansome. This was the street where heroic Italians made a last stand to rescue their little homes from the great fire of 1906. In desperation, according to the story, they broke out casks of red wine and doused their houses with vino, cooling and saving them from the flames. It's a pity the tactic didn't work with developers. Still, a handful of these wine-baptized houses reportedly survives. A likely candidate is 9 Upper Calhoun Terrace, which dates from 1854. Other 19th-century survivors can be spotted by walkers. If you like heights, take a look at the views from **Upper Calhoun Terrace** and the end of Alta Street. People with vertigo can't live on Telegraph Hill.

Below Montgomery, the Filbert steps turn to wood—rickety wood, with the nails sticking out. Unpainted and enchantingly cushioned in baby tears and ferns, it leads down to the rarest of San Francisco's country lanes, Napier. Last of the city's wood plank streets, **Napier Lane** seems to be heavily populated by beautiful cats, as well as a flock of feral parrots. By all means, clomp to the end of the lane and back for a look at the old houses, which survived the fire of 1906; but for the sake of the residents and their precious atmosphere, let us strangers keep our grosser presence fleeting. Below Napier Lane, the Filbert steps drop down to Sansome Street on a new concrete stairway.

The stretch of flat ground between Telegraph Hill and the Embarcadero wharves is covered landfill once given over to brick warehouses and train tracks. The industries have long since moved. Today many of the warehouses have been beautifully remodeled into designer studios, condos, restaurants, and offices, at least one with rooftop tennis courts. Even the old roundhouse engine shed for the San Francisco North Belt Railway, at the corner of Sansome and Lombard, has been converted to an attractive office called (somewhat contradictorily) Roundhouse Square. The area is known as Media Gulch for its abundance of graphic design, advertising, and broadcast TV and radio stations.

◆ LEVI PLAZA

Levi Plaza, between Sansome and Battery Streets at Filbert, is the corporate headquarters of Levi Strauss, manufacturer of blue jeans. During the Gold Rush, Levi Strauss came to San Francisco, where he no doubt met a good number of men with holes in their britches. He set about to invent some sturdier pants using rivet-studded tent canvas. Levi's blue jeans not only tickled forty-niners' fancies, but were destined to become perhaps the greatest fashion statement of the latter half of the 20th century. Like fortune cookies, steam beer, and cable cars, blue jeans rank as a San Francisco original.

Even without its historical context, the Levi Strauss headquarters should be seen for its admirable design. The staggered lines of the building, set against the staggered housing on Telegraph Hill, enhance the view, while its brick facade echoes the surrounding warehouse walls. Bookstores, bakeries, restaurants, and a cafe on the plaza have turned an erstwhile industrial zone into a stimulating and pleasant place to relax. But best of all is the splashing fountain in Levi Plaza, built of Sierra granite, inviting you to climb through it, as you might with a real mountain stream. Across Battery Street, this mountain "creek" flows through a grassy, boulder-studded "meadow" designed by landscape architect Lawrence Halprin. How much more civilized a corporate statement than a mammoth steel tower!

A SUPERMARKET IN CALIFORNIA

*W*hat thoughts I have of you tonight, Walt Whitman, for I walked down the sidestreets under the trees with a headache self-conscious looking at the full moon.

In my hungry fatigue, and shopping for images, I went into the neon fruit supermarket, dreaming of your enumerations!

What peaches and what penumbras! Whole families shopping at night! Aisles full of husbands! Wives in the avocados, babies in the tomatoes!—and you, Garcia Lorca, what were you doing down by the watermelons?

I saw you, Walt Whitman, childless, lonely old grubber, poking among the meats in the refrigerator and eyeing the grocery boys.

I heard you asking questions of each: Who killed the pork chops? What price bananas? Are you my Angel?

I wandered in and out of the brilliant stacks of cans following you, and followed in my imagination by the store detective.

We strode down the open corridors together in our solitary fancy tasting artichokes, possessing every frozen delicacy, and never passing the cashier.

Where are we going, Walt Whitman? The doors close in an hour. Which way does your beard point tonight?

(I touch your book and dream of our odyssey in the supermarket and feel absurd.)

Will we walk all night through solitary streets? The trees add shade to shade, lights out in the houses, we'll both be lonely.

Will we stroll dreaming of the lost America of love past blue automobiles in driveways, home to our silent cottage?

Ah, dear father, graybeard, lonely old courage-teacher, what America did you have when Charon quit poling his ferry and you got out on a smoking bank and stood watching the boat disappear on the black waters of Lethe?

—Allen Ginsberg, "A Supermarket in California," 1955

■ FISHERMAN'S WHARF

Before the Virgin Mary's name was ever invoked to bless San Francisco's fishing fleet, Tin Hau looked after her fishermen. The Chinese pioneered the business at Fisherman's Wharf. The Genoese came soon after, pushing out the Chinese, and in turn were edged aside by the Sicilians. The harbor of Fisherman's Wharf was known as an Italian lake for much of its life, and the daily sailings out and back of the fleet were a colorful sight in old San Francisco.

With over-fishing and pollution, San Francisco Bay fisheries grew slack after World War II. Though you can still find boats and fishermen at the wharf, the big money-earner today is tourism. Broad swaths of the neighborhood have been given over to the tawdriest kinds of schlock shops, buskers, clowns, metallic-painted "living statues," itinerant jewelry mongers, and honky-tonk and amusements. But don't be scared away. There is a lot to see and do at Fisherman's Wharf, even if the hucksterism turns you off.

◆ PIER 39 HIGHLIGHTS

Out-of-town tourists will have plenty of company at Pier 39, the epicenter of the Wharf. In a poll of San Francisco children, a majority once voted Pier 39 as their favorite place in the city—a ringing endorsement. Refurbished as an ersatz New England wooden fishing wharf in 1978, this erstwhile cargo pier now sports two decks of shops and amusements, including an aquarium, a carousel with a mezzanine, a calliope, street performers, and a resident colony of noisy sea lions. *Call 415-981-7437 for recorded information.*

Underwater World

Meet the sub-marine residents of the bay on a conveyor-belt ride through a transparent underwater tube, surrounded by sharks, rays, rockfish, and a host of other specimens usually served on platters in this neighborhood. *Pier 39; 415-623-5300.*

The Great San Francisco Adventure

Here's your chance to experience an earthquake, skate down Lombard Street, meet some San Francisco characters, and take in several other distinctly San Francisco experiences, without stirring from your seat in the Cinemax Theater. *Pier 39; 415-956-3456.*

Turbo Ride

If you haven't had enough virtual sightseeing yet, this contraption with hydraulically rigged seats and a giddy, high-tech graphics and motion picture backdrop simulates the thrill of a roller coaster. *Pier 39; 415-392-8872.*

Tourists aren't the only ones who enjoy a seafood dinner at Fisherman's Wharf (opposite).

The City Store

This curious store peddles bits of the city: road signs, pieces cable from the cable car lines, Lombard Street bricks, historic photos, etc. Nab a Haight-Ashbury corner street sign without breaking the law. *Pier 39, upper level; 415-433-7221.*

The National Park Store

This is the place for books or memorabilia on America's national park's, including an extensive selection on the Golden Gate National Recreation Area and Point Reyes National Seashore. *Pier 39, upper level; 415-788-5322.*

◆ PIER 41 & BOAT TRIPS ON THE BAY

Fisherman's Wharf sports the busiest docks on the bay, and not just owing to the fishing fleet. Locals and tourists alike enjoy getting out on the bay for ever-intriguing views of San Francisco, its hills, islands, and bridges. Whether you opt for a tour cruise, a dinner and dancing excursion, or a jaunt across the water on a ferry, you'll find something to meet your desires at the docks of Fisherman's Wharf. Ferries depart Pier 41 several times daily for Angel Island *(see page 221)*, Sausalito *(see page 218)*, Oakland's Jack London Square *(see page 241)*, and, with advance reservations, Alcatraz *(see page 138)*. As you amble through the crowds on Jefferson Street near the fishing fleet dock, you'll encounter a number of individual boats offering charter tours, often advertised by barkers barking at the top of their lungs. *The*

Boating on the bay is a favorite pastime of locals and tourists alike. (Kerrick James)

Blue & Gold Fleet offers cruises and charters from Pier 41 (415-705-5444) and trips to Alcatraz (415-705-5555 for reservations); while the Red & Gold Fleet offers a variety of excursions from Pier 43; 415-447-0597.

◆ HEART OF
FISHERMAN'S WHARF

The success of the famous Italian seafood restaurants of Fisherman's Wharf—Scoma's, Castagnola's, Alioto's, A. Sabella's, and others—demonstrates the relative profitability of cooking fish over catching them. In the hubbub of tourists and smelly crab pots cluttering the walks in front you can still find live and cooked shrimp and crabs for sale. Unfortunately, the shell-fish have

Crab vendor Tony Cresci is a Fisherman's Wharf fixture.
(Kerrick James)

to share the stalls with trinkets, postcards, and such unseaworthy snacks as chicken. To try the local specialty, Dungeness crab, come between mid-November and June; the peak of the season is around December.

If you want to see, hear, and smell the *real* Fisherman's Wharf, go behind the restaurants to the boat harbor, where wheeling gulls and barking sea lions try to bum free meals from the fish handlers. Walk out along the shore-facing side of Pier 45 to see the working boats. Many today are owned by Vietnamese and Korean fishermen. The fish-processing plant, one of the largest on the West Coast, hits its stride in the wee hours of the morning, finishing up most of its work long before the tourists begin their morning crawl along Jefferson Street, a great place to be if you came to San Francisco to buy a T-shirt.

The USS *Pampanito*

This fighting submarine sank six Japanese ships and damaged four others during the Second World War, narrowly escaping destruction on two occasions. She participated in the tragic raid that sank the Kachidoki Maru and Rakuyo Maru, which were carrying British and Australian POWs, though she managed to rescue 73. Keep in mind, as you squeeze through the tight passages, that this ship carried a complement of 10 officers and 70 enlisted men. The *Pampanito* gives new meaning to the word claustrophobia. It's open daily for self-guided tours. *Pier 45; 415-771-6188.*

Ripley's Believe It or Not Museum

If you've never seen a two-headed calf or met a gentleman with two pupils in each eyeball—and if this deprivation just happens to be burning a hole in you soul—then hie thee hither without delay. *175 Jefferson St.; 415-771-6188.*

Wax Museum

This ever-popular showcase of wax celebrities, ghouls, and other characters from the silver screen and the scary freaks of the Chamber of Horrors was undergoing renovation at press time. One can only surmise that, when it opens again in late 1999, it will retain some of the beloved classics, like Brigitte Bardot (if you don't know who she is, ask your grandpa) and Frankenstein. *145 Jefferson St.; 415-885-4975.*

The Cannery

This old Del Monte fruit-canning factory was one of the country's first brick factory buildings to be converted into a shopping mall. The present incarnation entices browsers to poke through its three levels of restaurants, clothing boutiques, galleries, and specialty shops selling such eclectic items as collector dolls, candles, designer fishing gear, and Native American arts and crafts. *Turn off Jefferson to Leavenworth; the Cannery is at 2801 Leavenworth; 415-771-3112.*

The Museum of the City of San Francisco

With a powerful theme but a wimpy budget, this serious museum is cheated of the venue and attention it deserves. The modest collection is made up of pictures and artifacts intriguing to aficionados, but unlikely to fire up much enthusiasm among the uninitiated. The current highlight is the gigantic head of the *Goddess of Progress,* a statue that used to stand atop the old City Hall until the 1906 quake knocked her off her pedestal. *Third floor of the Cannery; 415-928-0289.*

(right) Once a fruit-canning plant, the Cannery is now an upscale mall.

ALCATRAZ—"THE ROCK"

In 1775, Spanish explorer Juan Manuel de Ayala sailed into the bay on the *San Carlos* and named the 12-acre, guano-splattered hump *Isla de los Alcatraces* after the abundant pelicans (*alcatraces* in Spanish) he noted there. In 1853, construction of a military garrison began, and in 1861 the island was put to use for incarceration, becoming a military prison for Confederate sympathizers and unruly U.S. soldiers. Later in the century, Native Americans were held here as POWS from the Indian Wars of the West.

From 1933 to its closure in 1963, Alcatraz was the most notorious federal penitentiary in the country. Known as "The Rock," Alcatraz was a prisoner's prison, whose inmates were men unable to live by the rules of other penitentiaries. Famous guests included such superstars of crime as Machine Gun Kelly, Al Capone, Alvin "Creepy" Carpis, and Robert Stroud, the Birdman of Alcatraz who, in fact, did all his bird research at Leavenworth before being sent to Alcatraz for a prison murder. What did The Rock have that Sing Sing didn't? Aside from its terrible reputation, a tough and mostly silent regimen, and a tantalizing view of civilization at its most hedonistic, probably not much. True, Alcatraz was surrounded by a frigid bay, raked by powerful currents. On the other hand, it had good food and warm showers—the better, it was said, to keep prisoners too soft to escape.

After a scenic ferry ride from the Fisherman's Wharf, contemporary visitors are loosed on The Rock to explore on their own. Climbing up the grim hill through the sally port, most people head straight for the large cell block on the top of the island. There they wander quietly through the hospital ward (where the crazed Birdman spent much of his time), cafeteria, recreation yard, and solitary confinement in "D" block, where bullet holes in the wall testify to the bloody prison uprising in 1946. Most sobering of all is to stand among the tiers of empty cell blocks and imagine what life was like here. The rangers (whose ranks are sometimes bolstered by former guards and by ex-prisoners who served time here) have many stories to tell about life on The Rock.

One of the most mysterious stories involves Frank Morris (portrayed by Clint Eastwood in *Escape from Alcatraz*) and the Anglin brothers. After digging through the ventilation shafts in their cells, they prepared for their escapes by fashioning lifelike decoy masks from plaster and hair gathered from the barbershop. On the appointed night, they tucked the dummies into their beds and escaped to the roof. Having manufactured a raft from raincoats, they inflated it with an accordion bellows, and shoved off the island in the dark. They were never seen again. Officially, they are presumed dead—drowned and swept by currents through the Golden Gate—but intriguing reports of sightings still crop up from time to time. You can see a dummy setup in the main cell block (jocularly called Broadway), but the real masks are in the Maritime Museum archives at Aquatic Park *(see page 140)*. Their extraordinary getaway hastened the prison's closure a year later, in 1963. After the last prisoners were transferred elsewhere, The Rock was again left to the pelicans, until, in 1969, a group of Native Americans took over the island, citing an 1868 treaty granting them the right to claim uninhabited federal land. Without water or supplies, they had to end their occupation 19 months later. On October 12, 1972, Alcatraz fell under the control of the Golden Gate National Recreation Area.

Visiting Alcatraz
The Blue & Gold Fleet runs seven ferries a day to the island from Pier 41. Tickets for adults cost $11; for children, $6. Purchase tickets in advance by calling 415-705-5555, or buy them at the Pier 41 ticket counter. Price includes an excellent self-guided audio tour. *For other tour options and park information, call the Alcatraz ranger station at 415-705-1042.*

The dismal prison on Alcatraz now hosts only tourists.

◆ AQUATIC PARK

At the end of Van Ness, Municipal Pier hooks out like an arm into the bay, embracing the small harbor off Aquatic Park. Walk out to the end, enjoying the robust sea air and bracing views of the cityscape and the Golden Gate Bridge spreading out poetically all around you. Back on land, rows of bleachers above the beach provide seating for readers, bongo players, and day-dreamers. If you notice any swimmers plying the frigid bay, most likely they're a walrus-blooded member of the Dolphin South-End Rowing Club, headquartered on the rickety piers on the eastern edge of the beach.

Ghirardelli Square

The most sophisticated and attractive shopping mall in the Fisherman's Wharf area was converted from the redbrick factory buildings of Ghirardelli Chocolate, erected between 1900 and 1916. The Ghirardelli sign on the roof is a local landmark. The maze of passages, warm buildings, and sunny plazas are a delight for walking or sitting. There are more than 70 highly browsable shops displaying an array of crafts, foods, clothing, jewelry, books, and toys for grown-ups. The Ghirardelli Chocolate Manufactory, on the plaza below the Clock Tower, sells the famous chocolate, although it is now manufactured in San Leandro (in the East Bay). You can mull over the old chocolate-making machines while waiting for an expensive—and deliciously decadent—sundae. *On Beach St., uphill from Aquatic Park; 415-775-5500.*

San Francisco National Maritime Museum

Sitting like an ocean liner run aground in Aquatic Park, this excellent repository of ship models, nautical instruments, and old photographs and paintings recalls the spirited maritime history of San Francisco. The indoor collection is a great primer to the saltier collection of real ships down on the Hyde Street Pier. *Aquatic Park; 415-556-3002.*

Historic Ships at Hyde Street Pier

The heart and soul of the Maritime Museum are several great ships, permanently docked at the Hyde Street Pier. Old salts are on hand to answer questions and to demonstrate such practical skills as boat building, knot tying, and woodcarving. The flagship of the fleet is the *Balclutha,* a magnificent three-masted Cape Horn veteran launched in 1887. This venerable hulk used to make two round-trips yearly between the British Isles and San Francisco, trading California wheat for coal and whiskey. Later she worked in the Alaskan fish-packing trade, spending winters in San Francisco Bay. Walk the decks and explore the cabins and hold. Fans of the TV series *Nash Bridges* will recognize her as the police detective's floating office.

The handsome paddle-wheeler *Eureka*

was originally launched as a train ferry in the 1890s, and then ferried autos and people between her present berth and the North Bay from 1922 to 1941. The magazine store (for display purposes only) on the upper deck has some interesting period magazines.

The *C.A. Thayer*, another three-masted sailing ship, used to sail in the lumber trade along the Pacific coast. She retired in 1950. The tiny *Alma*, a lumber scow from the North Bay, is too small to allow landlubbers aboard. The *Eppleton Hall*, a British paddle-wheel harbor tug, is closed while awaiting restoration. Other vessels under care of the Maritime Museum are scattered at other berths. The *Wampama*, a steam schooner from the Pacific coast trade, is undergoing refurbishment across the bay in Sausalito. *Western end of Fishermen's Wharf, adjacent to Aquatic Park; 415-556-3000.*

The barque Star of Shetland *was one of many ships to sail into the booming port of San Francisco. (Photo by Gabriel Moulin, courtesy of the San Francisco Maritime National Historic Park)*

THE CULTIVATED
QUARTER

CULTIVATED
QUARTER

THE NORTHWESTERN CORNER OF SAN FRANCISCO encompasses some of the city's most opulent, poised, and cultivated neighborhoods. Sure, there are decrepit sections, too, but over all, the hard realities of urban life are less apparent here than in any other quarter. San Franciscans treat this section rather like their own backyard—jamming favored shopping and supping precincts, like Union, Clement, and Fillmore Streets; puttering around the museums; retreating to the solitudes of Golden Gate and Lincoln Parks. This is San Francisco's most romantic quarter, a bright collage of noisy markets and thundering seacoasts, Old Masters in silent rooms, spiked cannons, and overgrown gardens, haunted by cypress trees and foghorn music.

■ GOLDEN GATE NATIONAL RECREATION AREA

What other major American city comes boxed in a national park? Embracing San Francisco's northern and western shores, Golden Gate National Recreation Area (GGNRA) links a number of abandoned military properties in San Francisco with extensive tracts of the Marin Headlands, a semi-wilderness across the Golden Gate Bridge. With nearly 80,000 acres, the GGNRA is more than twice as big as the city itself, and receives 20 million visitors per year.

Park headquarters for the GGNRA is Fort Mason, western command post for the U.S. Army from the 1860s through the 1880s, and a major military depot during America's Pacific wars. Fort Mason still retains its fortlike mien, but the old quarters, warehouses, and docks are now given over to the fruits of peace. One of San Francisco's most important cultural centers, Fort Mason today shelters a host of museums, theaters, galleries, and nonprofit institutions promoting culture and conservation. A free monthly newspaper, Fort Mason Center, keeps track of events. A quarterly publication, Park Events, promotes the ggnra's activities. For up-to-the-minute news, maps, and information, go to the headquarters building near Franklin Street Gate; *415-441-5705.*

West of the Great Meadow from the information center (and down a flight of steps) lie the former fort's bayside wharfs. From these piers, where fishermen now try their luck, one and a half million U.S. soldiers embarked for the Pacific theater during World War II. The converted warehouses are a smorgasbord of curious sights, lively arts, delicious food, and noble causes. The vast halls on the piers are put to use for large social events, benefits, craft shows, and the like.

◆ FORT MASON SIGHTS

San Francisco Craft & Folk Art Museum

This tiny gallery features rotating exhibits of folk art and contemporary crafts from around the world. It also has a wonderful shop that sells quality handmade ethnographic goods such as toys and clothes. *Building A; 415-775-0990.*

Greens Restaurant

This famous vegetarian restaurant with ties to a Zen monastery serves imaginative and satisfying dishes in a setting graced with beautiful views of bobbing yachts and the majestic span of the Golden Gate Bridge. Reservations are highly recommended for dinner, but you might prefer lunch here anyway to enjoy the daytime view. Or buy something from the restaurant's bakery and eat outside. *Building A; 415-771-6222.*

Museo Italo Americano

This venue presents rotating exhibits of contemporary art by Italian and Italian-American artists. *Building C; 415-673-2200.*

African-American Historical & Cultural Society

With a library, gallery space, and exhibits of African arts, this museum honors African-American cultural contributions to California. Among the prominent San Francisco pioneers featured are William Alexander Leidesdorff, a Virgin Islands sea captain who sailed his ship, the *Julia Ann,* into San

THE NORTHWEST QUARTER

0   ½   1   1½   2

Miles

Map Area

OCEAN

Golden Gate
Bridge
(toll, south bound)

Golden

FORT POINT

To
San Rafael

Toll
Area

Guns

Batteries

Golden Gate
National
Recreation
Area

BAKER
BEACH

Battery
Chamberlain

MILE ROCK   Mile Rock
Lighthouse

N
W   E
S

LANDS END

CHINA
BEACH

MILE ROCK
BEACH

Palace of the
Legion of Honor

El Camino del Mar

S E A C L I F F

Lincoln
Park

Lincoln Park
Municipal
Golf Course

Lake

Rochambeau
Playground

Richmond
Playground

Lookout

Legion of Honor Dr

Club
House

California

POINT LOBOS

USS
San Francisco
Memorial

Fort
Miley

St Mary the
Virgin in Exile

Clement

Point Lobos Ave

43rd
42nd
40th
38th
36th
34th
32nd
30th
28th
25th
22nd
19th
16th

Geary

Sutro Baths
(Ruins)

Sutro
Heights
Park

R   I   C   H   M   O   N   D

SEAL
ROCKS

Cliff House

47th
45th

Anza

Balboa

La Playa

Ave
Ave
Ave
Ave
Ave
Ave
Ave
Ave
Ave

Cabrillo

Ave
Ave
Ave
Ave

Fulton

Queen
Wilhelmina
Tulip Garden

Archery
Field

Prayer
Book Cross

Petanque
Field

Model
Boat
Club

Spreckels
Lake

MARX MEADOW

Portals
of the Past

J.F. Kennedy

Dutch
Windmill

North
Lake

Chain of Lakes

Buffalo
Paddock

Llyod
Lake

Transverse Dr

Boat
House

LINDLEY MEADOW

Golden Gate Park
Municipal
Golf Course

Fly
Casting
Pool

Angler's
Lodge

SPEEDWAY MEADOW
West

STRAWBERR
HILL

OCEAN

Beach
Chalet

Dr

Middle
Lake

Polo Field

Dr

Metson
Lake

Elk Glen
Lake

Stow L

Stow
Lake

BEACH

Golden

South
Lake

Middle

Gate

Park

Way

Murphy
Windmill

Martin Luther King Jr

Dr

Lincoln

Mallard
Lake

J.F. Kennedy

PACIFIC

Great Highway

La Playa

47th
45th
43rd
41st
40th

Sunset Blvd

34th
31st
28th
25th
22nd
19th
16th

Irving

Ave
Ave
Ave
Ave
Ave

S   U   N   S   E   T

Judah

Ave
Ave
Ave
Ave

Kirkham

Golden Gate
Bridge

G
Fo
Nation

Blvd

Ma

Lincoln

Washington

Blvd

El Camino del Mar

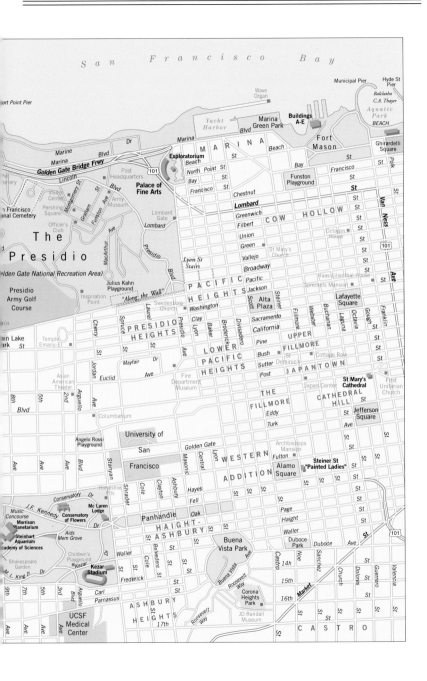

Francisco Bay in 1841. He liked the place, and stayed. Before his death at 38, he built a shipping empire, opened San Francisco's first hotel, and served as city treasurer, American vice consul of Yerba Buena, and administrator of the first American public school in California. His warehouses stood on the present site of Leidesdorff Street, in the Financial District. Leidesdorff is buried under the floor of Mission Dolores. *Building C; 415-441-0640.*

Mexican Museum

This unsung jewel houses a large collection of Mexican art ranging from preconquest and colonial artifacts to folk and contemporary arts and crafts. The vibrant rotating exhibits are filled with a fascinating blend of works by Mexican and Mexican-American artists and creations from ancient cultures of Mexico such as the Maya, Aztec, and Olmec peoples. Attached to the galleries is a fascinating shop selling pottery, masks, blankets, baskets, books, clothing, toys, a variety of colorful Mexican handicrafts. Pick up a free map of Mission District walking tours here, or inquire about guided tours. *Building D; 415-441-0404.*

The J. Porter Shaw Library

Exuding a nautical atmosphere, this orderly library stows more than 30,000 books, oral history recordings, archives, ship models, and other paraphernalia dealing with San Francisco's maritime and whaling industries. If you have a nautical question, they have a nautical answer. *Building E; 415-556-9870.*

Fort Mason Theaters

Some of San Francisco's premier experimental theaters are based at Fort Mason. The intimate, avant-garde **Magic Theatre** *(Building D; 415-441-8822)* has premiered the works of Pulitzer Prize–winning playwright Sam Shepard. **Young Performers Theater** *(Building C; 415-775-0252)* is both an acting school and playhouse for children, the perfect place to introduce your kids to the magical world of live theater. (Its counterpart in the visual art world, the Children's Art Center, is on the ground floor.) The **Cowell Theater** *(Pier 2; 415-441-3400)* and **Bayfront Theatre** *(Building B; 415-776-8999)* also host dance and dramatic productions.

Golden Gate Promenade

This scenic 3.5-mile pathway runs along San Francisco's north shore from Aquatic Park to the Golden Gate Bridge, cutting through Fort Mason. Linking San Francisco's urban core with its wild hinterlands, the Promenade traverses rocky coast, sandy beaches, historic army land, and exclusive city enclaves, ending at Fort Point, under the Golden Gate Bridge. From there, hikers can strike south on the 9.1-mile-long Coastal Trail, which passes Baker Beach, Lincoln Park, the Cliff House, Ocean Beach, and Fort Funston, or they can head north across the Golden Gate Bridge to ply the trails of the Marin Headlands, Muir Woods, Mount Tamalpais, and Point Reyes National Seashore.

■ THE MARINA

The Marina District is a flat, tidy, pastel neighborhood of wide, swept sidewalks, smacking of respectability. Because it was built on landfill, notoriously unstable in a tremor, the Marina was one of the two city districts hardest hit in the 1989 earthquake (the other being South of Market). Only minutes after the quake, pictures of collapsed Marina District housing and a fire were flashing across the country, and indeed the world, inadvertently leading many to believe that flames were engulfing the entire city. In fact, most of the scenes of greatest residential damage in San Francisco were shot in the Marina. Though the district's particular vulnerability in the next quake no doubt worries most residents, life has returned to normal here.

Chestnut, the Marina's main shopping street, was long considered exactly that—a chestnut—until the trendy commercialization of nearby Union Street taught Marina residents to cherish Chestnut Street's neighborly virtues. The quiet mix of delis, restaurants, cafes, and boutiques, with a homey bookstore and magic shop thrown in, still caters to a mostly young and upwardly mobile local clientele.

The nearby Marina Green is the promenade *par excellence* for the young mon-eyed set, who come from miles around to walk their dogs, play volleyball, in-line skate, or tend their boats moored at the adjacent St. Francis and Golden Gate yacht clubs. The Green also rates high among kite fliers for the unobstructed winds that blow fine and fresh from the Golden Gate. Views are superb.

At the west end of Marina Green, walkers can continue west on the Golden Gate Promenade to Fort Point, or they can turn east to the end of the West Harbor jetty to see the world's most peculiar musical instrument. Frankly, the **wave organ** resembles no Wurlitzer you've ever seen. What it looks like most, in fact, is a jumbled rostrum of broken tombstones strangulated by pipes crawling up from the sea bed. Waves striking the submerged ends of the pipes force air out through the other ends, moaning and gurgling, a true sea ditty if ever there was one. Stonemason George Gonzalez and the assistant director of the Exploratorium, Peter Richards, designed the wave organ to play loudest at high tides.

◆ PALACE OF FINE ARTS

If you turn south at Marina Green and walk south one block on Baker Street, you will come to the Palace of Fine Arts, San Francisco's last vestige of its most glorious fair. The Panama-Pacific International Exposition of 1915 officially marked the

The Palace of Fine Arts (right) was originally constructed for the 1915 Panama-Pacific International Exposition, depicted in the diorama above (top photo). Immediately behind the Palace stands the kid-oriented Exploratorium (bottom photo), where hands-on exhibits illustrate scientific laws and phenomena. (above photos, Kerrick James)

opening of the Panama Canal, but most San Franciscans knew it was really a monumental coming-out party for a city risen from the ashes of 1906. Its splendor was, by most accounts, unmatched by any world's fair before or since. Local poet Edwin Markham, admittedly fond of rhetorical hyperbole, deemed it "the greatest revelation of beauty that has ever been seen on earth," but even the sobersided *New York World* swore it was so "indescribably beautiful" that "it gives you a choky feeling in your throat as you look at it." Visitors delighted in the fairyland of brilliant electrical lighting, the Tower of Jewels, a five-acre working model of the Panama Canal, the "palaces" of Education, Horticulture, and Industry, and the fair's lovely centerpiece, the Palace of Fine Arts, designed by Bernard Maybeck as a colonnaded mock-Roman ruin built beside a reflecting pool. (A complete model of the Panama-Pacific fair, incidentally, is displayed at the Presidio Army Museum.)

When the fair closed and the buildings were dismantled, San Franciscans could not bear to raze the Palace of Fine Arts, sparing it for a half century's slow decay until a Marina resident generously donated the funds to rebuild it in 1962. A monumental salute to art for art's sake, the Palace of Fine Arts still rises enchantingly from its sylvan duck pond, a fantastic rotunda transported from a romanticized classic age. Sculptured maidens atop the colonnades weep piteously, filling the palace with a melancholy air of mystery.

◆ EXPLORATORIUM

Immediately behind the rotunda stands the Exploratorium, once dubbed the finest science museum in the country by *Scientific American*. Even people who find science a bore are engrossed by the Exploratorium, and no one has more fun than kids— older kids, that is. The Exploratorium was founded by Frank Oppenheimer (brother of A-bomb inventor J. Robert Oppenheimer) to encourage people to explore the wonders of physics and the human senses. Visitors do not merely learn *how* things work; they actually take hold of the more than 400 hands-on displays and experiments and *make* them work. You can custom-design a bubble, engineer a water spout, create fog or St. Elmo's fire in a vacuum, step into an optical illusion, or crawl through the sound- and light-proof Tactile Dome to test your reaction to an environment deprived of those sensations. Other experiments explain the behavior of light, color, motion, sound, plant and animal behavior, and electricity. There are also classes, a film program, and a marvelous store stocking scientific toys, maps, books, and experiments. *3601 Lyon Street; 415-561-0360.*

■ THE PRESIDIO

The main gate of the Presidio stands ajar on Lyon Street at Lombard, three blocks south of the Exploratorium. The Presidio was founded by the Spanish in 1776 to guard the entrance to San Francisco Bay. The Americans inherited the Presidio from Mexico when they annexed California, and turned it over to the U.S. Sixth Army. After more than two centuries as a military reservation, it closed in 1995 and was turned over to the National Park Service for operation. Although the most important features of the historic site are already open as part of the GGNRA, a large portion of the 1,480-acre Presidio cannot be maintained under the present budget, and remains in limbo while Congress debates its fate.

The Presidio contains the largest tract of forest in the city and more than 800 buildings. Among the most interesting attractions are the Presidio Army Museum, a National Cemetery, beautiful walking paths, rows of 19th-century officers' houses and barracks, El Polin Spring (revered by the Ohlone and the Spanish for its fertility-inducing properties), Fort Point, and the gun batteries above Baker Beach. A car is handy here. Get your bearings at the **Visitor Center**, housed in one of the brick Montgomery Barracks houses along the northwestern edge of the old Main Post parade ground. *Montgomory St., on the Parade Ground; (415) 561-4323.*

Pershing Square, at the southern end of the Parade Ground, was named for Gen. John Pershing, the first commander of American troops in Europe during World War I. He served at the Presidio for several years prior to departing for Mexico in pursuit of Pancho Villa, in 1916. General Pershing suffered a personal calamity here in 1915, when fire destroyed his house, killing his wife and three daughters.

The tragic heroine of San Francisco's most famous love story was born and raised on the Presidio. In 1806, when Concepcion Arguello was 15 years old, a seasoned Russian diplomat, Nikolai Rezanof, arrived in San Francisco Bay seeking aid for the starving Russian colony at Sitka, Alaska. As *comandante* of the Presidio, Concepcion's father entertained him with the best Hispanic hospitality, despite well-justified suspicions of Russian intentions. Completely green in the ways of the politic world, Concepcion fell in love with the Russian, who in turn proposed marriage. Before sailing through the Golden Gate with his hard-won supplies, he reminded her that since he was Russian Orthodox and she a Roman Catholic, he would have to get permission from both the czar and the pope. The journey, he noted, would take years, but Concepcion said she would wait.

Military animals and pets are laid to rest in the Presidio pet cemetery.

Rezanof never returned. In time, Concepcion retired to a Dominican convent, disavowing all connection with the world, and burying her sorrow beneath decades of silence and daily ritual. Then one day came bittersweet news: her fiancé had not abandoned her. He had frozen to death in the snows of Siberia some 40 years before, en route to petition the czar. Concepcion died in the convent, and is buried in Benicia, where strangers still strew her grave with flowers.

The Officers' Club on Moraga Avenue, at the southern end of Pershing Square, incorporates some of the adobe walls of the Spanish-era fort where Concepcion's father served (and indeed, where the young lady lived). The oldest complete building on the Presidio, however, is the handsome Old Station Hospital, now the **Presidio Army Museum.** Built in 1863 on the corner of what is now Funston and Lincoln, it is surrounded by spiked artillery and mothballed missiles. The Army carried away most of its property when it departed—including exhibits dealing with the American military era. The National Park Service will be working for years to reshape the focus and acquire new displays. In the meantime, the museum still recounts the Presidio's role as a refuge after the 1906 earthquake, displays a model of the 1915 Panama-Pacific International Exposition, and houses other exhibits of local military interest. *Funston at Lincoln Blvd.; 415-561-4331.*

The National Military Cemetery, where American war veterans are buried, lies farther west on Lincoln Boulevard. Less dramatic than the cemeteries of Normandy or Gettysburg, where every stone marks a life cut down on the field, the National Military Cemetery is nonetheless a compelling spot to reflect on the generations and individuals that bore the brunt of sacrifice in America's wars. The flag here is never lowered. Among the more famous gravestones, you will find the names of the Indian scout Two Bits and Union Civil War spy Pauline Cushman Fryer, an actress by profession.

Judging by the burgeoning number of new markers at the **pet cemetery** on Crissy Field Avenue, civilians have apparently usurped this graveyard once reserved for four-legged military personnel. Behind the white picket fence lies many a beastly hero, including General Pershing's horse.

Other military pets lie at rest here, with such epitaphs as "Trouble 1956–1965/ He was no trouble" and "Here lie our beloved rats/Chocolate/Candy" and "Skipper/ Best damn dog we ever had."

As guardian of the sea-approaches to San Francisco Bay, the Presidio hosts several abandoned artillery emplacements, some dating back to the 19th century. Its Pacific-facing ridge once bristled with the guns of batteries Marcus Miller, Godfrey, Dynamite, Crosby, and Chamberlain. This formidable pack, now defanged, are linked along the Coastal Trail, which runs south from the Golden Gate Bridge. The 1906-vintage **Battery Chamberlain** still contains a 95,000-pound disappearing gun carriage, designed to avoid incoming shells by ducking behind reinforced concrete walls. The mechanism still works. Rangers offer weekend tours.

Baker Beach, below, like many Northern California beaches, is dangerous for swimming. It does offer fishing, a long stretch of soft sand, and panoramic views of the Golden Gate Bridge and the Marin Headlands, while the planted forests of Monterey pine and cypress protect picnickers from the wind.

■ FORT POINT

The most spectacular fortress on the California coast is Fort Point, crouching with spine-tingling drama beneath the southern arch of the Golden Gate Bridge. You do not find too many Civil War–era forts west of Vicksburg, but Fort Point is the genuine article, built between 1853 and 1861 to guard the entrance to San Francisco Bay from marauders. Planted a mere 10 feet above the water, and exposed to

Army officers once inhabited the brick homes which line the Presidio's shady cul-de-sacs.

rough winds that sometimes whip the sea over the approach road, Fort Point is one of San Francisco's most exhilarating surprises.

Fort Winfield Scott, as it is officially known, once bristled with 126 cannons, but never fired a shot in anger; just as well, too, because it was obsolete almost before it was completed. Of similar design to historic Fort Sumter, Fort Point's brick walls were likewise rendered vulnerable to the new rifled-bore artillery barrels (which put a spin on fired shells) and heavier munitions developed in the Civil War.

Visitors enter through great, studded doors to a sally port, where defenders firing through gun embrasures could pick off storming parties before they breached the next door. The massive walls are built around a courtyard, where three tiers rise up on vaulting arches to a barbette roof. On the ground floor, southeast corner, the powder room is arranged much as it used to be, encased behind 15-foot thick walls. The extraordinary vaulting brickwork is a rarity in San Francisco, where the abundance of good timber encouraged wood-frame housing. Amazingly, Fort Point survived the 1906 quake with flying colors.

Living quarters occupied the east side, with officers on the second floor and enlisted men on the third, 70 to each barracks. Among their regular duties, the men were under orders to wash their feet twice a week, and to take a bath once a month. Their quarters now contain a small but interesting museum, with pictures, uniforms, and weapons. All in all, Fort Point must have been a cold, bleak, and very boring assignment.

Casemates overlooking the Golden Gate mark the business end of operations, presenting four tiers of formidable firepower to any enemy ship that got within a three-mile range. Climbing to the rooftop barbette, where rotating guns could fire over the parapets at moving ships, visitors are usually blasted with cold Pacific winds. It's worth every goose bump for the spectacular views of bridge, bay, rocks, and the craziest clique of windsurfers you've ever seen. Watching them skirt and dart about the hulking, frigid, green Pacific waves in the shadow of the gargantuan bridge piers makes for one of the most riveting and dramatic cityscapes in the world.

The fort is open daily, and entrance is free. Regular tours are given by docents dressed in Civil War garb, but you can wander about at will. Check the bookstore for schedules, information, and a terrific array of historical publications. *Fort Point Visitors Center; 415-556-1693.*

■ THE GOLDEN GATE

The skylines of New York, Paris, and Hong Kong are potent symbols of earthly power and order, but San Francisco at the Golden Gate is radiant beyond compare. The Golden Gate Bridge is arguably the Earth's most harmonious mastery of nature by mankind. What other structure radiates such majesty, such complexity of character? Viewed from any angle, or comprehended statistically, the bridge is marvelous both to rational minds and romantic ones, a symbol of serene grace in the midst of roiling clouds and open sea, a beacon of vaulting triumph, reason, beauty, and mathematical truth, and yet, a brooding mystery, a haunting presence, a siren song of suicides.

The view from Fort Point is awesome, from Lincoln Park, majestic, and from the Marin Headlands, almost unbelievably sublime. From the Berkeley Hills it is seen tenuously stretched, as if faintly threading a continental rift; looking up from below, it is overpoweringly vast. To motor across on a sunny day is to consort with elegance; to walk it on a windy one is pure exhilaration—or terror, if you fear heights. From the deck of a ship approaching from a long Pacific crossing, it can move a wandering native soul to tears, or cheers.

(following pages) The Golden Gate Bridge, scene here from the Marin Headlands with San Francisco in the background, is the perfect collaboration of man and nature. (Kerrick James)

Like most complex personalities, the Golden Gate Bridge is easier to appreciate when you know its history. Three miles long and one mile wide, the Golden Gate—the name of the bay entrance from which the bridge takes its name—is the largest gap in the Coast Ranges for many miles, and yet it was completely missed by Cabrilho, Drake, and other European explorers over the centuries. How could anything so big and important have been overlooked for so long? Perhaps it was foggy; but it's also true that from a distance at sea, the narrow gate appears solidly plugged by the Berkeley Hills behind it. Once discovered by Europeans, however, the excellent bay attracted envious scouts from many nations. When Washington finally sprang for it in 1846, some congressmen were calling it the greatest natural asset of the Far West.

An asset, yes; but no candy-asset. The tidal surge through the gate sucks out a volume of water equal to 14 times the flow of the Mississippi, at speeds up to 60 miles per hour. The currents have carved a deep canyon beneath the Gate. Wracked by storms and fogs, the rocky shores outside the Gate have claimed their share of shipwrecks. Against such extraordinary odds, bridging the Gate was un-thinkable to all but madmen and poets.

Appropriately enough, Emperor Norton was one of the first to propose it. He was followed by a poet named Joseph Strauss, who also happened to be an engineer. Strauss and his associates drew up plans and built models that showed it could be done. Yet even as the physical problems were solved, an unsympathetic public still scorned the idea of defacing such a magnificent work of nature. Over 2,000 lawsuits were filed to stop the bridge. (In the first half of the 20th century, it was still possible to win such a number of suits in a lifetime.) Bond measures were passed in 1930 by Bay Area voters willing to give it a try. The initial construction fees of $35 million were paid off by bridge tolls in 1971.

Actual work started in 1933 under supervision of engineer Clifford Paine. Eleven workmen were killed during construction, and storms once wrecked access piers, but the bridge was completed and opened in May 1937. When financier A. P. Giannini of the Bank of America asked how long it would last, Strauss replied "forever" if cared for properly. More levelheaded engineers say it's good for 200 years—which portends a bonanza year for scrap dealers in 2137.

The sheer size of the bridge is astonishing, especially if you walk out on it, as everyone should. Its art-deco towers rise 746 feet above the water, about as high as a 48-story building. If you include the underwater portion, the tallest tower is al-most as high as the Transamerica Pyramid. When it was built, its towers were the highest west of Manhattan, and the 4,200-foot main span was the longest in the world; it has now been surpassed on both accounts. The bridge can sway 27.5 feet from east to west in a wind (or earthquake). It takes four years to paint the bridge, a Sisyphean task that is necessary to prevent it from rusting.

You can park on either side of the bridge and walk across. On the San Francisco side, be sure to see the section of cut bridge cable displayed in the gardens near the parking lot. The cables contain enough wire to encircle the earth three times at the equator. The statue of Joseph Strauss, nearby, honors the tiny man who proved it could be built. Though Strauss was the force behind the bridge, he has too long received sole credit as *the* bridge builder. In fact, his assistants (like Clifford Paine) deserve much of the credit for the engineering feat.

Climb the steps to the Roundhouse store, where you can stamp a penny with an image of the bridge for 50 cents, or choose from a wide assortment of other mementos; no other American structure, save perhaps the Statue of Liberty, has inspired more schlock. Those who fancy flirting with their own immortality can have a brick inscribed with their name and a message, which then is used to pave the concourse.

The walk across the bridge is about two miles, one way. At 246 feet above the sea, it is like walking a catwalk around the top of a 16-story building. Looking down on Fort Point and on ships passing under the bridge, or looking up the precarious cable walkways, spotting dangling painters at work, a person with respect for heights can feel giddy. The bay gives scant cushion for anyone falling from such heights, but amazingly, a handful of attempted suicides have survived the jump. The number of those who have not surpasses a thousand.

■ Cow Hollow

The Marina District is walled in on the south by the rather abrupt rise of Pacific Heights. The trough at the foot of Pacific Heights, now engraved by Union Street, was once known as Cow Hollow for the score or so of dairy farms that operated here in the 19th century. Alas, the pastures, richly watered by springs, long ago disappeared with the advance of progress. In 1891, the last of Cow Hollow's namesakes was sent, kicking and mooing, into exile.

After six decades as a stodgy residential neighborhood, **Union Street** in the 1950s underwent a rejuvenation. With a paint job to the gingerbread and wrought ironwork, old Victorian houses were transformed into boutiques, coffeehouses, restaurants, and fine shops. Soon, Union Street was enjoying a reputation among cognoscenti as a chic shopping district. Word spread, and by the '70s, outlanders and tourists were arriving in droves to hobnob on Union Street, driving much of the chic set over the hill to Upper Fillmore.

Though sometimes verging on preciousness, one of San Francisco's hallmark pleasures is the eight-block stroll down Union between Van Ness and Steiner, poking through the courtyards, shops, and bookstores, idling in the cafes, chatting in the bars, expounding in the galleries, supping in the nosheries, and, in general, completely indulging one's lounger instincts. There's something for everyone: purveyors of crystals, pies, herbs, futons, masks, African jewelry, paper products, Afghan rugs, lingerie, bath potions, tribal art, down comforters, French pastry, ceramic cows, designer sunglasses, and metaphysical books. The fernier Union Street watering holes cater to a well-heeled singles crowd.

The **Octagon House**, at the corner of Union and Gough, is an architectural curiosity, built in 1861 with the idea that an octagonal shape allows maximum sunlight into a house. You won't have a chance to test that theory because the original interior has been altered. The house is now the only colonial museum west of Texas, and displays the decorative furnishings of the Colonial and Federal periods. A small donation permits you to wander among the antique tables and chairs, and to inspect the prize collection of autographs by the signers of the Declaration of Independence. *2645 Gough St.; 415-441-7512.*

Redwood-sheltered **Allyne Park**, next door behind the white picket fence, is San Francisco's most charming city park. Grab a mocha or a cappuccino from a cafe on glitzy Union Street, then let yourself in at one of the gates and enter another realm. The park has the feel of somebody's backyard, and you can lounge on one of the benches, taking in the fragrant gardens and watching the locals idly toss Frisbees to their dogs while they catch up on neighborhood gossip.

Another local oasis is the churchyard of **St. Mary's Episcopal**, where one of Cow Hollow's springs still flows up to water long-vanished pastures. The spring, hidden from the street by a hedge and lych-gate, endows the rustic scene with the peace and solitude of an English country churchyard. *2301 Union St.; 415-921-3665.*

Accommodations are available on Union Street in bed-and-breakfast houses, where the comfy flowers-and-sherry ambience matches the neighborhood character. For those who want to soak up one of San Francisco's most charming neighborhoods, if you have the budget, consider lodging in Cow Hollow.

■ PACIFIC HEIGHTS

The western end of Union Street halts at the Presidio wall, where **Lyon Street** bounds southward and upward to Pacific Heights. Here dwell San Francisco's bluest-bloods. It is by no means a small neighborhood. Pacific Heights commandeers the crest of a long, high ridge rising in the east from Van Ness Avenue and rolling 14 blocks west to the Presidio's eastern wall. On the north side, overlooking the bay, the mansions and apartments march down terraces as far as Green Street. On the south side, overlooking Hayes Valley and Twin Peaks, the streets drop more gradually to California Street. Presidio Heights, an even more exclusive enclave, takes up the torch at the Presidio wall, and runs several blocks farther.

The best way to get a feel for the Heights is to walk, enjoying the splendid architectural wealth of Gothic door-knockers, mansard roofs, fairy-tale turrets, gables, statuary, Tudor facing, wrought-iron fences, topiary, burnished lamps, carved doors, and clinging ivy. Bay vistas are the best that money can buy. By night, some half-opened curtain might treat you to a fleeting glimpse of a fine old library or a roaring fire, which you may, if you wish, enjoy vicariously. The Christmas holidays herald a tasteful profusion of lights and decorations.

Where to walk? If not quite aimlessly, let it at least be wherever fancy takes you. Certainly Lyon Street above Union is a good place to start. As you climb its landscaped steps, magnificent views open up over the Marina District to the bay, the Palace of Fine Arts floating like a magic castle in the foreground. At intersecting streets, like Broadway and Vallejo, avenues of mansions march solidly east. Finally, cresting the top, look west down Pacific at one of the city's most romantic views: the partially red-brick street plunges steeply down into a secluded kingdom known as Presidio Heights, whose rich hinterland embraces the parallel blocks of Jackson, Washington, and Clay. This particular stretch of Pacific between Lyon and Spruce is known as "along the wall," in deference to the low stone Presidio wall that separates civilians from warriors. "Along the wall" means old money and cultivated tastes. Governesses gather with their little charges at Julius Kahn Playground, beyond the wall at Spruce Street. Surrounding cypress woods, rolling across the Presidio hills, absorb the fog and hush the footfalls of passers-by.

A few blocks west along the Presidio wall, Presidio Terrace nurses a clutch of palatial mansions on a circular drive, in the shadow of **Temple Emanu-El**. Inspired by the grandiose dome of Santa Sophia in old Constantinople, this landmark synagogue was built by Arthur Brown, whose other works include City Hall and Coit

Tower. The temple is open to the public during the afternoon from Monday to Friday. *Enter at the corner of Arguello and Lake; 415-751-2535.*

A humbler, but still genteel, architectural statement is made by the **Church of New Jerusalem**, better known as the Swedenborg Church. Designed and assembled with loving care by architects and artists of the American Craftsman Movement in 1894, the church and its garden show the careful attention to detail and beauty that characterized much of Renaissance or classical Japanese workmanship. Yet, the tiny church is distinctively Californian. Its carved wooden beams, wood-burning fireplace, stained glass windows, and even its chairs handcrafted of hardwood and woven tule bulrush exude the cozy, yet reverent, atmosphere of a California forest. No wonder it's San Francisco's most popular wedding chapel. *2107 Lyon St.; 415-346-6466.*

The farther east you go in Pacific Heights, the more the old mansions have given way to apartment houses. Clusters of fine old Victorians still stand between the monoliths, hidden like Russian Easter eggs in the nooks of a garden wall. Many of these remaining mansions have become too expensive to maintain as dwellings, and

Climbing the Lyon Street stairs might cause you to lose your breath, but you'll be rewarded with this sweeping view of San Francisco Bay. (Kerrick James)

Pacific Heights is one of the city's wealthiest neighborhoods. (Kerrick James)

have been transformed into schools, nonprofit foundations, and even hotels. Lodging in a Victorian is an ideal way to get to the heart of San Francisco.

The **Haas-Lilienthal House** is one of the eccentric wooden Victorians that typifies old San Francisco. Owned and operated as a museum by the Foundation for San Francisco's Architectural Heritage, the house was built in 1886 with the jaunty bay windows, luxuriant ornamentation, fanciful gables, and Queen Anne–style circular tower so characteristic of the exuberant Victorian era. The rooms are still furnished with many of the Haas and Lilienthal family heirlooms. Foundation guides lead tours on Wednesdays and Sundays. *2007 Franklin St.; 415-441-3004.*

Two of San Francisco's prettiest hilltop parks are in Pacific Heights, surrounded by handsome architecture and elegant views. **Lafayette Park** is a delightful garden, flowery and well-wooded, smelling of pine and eucalyptus. **Alta Plaza**, on the other hand, rises in vigorously symmetrical terraces like a great, green Mayan pyramid—an oddly forceful monument in an otherwise well-groomed, genteel neighborhood.

The lights of nearby **Upper Fillmore**, the main shopping street of Pacific Heights, sparkle long into the night. Catering to a stable, well-to-do, and largely youthful clientele, urbane Upper Fillmore is the epitome of contemporary American trendiness, the domain of sushi and designer foods, luxury services, nail salons, import groceries, hot tubs, dessert boutiques, cafes, and rich young things with mannequin faces. The popular **Clay Cinema,** on Fillmore near Clay Street, shows art and international films. If Proust were alive and living in San Francisco, no doubt his Swann would have felt at home on Upper Fillmore.

■ WESTERN ADDITION

Ironically, until recently Fillmore was known as one of San Francisco's poorer streets. The Lower Fillmore (between Geary and Haight) still retains this intimidating cachet, though it is also known as an exciting neighborhood for music, especially with the Fillmore nightclub, on the southwest corner of Fillmore and Geary, and John Lee Hooker's club, the Boom Boom Room, just across Geary. The rising and falling fortunes of Fillmore Street are typical of the Western Addition in general.

The district acquired its name in the 1870s, when a spate of building to the east of Van Ness Avenue affixed a *western addition* to the old city core. Surviving the

Detail of a circular tower on a Queen Anne–style Victorian in the Western Addition.

1906 earthquake and fire virtually unscathed, it became the city's largest Victorian neighborhood.

Probably its most famous resident was a woman named Mary Ellen Pleasant, once better known as Mammy Pleasant, who lived in a house owned by Thomas Bell near the corner of Bush and Octavia. (The house is gone, but six venerable eucalyptus trees that she planted still grow in front, where a memorial plaque has been placed by the African-American Cultural Society.) Few figures in San Francisco history have inspired more mystery. Her notoriety followed hard on the death of her employer, Thomas Bell, who was killed in a fall from his third-floor balcony. Some claimed that he was pushed by Mary Pleasant, but no one ever claimed it in court or to her face. Nonetheless, rumors circulated until her death, and after, that she was a procuress, a murderess, and a witch. Modern accounts don't dispel the mystery, but are more likely to credit her as a consummate businesswoman, an ardent abolitionist, and a commanding, fearless person who demanded and received respect. The daughter of a black mother and Cherokee father, Mary Pleasant arrived in San Francisco during the Gold Rush. She opened a successful boarding house (which some say was a discreet bordello), and used her personal fortune to help finance the western terminus of the Underground Railway. Her San Francisco home was a sanctuary for runaway slaves. When John Brown was seized at Harper's Ferry, Maryland, a conspiratorial note signed with her initials was found on his person, but she escaped before any investigation could be mounted. Her interest in the plight of African Americans did not end with the Civil War. In 1865, she sued a San Francisco streetcar company over rude treatment to black riders, and won.

Of the many ethnic groups that have settled the Western Addition, among the most prominent were the Jewish community, which congregated here during the first third of the 20th century, the Japanese, who built "Little Osaka" around Post Street, and African Americans, whose community centered along Fillmore. Little Osaka was uprooted during World War II by Japanese-American internment, though many returned after the war. Conversely, the African-American community grew rapidly during the war as workers arrived from the South to build ships. When war jobs died out and unemployed black workers were passed over by private-sector companies, the neighborhood fell on hard times. The old Victorians deteriorated into slummy firetraps, and were replaced with ugly urban renewal projects.

Today, the Western Addition is undergoing rampant gentrification of its remaining Victorian enclaves. Modern city planners, wiser from their earlier mistakes, are designing with much more attention to aesthetics and social use. Still,

CULTIVATED QUARTER

many of the government housing projects of the Western Addition are plagued by high crime rates, especially in the blocks south of Geary.

One of San Francisco's most charming Victorian streets is **Cottage Row**, between Sutter and Bush, a half block east from Fillmore. Like Macondray Lane on Russian Hill, Cottage Row is another of those little country lanes so improbably spirited to the midst of the metropolis. While there, walk the extra block to **Marcus Books** *(1712 Fillmore, between Sutter and Post)* for a large selection of works by black authors and about African-American history and culture.

One block west of Fillmore, on the corner of Bush and Steiner, stands one of San Francisco's most popular religious shrines. Catholic pilgrims, many from Latin America, search out **St. Dominic's Church** to pay their respects to the statue of St. Jude, patron saint of lost causes.

◆ JAPANTOWN

Fillmore marks the western edge of Nihonmachi, or Japantown, a compact neighborhood loosely bounded by Geary, Octavia, and Pine. For persons completely unfamiliar with Asian cultures, the comparison between Japantown and Chinatown could serve to show that China and Japan are as different as, say, Italy and

Traditional costume, dancing, and a barrel of sake spice up a Japantown festival.

Denmark. Of course, Japantown does not attempt to be a faithful recreation of "the old country." Like Little Italy, it is a distinctively American hybrid, but harboring a treasury of details that can evoke a sense of Japan, much as a bonsai may evoke a whole forest, or a bite of *sfrappole* can bring back memories of old Bologna. Keep your senses primed as you walk through the district, and you may find such cultural touchstones in the hardware stores, the family-owned markets and bakeries, the Zen and Konko missions, and the comfortable, human scale of the streets and architecture. The one-block, open-air **Buchanan Mall**, between Post and Sutter, is the most self-consciously old-style Japanese street. Paved with riverine cobbles and lined by Japanese restaurants and shops, it is a comfortable, pleasant place to stroll or sit.

A more ambitious vision of modern Japan stands beyond Post Street. **Japan Center** is a three-block concrete mall, hemmed in by Fillmore, Geary, and Laguna, that many find ugly and impersonal. The interior, however, can be inviting, and certainly provides some fascinating cultural insights. Among the Japanese goods and provisions available are futons, cooking utensils, arts and crafts, clothing, furniture (including items specially designed for small-apartment living), antiques, fine paper products, pearls, tourist knickknacks, and a wide selection of Japanese books, videos, cassettes, and compact discs. The center also contains about 30 restaurants, from coffee shops to sushi bars, noodle houses to formal Japanese restaurants, some with tatami rooms. Visitors are fascinated by Isobune, where the sushi boats float by on a miniature river, and by the table-side chefs at Benihana, who put on skilled knife demonstrations while preparing meals. Casual **Sapporo-ya**, which makes its own noodles on an antique ramen machine, is popular for snacks. The adjacent **Miyako Hotel**, while blending Japanese trappings with Western comforts, also offers some genuine Japanese-style rooms with tatami floors and Japanese baths.

Japantown's sometimes sleepy facade belies its cultural vigor. Language and cultural classes, including such arts as cooking and flower arrangement, are advertised on the Japan Center community bulletin board. Seasonal festivals bring dancers, drummers, artists, and craftspeople from around the Bay Area. The **Kokusai Theater** (1746 Post) devotes itself to Japanese-language films. The AMC **Kabuki 8 Theaters**, anchoring the Fillmore end of Japan Center, offer first-run features; the Kabuki also hosts major San Francisco film festivals.

Downstairs, the **Kabuki Hot Springs** bathhouse mollifies the soul as it cleanses the body—or rather, *after* cleansing the body. The idea in a Japanese bath is to lather, scrub, and rinse yourself *thoroughly* before getting into the hot bath to soak. The Kabuki has traditional communal baths (hot and cold), as well as a sauna and a steam room, and is open to men and women on different days. As gentle New Age music soothes away stress, you can relax under an after-bath *shiatsu* (finger-pressure) massage. (And yes, sir, I mean a *real* massage.) The works aren't cheap, but you will come out feeling like a new person. *1750 Geary; 415-922-6000.*

♦ CATHEDRAL HILL

From Japantown, you can walk two blocks up Geary (east) to the top of Cathedral Hill, named for **St. Mary's Cathedral**, an unabashedly modern edifice rising at the corner of Geary and Gough. However peculiar the exterior (its likeness to a washing machine agitator has earned it the nickname St. Mary of Maytag) the vast interior is astounding, even in this atrium-jaded city. Built in 1971, it speaks boldly of an age of faith bolstered by the worldly powers of science and engineering. Enormous compound arches lift the cross-shaped dome 190 feet above the floor, opening the walls to expansive views out over the city. The majestic Ruffati organ explodes from the depths on an enormous concrete pedestal like a throne rising up to glory. If you like your cathedrals exuberant, you'll love St. Mary's.

The **First Unitarian Church** across the street is a much more staid, though handsome, stone structure dating from 1889. First Unitarian was the church of Thomas Starr King, the preacher credited with swaying California to the Union side in the Civil War. So enamored was California of this service that Thomas Starr King is one of the two statues that represent the state in the Hall of Fame in Washington. (The other is Father Junipero Serra.) King died before the war ended, in 1864. His tomb is outside the southeastern corner of the church.

♦ ALAMO SQUARE

South of Geary, Alamo Square anchors down another gentrifying section of the Western Addition. Many old Victorians line the park, including the famous row along Steiner Street so often pictured in books of the city *(see page 35)*. The old Imperial Russian Consulate still stands at 1198 Fulton; and the Archbishops' Mansion on the corner of Fulton and Steiner, once the official home of local Catholic prelates, has now been converted into a palatial B&B inn. Guests may sip sherry in the lap of Edwardian luxury, or play a few bars on Noel Coward's piano.

From the southwestern corner of Alamo Square, you can see the enchanting towers of St. Ignatius Church and the forested slopes of Buena Vista Park and

Mount Sutro. Though still a bit frayed in places, the neighborhood surrounding Alamo Square is one of San Francisco's most breathtaking. Look north across the valley for another view of Alta Plaza in all its Mayan symmetry.

■ THE RICHMOND DISTRICT

The name of Lone Mountain has struck a chord of terror in more than one generation of San Francisco children. That's because it stood for years at dead center of the city's necropolis, surrounded in all directions by acres of bone yards.

Where have all the graveyards gone? Gone to Colma, every one; at least the ones that they could find. Richmond District gardeners have been surprised more than once while planting their petunias.

In a city as small as San Francisco, the enormous cemetery plots were needed for the living, and so in 1914, Mayor Sunny Jim Rolph ordered all persons owning or claiming lots in the cemeteries to move their occupants to Colma, a city just south of San Francisco devoted to caring for the dead. Unclaimed bodies were buried in mass graves in Colma, and the stones were used, in part, to pave the city's sea walls. You can still see some on the jetty at the wave organ.

Today, Lone Mountain is crowned by a tower that is part of University of San Francisco. Founded by the Jesuits in 1855, USF is the oldest university in San Francisco, though it moved three times before settling on its present spectacular hilltop. The campus contains the most majestic church in the city, **St. Ignatius.** Its handsome dome and campanile, and its 210-foot twin spires, spectacularly lit at night, ennoble more than one city vista.

Only one remnant of Lone Mountain's cemeteries remains today—the **Columbarium**. Once surrounded by the Odd Fellows cemetery, it is now engulfed by buildings, and approached from the appropriately dead-end Loraine Street. The Columbarium is a splendid neoclassical rotunda filled with urns and memorial niches. Capped with a copper roof and decorated with precious vases and a Tiffany window, the four-story building keeps the cremated remains of some 6,000 people, many of them pioneer families. If you bring a companion, you can test the building's marvelous acoustics on any of the upper floors. Standing on one side, you should be able to hold a quiet conversation with someone hidden around the opposite side. The Columbarium is open to the public on mornings from Tuesday through Saturday.) *One Lorraine Court; 415-221-1838.*

(right) St. Ignatius is thought by many to be the city's most beautiful church.

CULTIVATED QUARTER

Firehouse buffs will want to visit the nearby **Fire Department Museum**, which stands on the other side of what was Lond Mountain. This museum captures the real veneration San Franciscans have for their fire companies—not a strange phenomenon for a city of wood. The paraphernalia here reflects the glory days when fire companies used to compete for the honor of extinguishing blazes. *655 Presidio Ave.; 415-861-8000.*

Clearing the cemeteries made way for San Francisco's Richmond District, by far a worthy trade-off. This western third of San Francisco, combined with the Sunset District south of Golden Gate Park, is known collectively as "the Avenues," because most of the streets running north and south are numbered avenues. At one time the Richmond was called the Outer Lands, and even the Great Sand Waste, for the obvious reason that it *was* a wasteland of shifting sand dunes and a few scraggly knolls. The land was opened for settlement largely through the efforts of a Prussian named Adolf Sutro, sometimes called the Father of the Richmond, who owned a good stretch of the Outer Lands. Sutro had made his fortune in the Comstock, and retired to a mansion across from the Cliff House, which he also owned. Next door he erected the largest bathhouse in the world, Sutro Baths, and connected it to the city with a steam railway. Thus, he built both the inducement and the means for people to go to the Richmond.

Today, the Richmond is a solidly middle-class neighborhood of great ethnic diversity happily sandwiched between the Presidio and Lincoln Park on the north, and Golden Gate Park on the south. The Russians were among the first major ethnic groups in the outer Richmond, when some 10,000 White Russians arrived in the years after the 1917 Revolution. Their passage to America was eased by the tireless lobbying of an extraordinary priest, known as John the Barefoot, who was to become San Francisco's first Russian Orthodox bishop. His bishopric was **Saint Mary the Virgin in Exile**, the golden, onion-domed church on Geary between 26th and 27th Avenues. The church opens for Mass in the morning, when visitors (long pants for men, modest skirts or dresses for women) *may* be allowed to view its enormous chandeliers, icons, and relics, including the *body* of St. John the Barefoot. Another notable landmark is Russian Renaissance, a restaurant at 5241 Geary. If you stop by in the evening and can stand a stiff drink, try an icy *zebrovka,* the house's buffalo grass–infused vodka. You can still find Russian newspapers in the stores, and a scattering of onion-domed buildings in the side streets. The 1990s are witnessing a resurgence of Russian immigration to San Francisco.

Mary the Virgin in Exile is the religious center of Russian life in the Richmond.

Many elderly Russians still congregate on the playground benches of **Mountain Lake Park**, a pretty spot on the Presidio's border near Park Presidio Boulevard. Anza camped here when he came to found the Presidio, in 1776. Thousands of refugees followed suit on the nearby golf course in 1906. Kids and adults alike will love the playground's large swings and rolling-pin slides.

The most prominent ethnic group in the Richmond nowadays is Chinese. The stretch of the Avenues between Arguello Boulevard and Park Presidio, especially along Clement Street, is known as **New Chinatown**, which lacks both the tourist glitz and squalor of Grant Avenue's Chinatown, while its markets and restaurants can beat it for quality and convenience.

Attracted by the strong Asian-American presence in the Richmond, the **Asian American Theater** has settled into a new home on Arguello at the corner of Clement. One of the premier small theaters in the country, it has produced works by Tony Award-winning playwright David Henry Hwang and other local artists. *403 Arguello Blvd.; 415-922-6841.*

The Richmond's restaurants attract more locals than tourists. The long stretch of Clement and Geary in the Richmond has long been known as San Francisco's premier restaurant row, celebrated for its great culinary diversity and quality. Nowadays the restaurants are more plentiful than ever, but the Richmond's once exceptional diversity now decidedly emphasizes East Asian cuisines. Chinese offerings are the most prolific, with *dim sum* and seafood (Cantonese), Mandarin, Shanghai, Hunan, Sichuan, Chaozhou, Hakka, and vegetarian. Vietnamese, Italian, French, Mexican, Japanese, Thai, American, and Korean are amply represented, but you can also find such rarer cuisines as Cambodian, Russian, Moroccan, Peruvian, Spanish, Danish, Laotian, Armenian, Indonesian, Singaporian, and Burmese—not to mention all the ubiquitous cafes, delis, dessert and ice cream parlors, and Irish pubs. You can idle away the hours between meals and late into the evenings at bookstores like Green Apple and Albatross II, on Clement; listen to live music at night spots like the Last Day Saloon or Plough & Stars; or hoist a pint of Guinness and have a heated debate on Irish politics at Ireland's 32 or the Pig & Whistle Pub.

All in all, the Richmond is nothing spectacular in the Disneyland sense of the word; but with good food, good drink, good books, and entertaining company, it is one of the most comfortable and stimulating neighborhoods in the city. And as if that weren't enough, it is well placed for escaping to the parks.

■ LINCOLN PARK AND LAND'S END

Seacliff, an exclusive neighborhood of stirring sea views, is incomparably coddled between the Presidio and Lincoln Park. The Coastal Trail from the Presidio passes through the streets of the neighborhood. You can hook into it on the east side at Baker Beach, at the end of 25th Avenue north, and on the west side near where El Camino del Mar meets Lincoln Park.

In Seacliff, devotees of Ansel Adams can take a small detour to the house at 129 24th Avenue, where the photographer grew up. In those days, this was out in the sticks. The house is not open to the public.

Another detour takes you to **China Beach,** named for the Chinese fishermen who used to camp here in earlier days. China Beach is an exception to the no-swimming rule of thumb at San Francisco beaches. The water is safe enough here, though never warm. The beach has changing rooms, showers, restrooms, and a lifeguard station.

San Francisco's most rugged stretch of seacoast is **Land's End,** west of Seacliff. Until closed by landslides, El Camino del Mar once ran through here to the Cliff House. Sutro's railway also passed through. Nowadays, both road and rail rights-of-way are footpaths administered by the GGNRA and Lincoln Park. Between the two parks, San Francisco enjoys both its wildest landscapes and its most rarefied vision of civilization, the Legion of Honor.

◆ CALIFORNIA PALACE OF THE LEGION OF HONOR

Few museums in all the world have a setting as magnificent as the California Palace of the Legion of Honor. Approached by car through Lincoln Park Golf Course from 34th Avenue and Clement, the Legion rises handsomely from its Lincoln Park hilltop like a classical French palace, fronted with colonnades, a triumphal arch, and heroic equestrian bronzes of El Cid and Joan of Arc. One of five original castings of Auguste Rodin's famous statue, *The Thinker,* cogitates in the formal courtyard at the front of a pyramidal skylight. A shockingly incongruous sculpture, George Segal's *The Holocaust,* clings half-hidden behind a corner of the balustrade. Its emaciated corpses and barbed wire shriek out with shameless effrontery amid the Legion's perfect setting—which, of course, is precisely the point.

Founded by Alma de Bretteville Spreckels, the French-born wife of a local sugar baron, the Legion was dedicated to American soldiers fallen in France during World War I. Marshals Joffre and Foch both attended the opening in 1924, each marking the occasion by planting a cypress on the Legion's southern side. For years

The Thinker *is one of several works by Rodin at the Legion of Honor. (Kerrick James)*

CULTIVATED QUARTER

devoted exclusively to the display of French art, the Legion of Honor absorbed the European collection from the M. H. de Young Museum in the 1990s, giving it a much broader scope. Francophiles may grumble, as indeed they do, but the Legion still exudes a staunchly Gallic air.

Surveying eight centuries of European art, the permanent collection contains works by El Greco, Rembrandt, Rubens, Van Dyke, Van Cleve, Renoir, Seurat, Cézanne, Degas, Boucher, Monet, Manet, Courbet, Cellini, and Rodin, who alone accounts for more than 70 sculptures. One of the most impressive pieces is an 11-foot-high bronze wine vase by Gustave Doré, depicting cherubs and vermin in drunken revel. Of special note are the period rooms, particularly the somber Medieval Mudejar ceiling from Spain, and the paneled French period room. The **Achenbach Foundation for Graphic Arts**, downstairs, cares for the largest collection of graphic prints in the western United States, including a splendid selection of Japanese woodblock prints.

Aside from the collections and exhibitions, the Legion of Honor organizes regular docent tours and hundreds of film, lecture, painting, and music programs, including weekly pipe organ concerts in the **Rodin Gallery**. Its **Florence Gould Theater**, one of the most intimate venues in town, hosts regular programs of chamber music, jazz, and dance, as well as demonstrations of historical musical styles and instruments. A small shop at the entrance offers a nice array of cards and books. On the lower floor, **Café Chanticleer** is a cheery setting for a light lunch. *For detailed exhibit information, call 415-863-3330.*

Outside again, if you like the Legion's facade, stroll around back for another perspective. En route, take note of the black engraved stone on the north side of El Camino del Mar. It is a monument to the *Kanrin Maru,* the first Japanese ship to arrive in San Francisco Bay bearing emissaries to America. Its American counterpart sailed simultaneously in the other direction. The year was 1860.

◆ COASTAL TRAIL

Behind that monument, a hard-to-find path cuts down the edge of the golf course to the Coastal Trail, which leads between the Golden Gate Bridge and the Cliff House via Land's End. (You'll find a second path to the west, at the end of the parking lot.) There are no roads here. Stay on the paths; the cliffs crumble easily, and someone falls or is swept away by freak waves nearly every year. The seas off Land's End are shipwreck waters. On foggy days, the sound of the horns and the smell of fog and the sea produce the kind of atmosphere that make Byronic hearts swoon with sweet melancholy. On clear days, the vistas sweep from Seacliff past the Presidio and the Golden Gate Bridge to rugged Point Bonita Lighthouse, in Marin County, the north channel's outside gatepost. In the foreground, Mile Rock Lighthouse blinks its lonely vigil through rough seas and calm. A spur off the Coastal Trail winds down to tiny Mile Rock Beach, a favorite of stalwart sunbathers.

As the Coastal Trail rounds **Point Lobos**, skirting thick, matted tunnels of cypress, it feeds into Merrie Way, near the Cliff House. Stairs lead uphill at this point to the bridge of the USS *San Francisco,* overlooking the sea at El Camino del Mar. Torn by shells, the piece of ship now stands as a memorial to 107 crew and officers killed in the 1942 Battle of Guadalcanal. The wooden observation house on the hill behind is the old Marine Exchange Lookout. Built to watch for ships entering the Golden Gate, it would announce the news to the more centrally located Telegraph Hill by semaphore. On the hill above the lookout, military buffs can explore Fort Miley's abandoned gun emplacements, built to greet less friendly ships.

■ THE PACIFIC SHORE

The **Cliff House** was one of the city's first tourist attractions. Mark Twain described a visit here in the 1860s, when it was already garnering a reputation as a fast place for fast people. When Sutro bought it in the 1880s, he stopped the hanky-panky and started to run it as a family resort. After the original Cliff House burned in 1894, Sutro erected a wondrous wooden castle on the site, bolstering business with a huge bathhouse next door. Unfortunately for lovers of the Gothic, the building burned in 1907. Be sure to see the pictures in the lobby of the contemporary Cliff House, which dates from 1908. *1090 Point Lobos Ave.; 415-386-3330.*

Still a tourist shrine, the Cliff House bars and restaurants mix warm repast with stirring views of sea stacks and rugged breakers. Downstairs, get your bearings, books, and maps at the GGNRA **Visitor Center** *(415-556-8642)*, with a view over

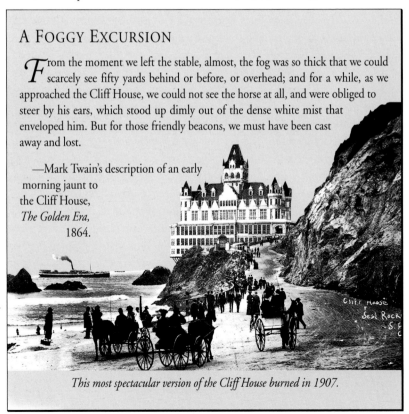

A FOGGY EXCURSION

*F*rom the moment we left the stable, almost, the fog was so thick that we could scarcely see fifty yards behind or before, or overhead; and for a while, as we approached the Cliff House, we could not see the horse at all, and were obliged to steer by his ears, which stood up dimly out of the dense white mist that enveloped him. But for those friendly beacons, we must have been cast away and lost.

　　—Mark Twain's description of an early morning jaunt to the Cliff House, *The Golden Era,* 1864.

This most spectacular version of the Cliff House burned in 1907.

(right) Ocean Beach is pretty to look at, but a menace to swimmers.

Sutro Baths. On the patio outside, visitors can enjoy the views of landscape, seascape, and plenty of fellow tourists. Barking sea lions play just off shore on **Seal Rocks**. Their ghostly roars take on added drama in fog or murk of darkness. On clear days, Point Reyes stands out clearly in the north, protected as far as you can see by state and national parklands. By night, the towns of Muir Beach, Stinson Beach, and Bolinas glow small and bright amidst the black hills and sea. Thirty-two miles to the west, you can sometimes pick out San Francisco's farthest outpost, the Farallon Islands, a rugged sanctuary for birds and sea lions. During the Gold Rush, enterprising businessmen used to collect murre eggs from there to sell for breakfast in the city.

The gulf between the Farallon Islands and the Golden Gate is part of the Red Triangle, a somewhat lurid name for a patch of ocean that the Great White Shark calls home. Recorded attacks on humans here are not overly common; but then, neither are swimmers.

The Cliff House also shelters the **Musée Méchanique**, a collection of coin-operated mechanical games and devices, the kind that used to be found in penny arcades around the civilized world. Plunk your quarters down to play the vintage pin-

Now a hole in the ground, Sutro Baths was once the world's largest bathhouse.

ball machines, mechanical fortune teller, miniature carnival, automated band instruments, and more. Admission is free, but bring plenty of change for the machines.

The ruins in the rocks north of the Cliff House are **Sutro Baths**, a Victorian pleasure palace opened in 1896. Its six salt baths and hundreds of dressing rooms had room for 24,000 swimmers under a soaring glass dome. An aerial cable car, the Sky Tram, once ran from the Cliff House to the rocks beyond, where visitors could view the crashing seas from a tunnel cut clear through the rocks. The baths burned in 1966, and the tram was dismantled soon after. You can still walk to the tunnel, and clear through the now-exposed opening above the rocks. Watch out for holes in the floor of the cave, where the surf pounds and gurgles through subterranean passages at high tide.

Sutro lived on an estate high on the hill across the road from the Cliff House. The house was torn down after his death, and his estate turned into **Sutro Heights Park**. Old walls and feral gardens lend a romantic air of ruin to the grounds. Views from high ground here reach to Ocean Beach, the Richmond and Sunset Districts, Golden Gate Park, Fort Funston, and beyond, a tremendous study in perspective— all the streets, the park boundaries, and the beach itself intersect at 90-degree angles.

The waters off **Ocean Beach**, running four miles to San Francisco's border and beyond, are not very hospitable. Chill winds usually render sunbathing uncomfortable, while severe undertow makes swimming perilous. Ocean Beach still pulls the crowds in on the hottest days, however, and almost always provides a magnificent backdrop for seashore strolls or horseback rides.

■ GOLDEN GATE PARK

Like the Golden Gate Bridge, Golden Gate Park was built despite a litany of naysayers who insisted that it couldn't be done. With 1,017 acres, it is probably the largest cultivated park in the United States, if not the world.

In a league with the Hanging Gardens of Babylon, Golden Gate Park is a work of art on a heroic scale, where lakes, forests, glades, waterfalls, streams, hills, and even the earth itself have been designed by human hands. Yet, what mankind nurtured, Mother Nature has now good-naturedly adopted as her own. A more botanically vibrant piece of ground would be difficult to find in any temperate clime.

When plans for a park first started tickling the fancy of boosters like William Ralston, the likeliest pieces of real estate near the center of town were already

(above) The great outdoors for many San Franciscans is Golden Gate Park.
(right) An aerial view of Golden Gate Park extending down to the sea at Ocean Beach.
(photo by Galen Rowell)

taken. Instead, the city acquired an oblong piece of the Great Sand Wastes, three miles long and a half-mile wide, at its closest point about three miles from downtown. It was the largest stretch of sand dune on the California coast. Such folly no doubt caused many a guffaw in the saloons and press-rooms of Montgomery Street. Even Frederick Law Olmsted, the landscape designer who built New York's 840-acre Central Park, threw up his hands in disgust at the site, which he thought incapable of supporting trees. He graciously admitted his mistake later.

In 1871, the contract for designing Golden Gate Park went to an engineer named William Hammand Hall, who had already surveyed the Outside Lands for the federal government. Hall went straight to work. First, he had to secure the blowing sand. He did this by sowing barley, then lupine on top of that, and grass on top of the lupine. With a mat of grass established, he planted trees. At the same time, he started building a wall on Ocean Beach to stop the dunes from blowing inland. He proceeded to grade, build roads, lay water pipe, and plant thousands of trees in the eastern section of the park, which had more promising soil than the coastal side. He also built the Panhandle, a long strip of park designed as an elegant carriage entry.

Hall's work was soon appreciated by San Franciscans, who started flocking to the young park for picnics and carriage races. But though San Franciscans loved the new park, government corruption and political shenanigans were eating at the park budget. After repeated attacks and trumped-up charges of extravagance and corruption, Hall resigned in disgust, in 1876. Funds were slashed, and Golden Gate Park drifted into a decade of decline. Plants and roads were neglected, crime and corruption flourished. Finally, in desperate straits, the government called Hall back again.

Hall took the job on the condition that he could appoint his own successor, a man capable of pressing on with the park's construction while fending off the rascally politicians. His choice, a Scotsman named John McLaren, took over as Superintendent in 1890 and served for the next 53 years. Fondly known as "Uncle John" by his staff and generations of grateful San Franciscans, McLaren was not only a master gardener who personally planted thousands of trees, but a canny handler of people.

McLaren believed that parks should be natural, beautiful settings where people can retreat from such urban trappings as buildings, statues, and roads. Under McLaren's trusteeship, Golden Gate Park blossomed into the masterpiece of landscape gardening that it is today. He brought in exotic plants from around the world and earned international fame for his extraordinary abilities to make them flourish. Against the pressures of developers he fought like a terrier, outplaying politicians at their own games. Once, for instance, when plans were hatched to bisect the park with another road, McLaren deftly nominated a plot in the planners' path for a police academy. The Police Department rushed to McLaren's support, and the road stopped dead in its tracks. The academy, of course, had to be built, but in due course it was reabsorbed back into the park as the Senior Center, as it stands today, at 37th Avenue.

McLaren eventually outlived all opponents, escorting his park beyond their reach into the middle of the 20th century. Until he expired, still superintendent, at the age of 93, his staunch loyalty to the vegetable kingdom never wavered. When asked what he wanted for his 90th birthday, the superintendent demanded without hesitation a load of manure to spread around his park. He was joking, of course; McLaren had been commandeering the city's manure supply for years.

The genius of Hall's plan and McLaren's implementation was that it was so well hidden. The land and woods appear so naturally lovely that it seems impossible to be by human design. Yet, nothing is by chance. Strategic pockets of fuchsias, camelias, roses, tulips, dahlias, cherry, magnolia, and other bright-blooming shrubs were placed to lend spectacular color to every season. The roads and walkways were laid out meanderingly, not only to discourage speeding, but to preserve the sense of exquisite seclusion. Even the prevailing winds have been checked and deflected by careful grading and planting. Golden Gate Park is a treasure; and yet more like a treasure hunt, for exploring it is quite as good as finding what you seek. The park never overwhelms. Rather it rewards quietly, with layer on layer of unlimited discovery for the visitor who can spend a lifetime or two getting at the heart of its mystery.

Golden Gate Park accommodates an amazing number of special activities without any one encroaching on another. Of course, all manner of sport—tennis, baseball, soccer, football, golf, bicycling, handball, jogging, basketball, horseback riding lessons, hiking, skating, archery, rowing, and lounging in the shade—is amply represented, but more obscure special interests are also royally cared for. Lawn bowlers have their lawns, fly-fishers their special casting pool, horseshoe pitchers their own elaborate grounds, card-players their designated shelter. (There is even a field for playing *petanque*, a French species of lawn bowling.) Children have three special playgrounds. Model yacht sailors have their own lake. Even dogs have four grounds set aside for their training and other personal needs.

Cultural activities are also well looked after: there are art museums, an aquarium, planetarium, museum of natural history and science, band shell, botanical garden, merry-go-round, and clubhouses for anglers, golfers, beach-goers, model boat sailors, and senior citizens.

CULTIVATED QUARTER

◆ GOLDEN GATE PARK HIGHLIGHTS

All this is put together in a setting of unrivaled botanical wealth. The richness and complexity of the park's special gardens are mind-boggling. Surely, the only way to do Golden Gate Park justice is to get a good map and follow your own interests. A tour can begin at McLaren Lodge, on the western edge of the park near the corner of Stanyan and Fell. In the days when park-keepers resided in the parks, Uncle John lived here. At the beach end of the park, the more ambitious **visitor center** now occupies the historic Beach Chalet *(415-666-7200),* designed by Polk. Drop in just to see Lucien Labaudt's Depression-era frescoes, which depict various tableaux of local scenes and personalities, such as John McLaren. The upstairs micro-brewery pays homage to another locally popular form of recreation.

There are many good ways to tour the park. A car is not the best of them, save perhaps on a rainy day. With 27 miles of footpaths and 7.5 miles of equestrian trails, walking and horseback riding are pure joy. Many roads in Golden Gate Park are closed to motor traffic on Sundays from 8 A.M. to dusk, providing a perfect place for bicyclists and skaters. (With up to 20,000 skaters swarming the roads on a sunny Sunday, walkers may prefer to deal with the cars.) You can rent bikes and skates from outlets on the edge of the park. Below are some highlights, moving roughly from the eastern edge to where the park meets the sea in the west.

Children's Playground

The most magical spot in the park for youngsters is the fantastic Children's Playground, the oldest public playground in the United States. Generations of San Franciscans have filled their imaginations in this enchanted sand-garden of swings and slides and make-believe fortresses. Younger kids especially love the 19th-century carousel—built in the style of a Greek temple—where storybook horses, cats, pigs, and other beasts prance to the music of a stirring band organ. Fittingly, adults are not allowed on the playground unless accompanied by children.

Conservatory of Flowers

The oldest and most stately building in the park is the Conservatory of Flowers, imported from Europe and assembled in 1878. A jungle of orchids, ferns, water lilies, tropical flowers, and even some sporadic birds thrive in the humid atmosphere. The gardens around the Conservatory are particularly lush. Paths lead through thickets of oak, blooming flowers, and a primeval glade of giant ferns. The nearby **John McLaren Rhododendron Dell** is enchanting in bloom. A small statue of Uncle John himself—a man who hated statues—poses in front, as if picking a pine cone from a tree.

To best sense the Japanese Tea Garden's subtle spell, avoid the crowds. (Kerrick James)

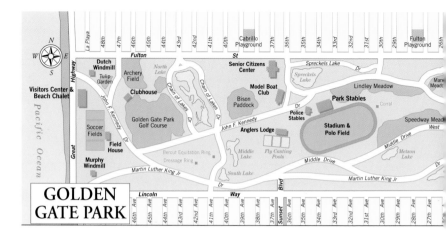

GOLDEN GATE PARK

◆ CALIFORNIA ACADEMY OF SCIENCES

Fronting the concourse on the south is San Francisco's oldest science museum, the California Academy of Sciences. With an aquarium and planetarium, natural displays of African and North American animals, and tens of thousands of reptiles, plants, insects, minerals, and fossils all under one roof, the Academy has long been the Bay Area's most popular science museum. A wonderful store stocks science and natural history books, art, and thoughtful games that attract parents and children alike. *Open daily, 10 a.m to 5 p.m.; 415-750-7145.*

African Hall

Sit near the (stuffed) zebras and giraffes at an African watering hole through a simulated cycle of day and night, surrounded by the sounds of unseen insects, birds, and roaring lions.

Wild California Hall

This spectacular exhibit centers on a huge diorama of Farallon Island cliffs, complete with churning surf, screeching gulls and enormous sea elephants. Other displays of California flora and fauna feature grizzly bears, condors, oak woodlands, salt marshes, and dioramas of kelp and seawater magnified 50 times to show plankton, shrimp, beetles, and flies the size of your Uncle Herman's hunting dog.

Steinhart Aquarium

In Steinhart Aquarium, 14,000 fish, crabs, turtles, dolphins, penguins, sea horses, eels, an octopus, and other specimens swim in lushly appointed tanks. Docents at the tide pool tank invite you to touch the starfish, sea urchins, anemones, and other animals.

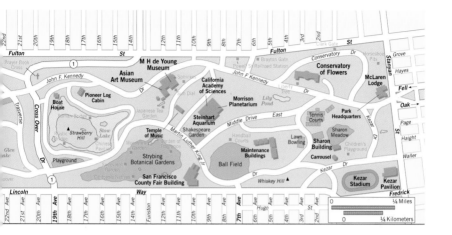

Morrison Planetarium

Walking up the spiral ramp to the Fish Roundabout, you will be completely surrounded by a doughnut-shaped tank filled with shoals of sharks, bass, snapper, rays, and yellowtail. **The Swamp**, an alligator pit bordered by the snake and lizard terrariums, always attracts a lot of attention. **Life Through Time** traces the history of evolution with models of prehistoric animals roaming through ancient habitats.

The galleries of earth and space sciences display model dinosaur skeletons, a piece of moon rock, a large revolving globe, a scale for measuring comparative weights on the Earth and its moon, and the hypnotic **Foucault Pendulum**, which slowly marks the Earth's rotation. The most dynamic display is the **earthquake platform**, which demonstrates how earthquakes of differing magnitudes feel, working up to the big one of 1906.

Morrison Planetarium
The star projector here was built in Germany before the Second World War, and it ranks as one of the best-crafted instruments of its kind. If you have never been to a planetarium, you will be impressed by the realism of the Morrison's night skies, glowing with stars of differing magnitudes and hues. Even if you are already familiar with planetarium shows, the high technical quality of the Morrison makes repeat visits always interesting. Sometimes the Planetarium is commandeered by the **Laserium**, a computerized krypton-gas laser synchronized to music, and played across the planetarium's ceiling. Music and patterns are always different, but the organizers preserve a choice between classical and modern. (Planetarium *(415-750-7141)* and Laserium *(415-750-7138)* tickets are purchased separately at the main entrance.)

M.H. de Young Museum

This fabulous museum shares a building with the Asian Art Museum *(see below)*, across the Concourse from the Academy of Sciences. The museums' forecourt contains the sculptor Earl Cummings' *Pool of Enchantment*—a young Indian boy piping to a pair of mountain lions.

The de Young offers a broad survey of American and British art, with a smattering of Mediterranean, Oceanic, African, and pre-Columbian American artifacts. Special galleries highlight Western landscapes, American furniture of the Federal period, still life, sculpture, and British decorative arts. Among the American artists featured are George Caitland, Frederic Remington, Albert Bierstadt, Thomas Moran, Charles Russell, Thomas Eakins, Grant Wood, John Singleton Copley, Benjamin West, James Whistler, Rembrandt Peale, John Singer Sargent, and silversmith Paul Revere. *M.H. de Young information: 415-750-3600.*

The Asian Art Museum

The Asian Art Museum houses the largest gathering of Asian art outside of Asia, a collection so vast (and a display area so small) that only 10 percent of it can be shown at one time. (Plans are afoot to move the museum to a larger location, at the old Main Library building in Civic Center.)

The arts of China and Korea occupy the ground floor, dazzling the eye against the lush, emerald backdrop of the Japanese Tea Garden. The collection draws from over 5,000 ceramic and lacquer articles, scrolls, sculptures, and other objects dating from as far back as the Zhou and Shang Dynasties (1400–1000 B.C.E.). Among the rarer items are scores of exquisitely translucent white ceramics, and other pieces of fluorescent blues and greens; the oldest known Chinese sculpture of Buddha inscribed with a date (equivalent to A.D. 338); Tang Dynasty (A.D. 618–907) earthenware animals; and a 17th-century bowl and pedestal decorated with dangling rings that was carved for a Qing Emperor from a single piece of white jade. The rest of the jade collection, ranging over 30 centuries, is no less astounding.

Upstairs, collections from Japan, India, Nepal, Burma, Kampuchea, and other countries include Khmer stone carvings, Indian gods and goddesses, a 16th-century suit of samurai armor, *netsuke* (small, carved pieces of wood and ivory), and an amazingly petite 19th-century wooden palanquin from Japan, decorated with red and black lacquer and gold leaf. *Asian Art Museum information: 415-668-8921.*

A single fee provides entry to both the Asian Art and de Young museums. Docent tours of special galleries run regularly through the day. A small but bursting shop sells art books, cards, and prints. Cafe de Young offers light refreshments, sandwiches, and hot meals either indoors or in the Oakes Garden, surrounded by camellias and classical statuary.

Japanese Tea Garden

The has been one of San Francisco's most enduring attractions since the 1894 Midwinter Fair. When the fair ended, the park commission hired a full-time gardener, Makota Hagiwara, to tend the gardens and operate the tea concession. The Japanese Tea Garden flourished under the Hagiwara family's care until politicians, goaded by anti-Japanese sentiments, forced their removal at the turn of the 20th century. McLaren, who valued good gardening more than bad politics, asked them back, and the family kept the garden until they were interned during World War II. A plaque honoring the Hagiwara family stands by the main gate.

The garden's carefully tended paths and shrubbery, ornamental gates and lanterns, and pools swarming with gold and black carp are delightful, provided you visit early on a weekday morning, or on a rainy day. During weekends, the garden can be almost too crowded to appreciate, with tourists clamoring to be photographed on the famous steep-arched bridge, or in front of *Amazarashi-no-hotoke-Buddha*, alias *The Buddha Who Sits Through Sun and Rain Without Shelter*. Cast in Japan in 1790, he is probably the largest bronze ever exported from Asia. The cherry trees bloom in April, a special sight.

A small souvenir shop and a pavilion serving green tea and cookies stand in the garden. San Francisco's most famous culinary invention originated here in 1909— the fortune cookie. Although Makota Hagiwara was the first to make them, the fortune cookie was popularized by Chinatown restaurants as a *Chinese* "tradition," though you won't find fortune cookies at all in China. *For Japanese Tea Garden information: 415-666-7200.*

Strybing Arboretum and Botanical Gardens

Golden Gate Park's most concentrated collection of rare and exotic plants features species and gardens from Australia, New Zealand, Africa, Asia, and the Americas. Several gardens maintain special themes, including the New World Cloud Forest, and the succulent, dwarf, Biblical, and California gardens. Medical and culinary herbs grow in the Garden of Fragrance, designed for the blind to appreciate through touch and smell. Plants are labeled in Braille. The Asian Garden, built around the simple Moon-Viewing Pavilion, is lovely and quiet even when the Japanese Tea Garden is overrun with tourists. Nearby, a small stream winds through a grove of stately California redwoods. Look for the rare Dawn Redwood from China, the only species of redwood that grows outside of California and Oregon. You can buy wildflower seeds, cards, and books on nature and botany at the store near the main entrance, or peruse some of the 12,000 volumes on plants at the Helen Crocker Russell Library, housed in the adjacent County Fair Building. *415-661-1316.*

Shakespeare Garden

This very special English garden grows across the road (Martin Luther King, Jr. Drive) from the arboretum, beside the Academy of Sciences, and it contains only flowers and plants mentioned in Shakespeare's works. In case you forget your lines, the relevant ones are cast in bronze on the garden wall. A rare bust of the Bard himself is kept in a box under lock and key. It's a copy of a cast made in 1814 in Stratford-Upon-Avon, from a stone bust which was itself hewn by Gerard Johnson upon Shakespeare's death. Being only thrice removed from the actual face of Shakespeare, it is thus reputed to be one of the most realistic likenesses. If you want to see it, ask at McLaren Lodge.

Stow Lake Area

Encircling 428-foot-high Strawberry Hill, man-made Stow Lake is the park's largest lake, and a favorite for rowers, who rent their boats at the northwest corner of the lake. A circumnavigation of Strawberry Hill Island takes in its two bridges, Huntington Falls, and the Chinese pavilion. A gift from the city of Taipei, the pavilion was shipped in 6,000 pieces and assembled on the island. Prayer Book Cross, a copy of a Celtic cross from the British isle of Iona, stands on a hill above Rainbow Falls, a McLaren-made creek inspired by a California mountain stream. The creek flows into Lloyd Lake, in which is reflected San Francisco's sentimental monument to the 1906 earthquake—Portals of the Past. The portals were all that was left standing of a Nob Hill mansion after the fires were quelled.

Western Half

The western half of Golden Gate Park is far quieter than the busy eastern half. Here, during the week, a stroller on Speedway, Marx, or Lindley Meadows, or along the Chain of Lakes, meets few passers-by. A curious surprise is the Bison Paddock, where a small herd—relocated from Wyoming in 1984 to replace the original stock first brought here in 1894—stands around looking fairly bored under the eucalyptus trees, no doubt dreaming of their long-lost home on the Plains. Holding down the westernmost corners of the park are two windmills from Holland, installed at the turn of the century to irrigate the park. It has been said that the southern one, the Murphy Windmill, is the largest of its kind in the world, though it is in want of renovation. The northern Dutch Windmill has been restored. The Queen Wilhelmina Tulip Garden blooms in spring at its foot.

■ THE INNER SUNSET

Something about Golden Gate Park makes a person hungry. Of course, you can eat in the museums or pack a picnic, but two commercial districts are also handy to the park's eastern end. Everyone has heard of Haight Street, of course, but the other little neighborhood just beyond the **Ninth Avenue gate** is a local secret that's fast becoming a higher-rent district.

Most people think of the Sunset District as boring—a nice place to live, but you wouldn't want to visit there. Some of Golden Gate Park's magic seems to have rubbed off on its northeastern corner, however, where Irving and Judah cross Ninth Avenue. Just a 10-minute walk from the Music Concourse, this homey little neighborhood offers several excellent restaurants, cafes, and shops. Come for a hearty breakfast, pop in for lunch, or browse through the bookstores till late at night. If you're heading back downtown, the N-Judah MUNI streetcar runs right through the neighborhood. But what's the rush? Just outside the Ninth Avenue entrance stands the Little Shamrock Pub, established in 1893, when the Sunset was a giant sandflat. Have a pint of Guinness and check out the historic photographs.

On the thickly wooded slopes of Mt. Sutro, the gargantuan University of California (UCSF) Medical Center sets the serious mood of Parnassus Avenue. One of the last cobbled streets in the city, **Edgewood Avenue** climbs up UCSF's eastern boundary, ending in a eucalyptus forest. Walkers can reach it via **Farnsworth steps**, enjoying a grand view over the Richmond District and the red, steep roofs of Haight Street. Walking east on Parnassus, you'll soon hit Stanyan Street and, two blocks later, Cole Street, both fair and friendly prospects of thriving restaurants and little shops which serve **Cole Valley,** a cozy and inviting neighborhood with a small-town feel. Turning left onto either will guide you into the district known to San Franciscans as **the Haight,** and to everyone else as Haight-Ashbury.

■ HAIGHT-ASHBURY

Like North Beach, Nob Hill, and the Barbary Coast, Haight-Ashbury is a name that transcends mere geographical designation. A mishmash of images comes to mind when one hears it: pop Zen, black-light posters, incense, flowers, purple velvet, buckskin, proffered joints, tambourines, Victoriana, long hair, psychedelia, acid rock, free love, peace signs, cosmic harmony, and bongos in the park. No one can ever forget Haight-Ashbury in the '60s, even those who never saw it. The 1967 Summer of Love lasted a scant three months, but it defined the city for the generation who came of age at that time, and it still generates its own pervasive mythology. Some 200,000 young people came to San Francisco that year, drawn by an enchanting vision of freedom and social harmony.

Haight-Ashbury started life as a solid family neighborhood along Haight Street, a commercial center for the new Golden Gate Park. Large, rambling, wooden houses sprouted on its cross streets, named for city supervisors Stanyan, Cole, Clayton, Shrader, and Ashbury. The wide, green **Panhandle**, designed as a carriage entry to Golden Gate Park, was lined by Victorian rows of Queen Anne towers and gables that lent a kind of Parisian grandeur to a city otherwise choked by dense housing. After the streetcar tunnel under Buena Vista Park was completed in 1928, however, middle-class citizenry started departing for the suburbs in the Sunset, and the bypassed Haight-Ashbury began its long, slow decline in fortune. By the early 1960s, it was a run-down district of cheap rents in subdivided Victorians. Still, the almost exotic beauty of its architecture and grand planning remained.

Almost completely surrounded by parks, and haunted throughout by decaying stateliness, Haight-Ashbury seemed a lyrical, almost magical setting to the generations raised in insulated suburbs and small towns. Seeking to shed the restraints of The Establishment, they came to indulge their senses through communal living, drugs, music, free love, and outright fantasy, to *live* their protest against materialism, the war in Vietnam, racial strife, social inequality, and parental control. The *San Francisco Examiner* called them "hippies." Decked out in scruffy clothes and long hair, they were not, of course, an exclusively San Franciscan phenomenon, but "Hashbury" (as it was called in the press) became their most celebrated mecca. The music industry spread the gospel. Local rock groups like Jefferson Airplane and the Grateful Dead played free around the Haight and Golden Gate Park, and scores of other stars were made in the nearby Fillmore West and Winterland auditoriums by rock impresario Bill Graham. Psychedelic concert posters from the Haight appeared on bedroom walls across the country, and across the Atlantic. Songs like Eric Burdon's "San Francisco Nights" inspired many to come and experience the "street called Love" for themselves. (And taking a cue from the Scott MacKenzie ode, many really *did* wear flowers in their hair.)

By autumn, the Summer of Love was already changing. Tourist buses and media exposure soured the novelty. Thousands of curious wannabe flower children swelled the Haight population, straining the resources, easy prey for streetwise manipulators. Drugs and pushers took their toll. The war in Vietnam blazed on, intruding on the celebration of life. Many true believers left the district for communes and small towns. The Haight lurched toward decrepitude and violence.

Like much of Victorian San Francisco, the Haight today has once again gentrified.

"It's better to burn out..." (Kerrick James)

It's hardly surprising. Few neighborhoods harbor such beautiful homes, and none can match its bosky parkland "backyard." Many of the pre-'60s businesses—like the bike rental outlets—are prospering. New bars and restaurants along Haight cater to a politically aware *and* financially secure clientele—a contradiction of terms in the old Hashbury. The head shops have closed, having been replaced by increasingly hip and decreasingly hippy boutiques and cafes. But you can still have your mind expanded at places like Pipe Dreams, where water pipes and Grateful Dead paraphernalia are sold. The scores of street people who congregate on the edge of Golden Gate Park, at the head of Haight, are not a community of quaint, aging hippies.

◆ BUENA VISTA PARK

Six blocks down Haight from Golden Gate Park, a forest of twisting, matted trees rises abruptly, like some fantastically overgrown Tuscan hillside. When seen from below, or from a distance, Buena Vista Park presents one of the wildest, most enchanting aspects of San Francisco. Climbing up the steep paths into the park is less exalting, except for the views, if you can find the holes through the trees. From the middle of the hill, where the pitched roofs of Ashbury Heights tumble down toward the Panhandle, look north across the marble-white city and the parks' green rectangles, beyond the church towers of St. Ignatius to the bridge-spiked headlands of the Golden Gate, as exotic as Istanbul, more beautiful than Paris. You can almost understand how such an enchanting place might inspire tangerine dreams of a New Jerusalem.

■ ASHBURY HEIGHTS

Now you are climbing into real hill country, where winding streets finally start to shake the standard San Francisco grid. Submerged under an aging but respectable neighborhood, the little peak of **Mount Olympus** still nurtures a curious pedestal, where Sutro once erected a statue of the goddess of liberty, entitled the *Triumph of Light*. Sadly, the lady was vandalized and carted off years ago, and even the views are blocked by buildings.

Like Mount Olympus, **Corona Heights** is a purely local curiosity, an ugly red hill gouged out by brick-making operations in the last century. Excellent views from the Heights bore straight down Market Street, and south to Eureka Valley.

Avoid the cliffs on the eastern edge. Below the peak is a nifty little museum for city kids to learn how Mother Nature runs her show. The **Josephine Randall Junior Museum** keeps a menagerie of snakes, owls, raccoons, lambs, goats, and other animals for youngsters to touch and care for. Summer classes and simple displays make science fun for kids. *199 Museum Way; 415-554-9600.*

Leaving Ashbury Heights by the back door, you can descend toward Market Street and the Mission District via **Vulcan Stairs**, one of the more exotic city walks. Departing from Levant Street, Vulcan enters another country, where quiet, almost *rural* houses peer out from behind small gardens of dangling fuchsias, stalks, pines, roses, daisies, succulents, and fennel. In summer, plump blackberries and plums hang ripe for the picking—I mean by the residents, of course. The views fall dramatically from craggy Corona Heights down to the Castro, where rainbow-striped "Freedom" flags festoon the Victorians with an air of fantasy; and indeed, it is something of a brave new world.

The towers of St. Ignatius Church bathed in the glow of sunset and framed between cypress trees on the steep, wooded slopes of Buena Vista Park. (photo by Michael Oliver)

CULTIVATED
QUARTER

THE CITY'S SOUTHERN EXPOSURE

SAN FRANCISCO'S SOUTHERN HALF is left pretty much to those who live there. Every day, to be sure, a few tourist buses can be found parked in front of Mission Dolores or inching around the heights of Twin Peaks. But of these, how many of their passengers stop to smell the *flores* along thriving 24th Street, or sidle down the secluded stairways that hang from the city's highest slopes? Almost none.

The tourist industry's neglect of the southern neighborhoods is, for better or worse, a situation that will probably reverse itself in time. It just so happens that the gentrification of San Francisco's "quaint" neighborhoods started at Telegraph Hill, working its way across the city by slow degrees. The Upper Fillmore, South of Market, Western Addition, and Haight-Ashbury, each in their turn, have braced against the tide of higher rents and wealthier tenants that followed their "discovery," washing up a flotsam of boutiques and restaurants, and a reputation among the trendy as a fashionable "new" neighborhood.

For now, fortunately, most of San Francisco's southern half simply does not appeal to the sight- and action-oriented tourist. The southern half contains the city's most desolate post-industrial zones, its largest stretches of residential poverty, and its greatest concentration of neighborhoods just bland enough to discourage exploration. But it's also true that you will find a lot of what has already been celebrated in the northern half, mercifully unprettified by three decades of rampant tourism. For the traveler who appreciates vibrant cultures and cuisines, enchanting cityscapes, neighborly folks, and a good cup of coffee in a cultivated setting, the southern half deserves to be discovered.

■ THE MISSION DISTRICT

The most *naturally* hospitable spot in San Francisco is the Mission District. Like the Spanish clerics who followed them, the local Ohlone tribe (they called themselves the Ramaytush) chose this broad, sheltered valley to build their largest settlement. The mercantile Americans shifted the focus of settlement to the harbor at Yerba Buena Cove, now the Financial District, leaving the Mission Valley largely undeveloped until the 1860s. The district became one of San Francisco's first suburbs. By the early part of this century, a preponderance of Irish immigrants in this neighborhood even gave it a distinctive accent, called "Mish," which was said to sound something like Brooklynese. The greater portion of the Mission District was spared destruction in the 1906 fire, and today retains some of San Francisco's finest examples of Victorian architecture.

Ironically, the predominant ethnic flavor of the Mission today is once again Hispanic. Since the 1960s, increased immigration from Mexico and Central and South America has made this San Francisco's largest Latin American neighborhood. Spanish alternates freely with English in the shops and on the streets. About

Colorful murals adorn many a wall in the Mission District.

Sunbathing at Mission Dolores Park: a beach towel with a view. (Kerrick James)

half the residents are Hispanic; of these, roughly half trace their roots to Mexico and the rest to other Latin countries, including El Salvador, Panama, Nicaragua, Colombia, Peru, and Guatemala.

The Mission District is San Francisco's most visually colorful district—culturally vibrant, yet down at the heel. Twin Peaks blocks the Pacific fogs, making it the brightest and warmest neighborhood in the city. Its low rooflines and wide streets seem to catch the sun. Crowds of people fill the streets in a way that never happens in the Sunset or Marina: shy country folk, fast-talking businessmen, panhandlers, dancers, artists, mothers with babies, muscle-bound teenagers, aging revolutionaries, the walking wounded. Market fruits and vegetables, pounding music, and deep, rich aromas of cooking food spill out onto sidewalks. Higher up, brilliant murals ignite the walls in monumental tribute to families, community, work, the harvest, political strife, and dreamier, fanciful themes. Tour these colorful murals—a major Mexican art form—with a free walker's map from the Mexican Museum at Fort Mason.

The largest public festival of the Mission District is Cinco de Mayo—the Fifth of May, which celebrates the victory of Mexican troops under command of General Zaragoza over the French invasion forces of Napoleon III, in 1862. Highlight of the festivities is a parade through the Mission. It is followed in late May by Carnaval, a good excuse to dress up in exotic costumes and parade through the streets. Another colorful festival, the Day of the Dead, culminates on November 2 with a nighttime candlelight parade of skeletal celebrants. It might be called a Latino version of Halloween, but more macabre, though with a streak of graveyard humor, and religious roots intact. Local shops prepare for the festival days beforehand with eerie (or gaudily devotional) altars, skull candies, and bone-shaped breads called *calaveras*.

The Pan-American character of the Mission is enshrined in its restaurants. Mexican sets the tone, but you can also find authentic Argentine, Nicaraguan, Brazilian, Cuban, Puerto Rican, Salvadoran, Peruvian, and other Latin American kitchens, many of them intimate, hearty, and cheap neighborhood establishments where expatriates gather to eat and socialize.

The Mission around 16th and Valencia is the likeliest candidate for San Francisco's reigning bohemian district, a perfect example of how alternative intellectual strains prosper best amidst cheap eats and rents, *not* quaintness. Bohemia isn't tidy; but that doesn't mean it can't comfortably entertain its guests with good cof-

The Mission District's 16th Street is a hotspot of cafes, restaurants, and nightclubs. (Kerrick James)

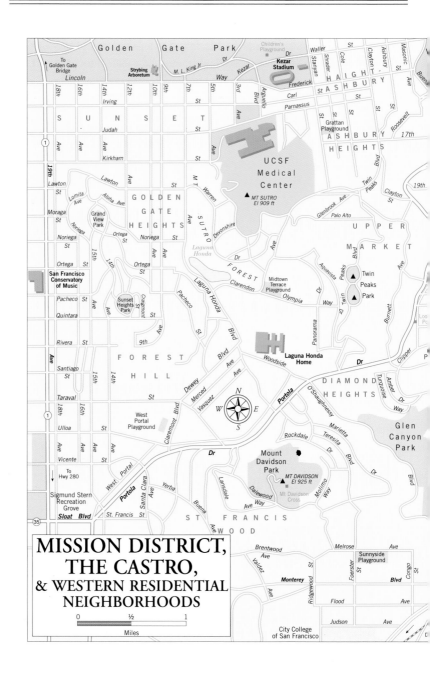

MISSION DISTRICT,
THE CASTRO,
& WESTERN RESIDENTIAL
NEIGHBORHOODS

0   ½   1

Miles

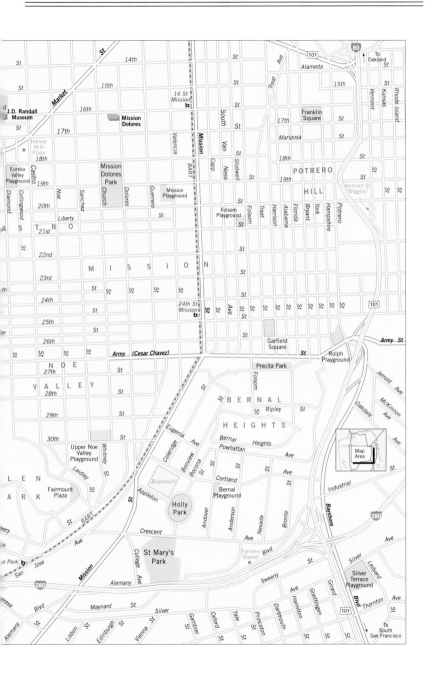

fee and company, and evening poetry readings. On any given evening, patrons of neighborhood bars, bookstores, and coffeehouses will likely enjoy (or revile, as the case may be) the company of off-duty dancers, writers, and artists, as well as on-duty pool hustlers, chess players, and poets. Eat and drink today, for the yuppies are quickly driving it down beyond 24th Street.

◆ MISSION DOLORES

Built in 1791 and standing at the corner of 16th and Dolores Streets, as it has since before the streets existed, this is the oldest standing building in San Francisco. It was the sixth mission to be founded in California, on orders from Father Serra, whom California honors with a statue in Washington's Hall of Fame. Father Serra was beatified by the Catholic Church in September 1988, and may yet become California's first Roman Catholic saint—though he remains controversial as the symbol of Native California's demise.

Visitors are charged a small fee to enter the walled mission compound to see the church, a small museum, gift shop, and the beautiful graveyard. The walls were built of adobe, brick made from sun-dried mud and manure. Though adobe is not the strongest material, Mission Dolores survived the 1906 earthquake, while the American-era basilica next door crumbled. On rare hot days, Mission Dolores exudes a musty coolness. Its beautiful painted ceilings are based on original Ohlone designs done and with vegetable dyes. The bells, altars, and statues were carried from Mexico by mule.

The peaceful, overgrown cemetery, watched over by a brooding statue of Father Serra, has many a tale to tell. (One of them is not, as fans of Hitchcock's *Vertigo* might wish, the whereabouts of Kim Novak's double.) A number of mostly Hispanic, Italian, and Irish pioneers are buried here and in the church, including William Leidesdorff; the Noé Family; Don Luis Antonio Arguello, first Mexican governor of California; and San Francisco's first mayor, Don Francisco de Haro. It was said that de Haro died of lingering heartbreak after Kit Carson, while in the service of Captain John C. Frémont, shot his twin sons during a poor excuse for a revolutionary skirmish.

Another poignant story is buried with Charles Cora, who was hanged by vigilantes in 1856. His wife of one day, Arabella, lies at his side. The couple were married at the prompting of the priest who had come to deliver last rites before Cora's execution. Arabella had played an unintentional part in Cora's downfall. As Cora's mistress, she was snubbed one evening at the opera by U.S. Marshal William

Richardson. Cora and the lawman exchanged words over the incident, which escalated to a fight, during which the gambler shot the marshal dead. By all accounts, including the one accepted by the jury, Marshal Richardson was the aggressor and the homicide justified. The vigilantes did not accept the jury's verdict, however, and the fruits of their justice lie here for all to see. Aside from Cora, two other victims of vigilante justice, James Casey and James "Yankee" Sullivan, are also buried here.

The most tragic tale of Our Lady of Sorrows is also the one least known. In this quiet churchyard, about 5,000 Ohlone men, women, and children are buried in unmarked graves; the large rock grotto in the middle of the cemetery is their memorial. Most died of measles in the early 1800s. In 1850, when California's first U.S. Indian agent came here to take a census, he found only one Native American left, a man named Pedro Alcantara, who spoke of his love for a missing son, and said that he was the last of his tribe. *Mission Dolores; 415-621-8203.*

Lively, low-rent Mission Street is the district's main thoroughfare, but the stretch of **24th Street** between Mission and Potrero has a more neighborly Latin ambiance. Restaurants and piñata-hung family grocery stores cater to the local community. This is the place to go for such Latino specialties as *nopales* (cactus leaves), fresh and dried chilies, *paletas* (frozen fruit-juice bars), Mexican cheeses, tropical American fruits (including a wide variety of bananas and plantains), and ready-made burritos, tamales, tacos, and pies. If your nose leads you to the corner of Alabama and 24th, stop in for cake, cookies, *churros* (twisted, fried-dough snacks), or pastries at La Victoria, a wonderful Mexican bakery. The **Galeria de la Raza**, on the corner of Bryant, exhibits the works of Hispanic artists, and is a good place to find the often bizarre altars for the Day of the Dead; *415-989-6015.*

The southern edge of Mission Valley is marked by the rise of **Bernal Heights**. It is, in fact, one of the homelier hills of the city—but homely doesn't mean we don't love it, for its character is endearingly San Franciscan. One story says that Bernal Heights was settled by a clever ruse in 1876, when developers triggered a miniature gold rush (and raised land prices) by lacing the summit with gold. Bernal Heights has an almost rural feel in places. Take Franconia Street, for instance, as it rambles around the side of the hill, angling in and out in ways that genteel city streets are taught not to do, and even going so far as to turn to gravel around the middle. Plunked down on the heights are big, fiercely independent, hillbilly houses that sit askew, with land around them. Some were built after the earthquake of 1906 with timbers salvaged from wreckage. Long considered a bit of a bumpkin, Bernal Heights has been able to preserve its comfortable and affordable lifestyle up to now. But alas, in the San Francisco scheme of things, yesterday's rustic neighborhood is today's quaint victim of gentrification—and tomorrow's exclusive district. Residents of Bernal Heights are worrying that the secret may be out.

■ THE CASTRO DISTRICT

The slope of Twin Peaks rises abruptly to the west of Mission Valley. In the best San Franciscan tradition, its hillside streets below Market were built on a right-angle grid, so that they appear on a map to be as flat as Mission Street. Don't be fooled—Noe Valley and the Castro are two of the hilliest neighborhoods in the City. This natural barrier to easy public access has kept them remote from major transport arteries, and therefore quiet, stable, middle class, and Victorian in appearance, though not in character. Still, Noe Valley and the Castro are very different from one another.

The Castro, known to old-timers as Eureka Valley, is the city's largest gay neighborhood. Its standing in the Gay Rights Movement is of international scope, for in no other major city do gay men openly comprise such a large percentage of the population, enjoying such social freedom and political clout. The exact population of gay men and women in San Francisco is wildly disputed (and impossible to count), but 100,000 is a commonly quoted figure that *seems* reasonable.

The neighborhood's main commercial crossroads is the corner of **Castro and Market Streets**. Harvey Milk Plaza, on the southwest corner, is named for San Francisco's first openly gay supervisor, who, with Mayor George Moscone, was assassinated by a disgruntled ex-supervisor, Dan White, on November 28, 1978. When White was convicted the following May of an incredibly lesser offense (voluntary manslaughter by reason of "diminished capacity"), thousands of

Halloween in the Castro is an all-day costume party. (Kerrick James)

Cafe Flore (known locally as Cafe Hairdo) is a Castro institution.

protesters besieged Civic Center in riotous anger. Every June, the annual Gay Freedom Day parade marches from City Hall, scene of the murders, to downtown.

The Castro has a strong sense of community. All goods and services necessary for a happy and fulfilling urban life are locally available, so that it can be a world unto itself for those who wish it. Bars, restaurants, cafes, furniture stores, hair salons, delis, bookstores, and scores of other shops cater to a predominantly gay clientele. The **Castro Theater**, a vintage movie palace with an Arabian-nights interior and a Wurlitzer on a hydraulic lift, shows classic films. The neighborhood hosts a "Pink Saturday" party the day before the Freedom Parade, as well as a flamboyant and festive street fair in August. While the Castro no longer officially hosts its legendary Halloween party, shopkeepers and customers alike dress in costume on October 31.

The Castro is a beautifully maintained neighborhood, stylish in that a good deal of money and effort go toward cultivating a distinctive ambience. Along Castro, Victorian parody vies with avant-garde, and fine taste clashes with the outrageous. Shop signs pun cleverly. Patrons stroll in and out of hip boutiques and crowded cafes. Beyond the commercial district, pitched-roof Victorians leapfrog

(following pages) This panoramic view of downtown can be had from Diamond Heights.
(Kerrick James)

up the hillsides, brilliantly decorated and wrapped in well-tended gardens. Even the cats lounging in the sunny windows seem placed there by design.

■ NOE VALLEY

If you climb up Castro Street to the ridge above, a long, steep haul, you will crest the hill near 22nd Street before dropping into Noe Valley. This dividing ridge between Noe and Eureka Valleys—where 21st, Hill, and Liberty cross Collingwood, Castro, Noe, and Sanchez—is one of the prettiest residential enclaves in the city. Quiet, attractive streets and stairs lead to views that tourists seldom see.

Noe Valley is the Switzerland of San Francisco. Hilly, clean, prosperous, and stable, it cherishes its lofty seclusion high above the teeming flatlands. Overhead, the barren summits of Twin Peaks, with their bone-chilling winds, will put you in

mind of the Alps—on a foggy day, of course, and better yet, with a nip or two of brandy. Even the steep-pitched Victorian rooftops seem to be eternally awaiting snow, which never comes. Its residents are loyal to their community. They do not maintain a standing army, but they do have a neighborhood library on Jersey Street, where lectures, films, seminars, local art shows, and publications keep everyone abreast of community affairs. A free neighborhood newspaper, the *Noe Valley Voice*, is published in a wooden church built in 1888 at 1021 Sanchez. At night the church becomes Noe Valley Ministry, an intimate venue for offbeat but consistently high-quality folk, world, and jazz concerts.

Noe Valley's stretch of **24th Street** contains all the conveniences of big-city life with the scale and character of a small town's Main Street. The heavy concentration of cafes and breakfast spots along here rate high from people with time on their hands and change in their pockets. The neighborhood boasts several good restaurants,

clothing boutiques, toy stores, and even an old-fashioned grocery or two, where you may find the proprietor sitting at the counter watching the ball game on TV.

■ TWIN PEAKS

As you climb toward Upper Market and Diamond Heights, the city spreads out like a child's counterpane, with toy houses stacked in the tucks and ridges, their roofs of black, gray, red, blue, and green. Romantics say that San Francisco has seven hills. Nit-pickers, in fact, have counted a total of 43. The most famous ones—Russian, Nob, and Telegraph—are midgets compared to the range of hills that rise in the geographic center of the city. Of these, Twin Peaks, Mount Sutro, and Mount Davidson all top 900 feet.

When Daniel Burnham required a View of Views from which to make his master plan for San Francisco, he retreated for two years to the top of **Twin Peaks**. Burnham and his plan have long blown town, but Twin Peaks and its view are still there, more magnificent than ever—the night expanse of lights was never so magnificent in Burnham's day. Twin Peaks Boulevard encircles both peaks near their summits and offers amble places to park and gawk.

Wooded Mount Sutro is the platform for San Francisco's tallest structure, a much-hated (because very obtrusive) radio antenna called Sutro Tower. Red-striped and gigantic, it's visible from all over the Bay Area.

Mount Davidson is the highest hill in the city. Thick woods obstruct the views afforded from naked Twin Peaks. Paths from the surrounding neighborhood wind to the top, where a huge cross stands, visible from miles around. At 103 feet (31 m) tall, it just might be the largest cross in the New World. Every Easter, thousands of people gather here for sunrise services. The cross also attracts its share of detractors, who demand that it be dismantled because it stands on public land in violation of the constitutional separation of church and state. Legalistically, they may have a case; let's just hope nobody tells them where the city of San Francisco gets its name.

Between Mount Davidson and Twin Peaks, a wilder aspect of pre-Yankee San Francisco still survives in **Glen Canyon Park**. Once part of a Spanish cattle ranch, the rugged canyon is now a day camp and playground for local kids.

The neighborhoods on the slopes of these peaks are newer than most in the flatlands, and their streets were built to follow the contours of the hill, not a surveyor's grid. Were it not for their spectacular views, many of these neighborhoods would be rather plain. Some of the terraces are linked by stairways. Partly overgrown Pemberton stairway is the best in the Upper Market area. Wooded Mount

Sutro supports Oakhurst Lane, the longest, highest stairway in the city, as well as the Ashwood, Blairwood, and Glenhaven stairs. One of the least-known stairway walks is Harry Street, a ramshackle affair that clambers between Beacon and Laidley Streets, on Glen Park's eastern edge, with a bird's-eye view of Noe Valley. San Francisco's most elegant stairway sweeps up from near Dewey Boulevard into sheltered Forest Hills, an affluent enclave on the western slopes of Twin Peaks. Adah Bakalinsky's *Stairway Walks in San Francisco* is an excellent guide for searching out these and other hidden steps.

In a city of outstanding views, some shock even natives, mainly because they have not been snapped to death by photographers. **Sunset Heights** is one example. Fantastically situated on high, steep, exposed hills west of Mount Sutro, the area offers surprise views around almost every corner, with steep stairways connecting different levels. Looking west, the cross-hatched Richmond and Sunset districts resemble an unfolded map, on which you can pick out Seal Rocks, the Farallon Islands, Golden Gate Park, Point Reyes, and other landmarks. Climb the stairway to the lofty knob of **Grand View Park** for the best views.

■ WEST PORTAL

Saint Francis Wood is yet another of San Francisco's moneyed neighborhoods. Frederick Law Olmsted, who designed New York's Central Park, helped John Galen Howard lay out these urbane streets, with their fountains and gateways, in 1912.

West Portal, next door, is the area's main shopping street. West Portal refers to the western entrance of the 2.25-mile streetcar tunnel under Twin Peaks. The tunnel opened in 1917. Until the Market Street section was put underground in the 1970s, the tunnel's eastern portal was on Market Street at Castro. Nowadays, when you ride the K-Ingleside, L-Taraval, or M-Ocean View streetcars from downtown, your first glimpse of sunlight is at West Portal.

There is something vaguely romantic about West Portal. Imagine sitting in a restaurant overlooking the street at dusk, perhaps with streaks of rain on the window, watching the streetcars come and go. Commuters returning from downtown rush off to do their grocery shopping, while others scurry aboard for the ride back—perhaps for an evening at the theater. All the hallmarks of San Francisco chic are here, the tidy shops and ethnic restaurants. Despite its cosmopolitan airs, West Portal most resembles some nondescript Central European streetcar suburb. It's a great place for a romantic rendezvous, not least because it provides an expedient getaway should that prove necessary.

■ THE SUNSET DISTRICT AND POINTS SOUTH

As mentioned earlier, the Inner Sunset where Ninth Avenue crosses Judah and Irving is by far the most interesting section of the district for outsiders. *(See page 192).* Otherwise, the Sunset is an orderly, middle-class residential area sandwiched between the peaks and Ocean Beach. The summer fog here is relentless. San Franciscans from other neighborhoods occasionally find their way out to a Sunday concert in Stern Grove, a recital at the San Francisco Conservatory of Music *(1201 Ortega)*, or a Chinese dinner on Taraval (which has been christened by some as *new* New Chinatown!). But on the whole, the Sunset keeps pretty much to itself.

Once upon a time in what is now **Stern Grove**, there was a roadhouse of ill repute called the Trocadero Inn. It achieved its greatest notoriety as the place where Abe Ruef, the corrupt political boss of Mayor Schmitz's regime, was captured after a gunfight with police. For better or for worse, the Troc has long since been rehabilitated.

◆ SAN FRANCISCO ZOO

The main gate of the zoo is on Sloat Boulevard, a stone's throw or two from Ocean Beach. Though not ranked as one of the best American zoos, some of the individual animal habitats themselves do rank quite highly. The gorillas' new home gives them room to roam, rocks and trees to climb, and a thick window through which they may safely observe the homo sapiens at close range. Silkworms, tarantulas, black widows, termites, beetles, crickets, scorpions, and other vermin dwell in the Insect Zoo, where you can also observe bees at work in a living hive, without getting stung. The Children's Zoo lets kids feed and touch barnyard animals. In the Kresge Nocturnal Gallery, visitors can study a bush baby, slow loris, and other nocturnal animals in their natural settings. The Phoebe Hearst Discovery Hall uses computers to stimulate questions and answers about primates. Other zoo attractions are Wolf Woods, Koala Crossing, the Lion House, the Gorilla Habitat, Musk Ox Meadow, and a host of rhinos, elephants, hippos, tigers, giraffes, zebras, bears, penguins, and other birds and beasts. A roaring good show is feeding time in the Lion House, daily at 2 p.m., except Monday. The zoo operates guided tours, snack bars, a gift shop, a popular playground, and a magnificent carousel, built in 1921 by William Dentzel. *Sloat Blvd. at 45th Ave.; 415-753-7145.*

The last of the exposed sand wastes that once overspread the Richmond and Sunset Districts survives at **Fort Funston**. Now part of the GGNRA, this old military property on San Francisco's southernmost coast was once used for trial beachhead landings by the Army. The barren, windy cliffs are popular for hang gliding.

Lake Merced is another natural area that has miraculously survived the city's expansion. Now protected as a park, San Francisco's largest lake provides a natural habitat for wildlife, as well as recreation for fishermen, boaters, joggers, golfers, and birdwatchers. Bring your own (non-motorized) boat, or rent one from the Boat House on Harding Road.

San Francisco State University's modern campus stands on the eastern shore of Lake Merced. One of the most academically acclaimed schools in the state university system, the school is home to the Sutro Library (480 Winston Drive), inherited from the Sutro estate, and one of the West's earliest and largest collections of books. Another intellectual property of note on campus is the American Poetry Archives, the world's largest videotaped collection of poets reading their works or being interviewed. The archive is open to the public in room 117 of the Humanities Building.

Beyond "State" is **Ingleside**, the neighborhood whose greatest claim to fame is the world's second-largest sundial—or is it the third? Sundial worshippers can make the pilgrimage to Entrada Court to genuflect before the 26-foot-high device.

■ THE BORDER NEIGHBORHOODS

The residential districts along San Francisco's southern border—Hunters Point, Visitacion Valley, Bayview, Ocean View, and the Outer Mission—are *terra incognita* to most San Franciscans who do not live there. That's not to say that they aren't interesting, so long as you realize that they are working-class or poor residential neighborhoods that do not cater to tourism.

The Excelsior and Crocker-Amazon neighborhoods, lumped together with the **Outer Mission**, are down-home cosmopolitan places. The residents trace their roots in roughly equal numbers to Asia, Africa, Europe, and the Americas. Unlike the prosperous and international Richmond District, the Excelsior is the poor-man's polyglot, vibrant in a colloquial, unflamboyant way. Sure, it needs a little "softening up" before it's ready to entertain visitors. In the meantime, local residents take it for granted and enjoy the lower rents.

Sandwiched between the Excelsior and Visitacion Valley, **McLaren Park** preserves a large hill from development. Most of the park has been left alone as natural, uncultivated grassland. The views are unique. Look south across Visitacion Valley to Mount San Bruno; the hulking Cow Palace, an all-purpose auditorium, dominates the valley from the Daly City side of the city line. Look north, and the towers of San Francisco rise like an Emerald City behind the grid of the Bayview District, tossed over its hills like a checkered quilt.

Bayview–Hunters Point has strong name recognition among San Franciscans, almost none of it favorable. Outsiders don't come here much, except en route to Candlestick Park to see the Giants or 49ers play, or to the Cow Palace for rodeos and stock shows. During World War II, Hunters Point was the largest shipyard on the West Coast, drawing large numbers of out-of-state workers, who settled in makeshift housing beyond the docks. Hunters Point became, and remains, the largest predominantly African-American district in the city. Since the war, the speed and quality of urban renewal has not been universally inspiring, though many of Bayview's hills and old houses, punctuated by wooden church steeples, retain distinctively San Franciscan qualities admired by visitors to other districts. Unfortunately, Bayview-Hunters Point is ravaged by high unemployment, drugs, and violence. Parts are heavily industrialized, and many residential neighborhoods are extremely depressed. Many artists have retreated to studios at the old navy base on Hunters Point. Once a year, the Open Studio program offers a peek to the general public. *For Open Studio information, call 415-822-3809.*

◆ GOLDEN GATE RAILROAD MUSEUM

This museum's ever-growing collection stands amidst the weedy grittiness of a once-working trainyard. The most impressive piece of equipment is an enormous steam locomotive that used to chug along the Coast, Sacramento, and San Joaquin Routes until its retirement in the 1950s. If you've ever hankered to spend an hour at the throttle of an old steamer or diesel locomotive, the museum also offers locomotive driving lessons. *Hunters Point Shipyard; 415-822-8728.*

■ POTRERO HILL

Long a quiet backwater in the midst of the city, Potrero Hill is one of the latest districts to feel the winds of gentrification. So far, the southern half of the hill, closest to Hunters Point, remains in the lee, but the northern half is very much a community like Noe Valley, with a quiet, pleasant shopping street along 20th. Views to the west over the Mission, and north toward downtown, are inspiring. Vermont Street from McKinley Square squiggles down the hill like a miniature Lombard, but without the tourists. Potrero Hill even has its own library (on 20th), newspaper (*The Potrero View*), playhouse (Theater Artaud), and brewery (Anchor Steam).

Anchor Steam Brewery, at 1705 Mariposa Street, ranks as a San Francisco original. Unlike all other lagers, steam beer is made without ice—a rare commodity in

Until the new stadium in China Basin is completed, the Giants and the 49ers play at 3Com Park—the ballpark formerly known as the "Stick,"—in Hunters Point. (Kerrick James)

San Francisco at the brewery's founding in 1851, when Gold Rush thirsts could not be quenched by imported stock. The founding family had to devise a cooling method that used air instead of ice. As the idea caught on, other steam-beer breweries started up, but all disappeared with the advent of refrigeration, except for Anchor Steam (which actually adopted its present name a half-century after its founding—in 1896). The modern plant now brews three ales, two lagers, and a delicious wheat beer by their special methods. They also partake of the old brewers' custom of making a special Christmas vintage ale (it's actually a barley wine). Beloved by San Franciscans, Anchor Steam has a devoted following. Beer fanciers who want a taste of the Gold Rush should seek it out, and tours are a special treat.

Eastern Potrero Hill drops down to the docks, a working mixture of old brick warehouses and modern cranes. If you like the smell of the docks, the sight of ocean-going vessels, and the sounds of a solid Miles Davis tune, go to the Ramp, an outdoor jazz bar on the southern end of China Basin Road. On sunny weekend afternoons, patrons crowd the deck's tables to imbibe huge margaritas and take in the view across Central Basin to huge ships draining their bilge at the docks.

■ THE BAY BRIDGE

Bay Area residents love their bridges. The span across the Golden Gate inspires a virtual cult following, who garland it with all manner of glorious praise. Fans of the **San Francisco–Oakland Bay Bridge** don't have much truck for that kind of hogwash. And why should they?

The Bay Bridge is a big old hairy-chested roustabout span that does the work of two Golden Gate bridges. Five lanes wide, two decks deep, it joins causeway, truss, cantilever, tunnel, and double suspension spans to make the largest high-level steel bridge on Earth. About 2.25 billion vehicles crossed it during its first half-century of work. Today, the rate is about 250,000 *daily*. When it was completed in 1936, there was none bigger. How big? In length, about 8.25 miles, of which 4.25 miles are over water. The tunnel bored through Yerba Buena Island was the world's widest when built. The massive center anchorage alone, which anchors the ends of the two suspension spans in the middle of the bay, is bigger than the Great Pyramid at Giza. The bridge was designed by Charles Purcell, who called it a tribute to the intelligence of the American workingman. When you consider that the Bay Bridge and the Golden Gate Bridge were built *simultaneously*, who can fail to marvel at the vigor and confidence of the San Franciscans of yore!

The earthquake of 1989 severed the bridge where the cantilever section and the Oakland approach ramp join, knocking out 50-foot sections of both decks. Fortunately, neither section dropped into the water, but the crossing was closed for one month of repairs. While engineers rejoined the sections, road crews completely resurfaced the decks, a job that normally takes two years to do.

The Bay Bridge is closed to walkers and cyclists, but drivers can exit the bridge midway at **Yerba Buena Island** to hunt for the classic view of the suspension span marching into San Francisco. Another stupendous view is from adjacent **Treasure Island**. When completed in 1937, it was the largest man-made island in the world. It was originally intended as the site of San Francisco's first airport, but only Pan Am's *China Clipper* flights to Asia and the Pacific ever flew from here. Instead, the city gave Treasure Island to the U.S. Navy in exchange for the site of the present airport. The Navy has since given it back, and the city is wondering what to do with it.

The **Treasure Island Museum** remains as a vestige of its military past. On permanent exhibit are mementos of the Golden Gate International Exposition, a world's fair held here in 1939 and 1940 to celebrate completion of the bridges. Uniforms, weapons, nautical instruments, paintings, murals, and other treasures illustrate the history of the maritime services. *In the old* China Clipper *terminal; 415-395-5067.*

The eight-mile-long Bay Bridge is the region's busiest span, carrying more than 250,000 commuters between the East Bay and San Francisco every day. (Kerrick James)

E X C U R S I O N S

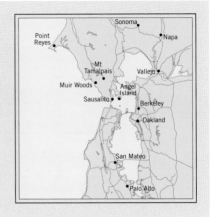

AMONG SAN FRANCISCO'S MANY RARE ENDOWMENTS, there's none more wonderful than the ease with which you can leave the town. You can quickly slip away north, south, or east—by bridge or by BART—to enjoy the earthly pleasures of California's renowned Wine Country; the intellectual stimulations of Berkeley and its university; or the museums and monuments that populate Silicon Valley, the epicenter of the Technological Revolution.

———◄◦►———

MARIN COUNTY

The perfect escape is north, across the Golden Gate or on the splendid little ferries to Marin County. Whether your tastes run to seascape or mountain scenery, backpack trails or tea in a cultivated setting, birdwatching or oyster shucking, you can start your vacation within minutes of leaving San Francisco.

■ SAUSALITO

Tourist promoters like to compare Sausalito to the Riviera. A certain visual similarity exists, but don't expect warm beaches and bikinis. Built on a steep, wooded hillside tumbling straight into the deep, blue bay, Sausalito is a pretty sight. Yachts and houseboats crowd its harbors, and a carefree air of leisure plays about its shops and restaurants.

Sausalito has not always been thought a pretty face. During World War II, it was a major shipyard. At the turn of the century, it was full of rough-and-ready waterfront bars and gambling parlors. In the Depression, the town was a haven for bootleggers. Today, Sausalito has become a little precious. The colorful old buildings remain, but too many of them are in the T-shirt and knickknack business. Still, Sausalito has managed to keep its charm.

Avoid parking problems by coming from San Francisco by ferry. Near the pier, the old town center of Plaza Vina del Mar is dedicated to Sausalito's Chilean sister city; the twin elephants holding up the lampposts were salvaged from San Francisco's 1915 Panama-Pacific International Exposition. Sausalito's main street is **Bridgeway**, a charming gauntlet of shops, galleries, restaurants, and watering holes, intersected by stairs and steep residential streets from on high, and opening to spectacular views of San Francisco's spires and towers on the shore side, where scuttling crabs and a bronze seal rule the rocks. The boutiques, toy stores, and other shops of the central Village Fair mall, converted from an old garage, climb interior stairs to pretty little patios and overlooks.

Houseboats at Sausalito.

◆ BAY MODEL

Built by the Army Corps of Engineers to study the effects of engineering projects in the bay and local river systems, the Bay Model is a gigantic working map of the Bay Area. You won't see all the familiar landmarks, but the shape and dynamics of the bay and its tributaries are produced accurately, right down to the tides, currents, salinity, and sedimentation. (The only compromise in accuracy is that the Delta and the Sacramento and San Joaquin Rivers had to be bent above the Carquinez Straits to fit into the building.) Nonetheless, it is a fascinating piece of engineering, and its scale and complexity are downright amazing. As the rivers and streams flow at one-tenth their actual velocity, the tide rolls through an entire cycle in 15 minutes, a month of tides in 7.2 hours. You can watch the salt collecting on the mud flats of the South Bay, or inspect the prevailing flow of water through the bay's shipping channels and submarine canyons. A look at the sunken islands of the delta will show in an instant the disastrous effects of a broken dike. The Army Corps of Engineers has done a magnificent job of presenting the model to the public, with interpretive displays, elevated walkways, and recorded explanations. *2100 Bridgeway, Sausalito; 415-332-3870.*

◆ ANGEL ISLAND STATE PARK

The largest island in San Francisco Bay, this bosky state park is reached by private boat or ferry from San Francisco, Oakland (weekends only), or Tiburon in Marin County. Port of entry is **Ayala Cove**, a pretty, crescent-shaped bay on the protected northwest side of the island. Hikers and bicyclists circumnavigating the island on its fire roads and trails pass alternately through forests and grasslands, enjoying spectacular views of the city and the bay. Several historic sites around the island invite exploration. The old immigration station on the north side, sometimes called **Ellis Island of the West**, was the main entry for immigrants from Asia and South America during the early part of the 20th century. On the east side of the island stands a ghostly military hospital above a collection of dilapidated buildings that served as an army post and military quarantine station through the 1940s. The summit of 781-foot-high Mount Livermore, the island's high point, serves up one of the most striking panoramas in the Bay Area. To really soak in the spirit of Angel Island, reserve one of the nine "environmental" camp sites that are sprinkled about the island. Sites 3, 4, and 5 offer amazing views of the city. *For general park information, call 415-435-1915; or 800-444-7275 for camping reservations.*

■ MARIN HEADLANDS

The dramatic cliffs of Marin County, rising above the northern shore of the Golden Gate, are known as the **Marin Headlands**. The military early on commandeered these strategic heights, closing them to the public, and thus preserving them from development. When modern technology rendered their gun batteries obsolete, the army retreated gracefully, leaving the land most fortunately in the hands of the Golden Gate National Recreation Area. Hikers here can hook into an extensive trail system that leads from Fisherman's Wharf clear to Point Reyes.

Stark, windy, and rugged, the Marin Headlands offer ravishing views, solitude, seasonal wildflowers, and a handful of interesting military sites to explore. There are hike-in campgrounds, wildlife tours, and guided walks through the bunkers and garrisons. For information about park sites and events, inquire at the visitor center in Fort Cronkhite's converted chapel on Field Road, or at park headquarters in Fort Mason, San Francisco. *For detailed information, call 415-331-1540.*

◆ MARIN HEADLANDS HIGHLIGHTS

Bay Area Discovery Museum

Some of Fort Baker's old, white-frame officers' houses have been converted to house this educational children's museum featuring hands-on exhibits that include Bay Area history and ecology. Kids can climb over a make-shift fishing boat, crawl through an "undersea tunnel," investigate glassed-in, working models of plumbing fixtures, and sketch on a drafting table. There's also a science store and cafeteria. *415-487-4398.*

Conzelman Road and Hawk Hill

The only way into the western headlands is by serpentine, cliff-hugging Conzelman Road, reached by following the signs from the Alexander Avenue exit off Highway 101. The road provides, quite simply, the most sublime cityscape this side of Jupiter:

the great Golden Gate Bridge looming in the foreground, San Francisco's skyline framed poetically between the huge red towers. There are pullouts all along the road for gawking. Stop and walk up **Hawk Hill**, where, during migration in September and October, thousands of birds of prey can be seen soaring and wheeling on the wind.

Rodeo Beach

Rodeo Beach is washed by seas too rough for all but expert swimmers. Trails head north and south from here, and around Rodeo Lagoon, a favorite of bird-watchers. Guano-covered Bird Island glowers offshore like a great white whale. On the rise above the lagoon, the California Marine Mammal Center operates a hospital for sick and orphaned seals and sea lions.

Point Bonita Lighthouse

The most exhilarating short walk in the Marin Headlands leads to Point Bonita Lighthouse, the last lighthouse in California that was tended by a human keeper. This half-mile trail starts at the marked parking area on Field Road, a short drive from the visitor center. Descending a good path on the rocky cape, stupendous views of the sea and the Gate fall away on either side. Passing through a tunnel chiseled by hand in 1877, you emerge on the ocean side of the rocks, then cross to Point Bonita on a shaky wooden suspension bridge built over crashing waves in 1954, after waves washed away the original path. (A Coast Guard officer reported 130-foot waves breaking over the stubby lighthouse in 1967.) The present lighthouse was built in 1877 on a rocky ledge above rough seas at the mouth of the Golden Gate. It is now controlled automatically and sports a 300 ton lens—built in France by Frensel in 1855—and an automatic foghorn The powerful light is visible from 18.5 miles out to sea. When it was first built, the lighthouse keeper had to fire a cannon every 30 minutes in foggy weather.

The Marin County coastline is often shrouded in fog.

◆ MOUNT TAMALPAIS STATE PARK

Here lies San Francisco's Mount Olympus—a sylvan backdrop to countless cityscapes, an inspiration to writers and artists, an almost pagan symbol of nature worship for generations of city hikers. A road winds up to a point near the 2,571-foot summit of East Peak, with extraordinary views down western canyons to Point Reyes and the Pacific, and south to San Francisco and beyond. The best of the park are the meadows, mountain creeks, and redwood canyons reached only by trail. In the best old-world mountaineering traditions, **West Point Inn** offers tea (and lemonade) to hikers on its wooden porch. Floating far off to the southeast, the inconsequential towers of San Francisco fade before the more demanding flurry of a blue jay, begging for your sandwich. The park also offers camping and picnicking, and is popular with mountain-bike riders. *For park information, call 415-388-2070.*

◆ MUIR WOODS NATIONAL MONUMENT

Muir Woods is a mossy treasure, a grove of ancient redwoods untouched by lumberjacks. Being the closest grove to San Francisco, Muir Woods receives a huge

(above) Muir Woods contain the area's most impressive virgin redwood stands.

(opposite) In summer, fog rolls past the Marin Headlands and under the Golden Gate Bridge, creating surreal pictures such as the one shown here. (Kerrick James)

number of visitors throughout the year, though if you come early on a weekday, or on any rainy day, it is an enchanting place. In some ways prettier than the Santa Cruz mountain groves at Henry Cowell and Big Basin State Parks, Muir Woods lacks the spectacular specimens and grotesque shapes that titillate the minds of statisticians and exercise the trigger-fingers of amateur photographers. Redwoods can live beyond a thousand years, but few of the trees in Muir Woods are a day over 800. Likewise, coast redwoods are the tallest living things, but the loftiest tree in Muir Woods—a paltry 252 feet—is a good hundred feet shorter than the noblest specimens growing in Redwood National Park, up the California coast. Still, it's impressive to keep in mind that if this same 252-foot tree were growing on the surface of San Francisco Bay, it would poke about 32 feet higher than the roadway of the Golden Gate Bridge.

Muir Woods National Monument has a small visitors center, gift shop, and cafeteria. The short, gentle walks through the groves along the valley floor are easy for just about everyone. More strenuous hikes connect the park with Mount Tamalpais State Park and the GGNRA. *For park information, call 415-388-2595.*

■ POINT REYES NATIONAL SEASHORE

Point Reyes is an enchanting mystery, a world quite removed from the rest of the Bay Area. It moves to a different rhythm; the natural cycles of bird migrations, rising and falling tides, the crash of waves, the passing of storms, and quiet stretches of utter solitude. The human side also lives in conscious respect of nature—the ranchers tending dairy herds, the fishermen following the shoals, the tourists who migrate in summer and on weekends, and who disappear back down the coast when the big Pacific storms blow in. Point Reyes has an air of big things that happened long ago, mysterious things—of vanished tribes and Elizabethan privateers, sunken Spanish galleons, an English ghost-fort, Russian pelt-hunters, traces of Ming China washed up on the beach. It is the most thoughtful and thought-provoking of landscapes, hauntingly beautiful, often stark, humbling to city people used to bullying around seasons to fit their busy schedules.

Part of Point Reyes' feeling of separateness from the rest of the world is that it *is*, literally, from someplace else. The peninsula is separated from the "mainland" by the San Andreas Fault, which runs up the rift of Bolinas Lagoon, the Olema Valley, and

The moor-like landscape of Point Reyes.

Tomales Bay, making it the most clearly visible section of the fault in the Bay Area. The peninsula, on the western plate, is moving north at a good clip. Its origins have been traced to some 300 miles south of its present location. During the 1906 earthquake, the Point Reyes peninsula lurched north by some 16 feet in one movement, displacing roads and fences, and destroying buildings. The Earthquake Trail near the park visitor center at Bear Valley makes a short loop past one of these displaced fences, while interpretive displays point out other signs of the earthquake's impact.

◆ POINT REYES HIGHLIGHTS

Bear Valley Visitor Center
This barn-like building displays dioramas of Point Reyes animals, plants, and birds, and provides a detailed introduction to the area's ecology and natural history. This is the place for maps, books, postcards, and park info such as tide tables, which are extremely important if you intend to hike the beaches, because most of the beaches at Point Reyes are backed by cliffs and can be covered at high tide. *Bear Valley Rd.; 415-663-1092.*

Trails

Outside the visitor center, the half-mile **Earthquake Trail** straddles the San Andreas Fault, which is explained along the way. You can see the spot where the peninsula moved 16 feet north in the 1906 quake.

Another short path leads from the visitor center to the bark-slab houses, sweatlodge, and other structures of **Kule Loklo**, a replica of a native Miwok village.

More than 70 miles of other trails lead through pristine forest and marsh land, to less-frequented beaches and remote campgrounds. The park contains designated wilderness areas covering 32,000 acres. Rangers at the visitor center can assist in route planning, but be advised that reservations are needed well in advance for the seashores' campgrounds. (They can be made by calling: *415-663-1092.*)

Limantour Beach

A good cross section of the park is visible along Limantour Road, which runs from Bear Valley Road through Douglas fir forests and rolling coastal meadow to Limantour Beach. Bracing winds consistently buffet the walk to the end of sandy Limantour Spit, where you'll have Limantour Estero on one side of you and Drake's Bay on the other.

Point Reyes Beach

Sir Francis Drake Boulevard leads from the bosky inland reaches of the park to the windswept, almost moor-like swath of coastal grasslands on the west side of the peninsula. The bulwark of the peninsula is 13-mile-long Point Reyes Beach, divided (by virtue of parking lots) into North Beach and South Beach. The wild breakers that roll in across the wide Pacific crash with such force that swimming is lethal, but the sandy beach is long, with fine white sand, and you can always find solitude there.

Drake's Beach

A well-marked spur road from Drakes Boulevard, near the tip of the peninsula, leads to the pleasant sands of **Drake's Beach** and the white cliffs fronting Drake's Bay. According to historians, the English privateer Sir Francis Drake probably anchored there for repairs in the 16th century, stayed a month and claimed the land for England. He christened it Nova Albion. (Albion was a poetical name for England derived from the Latin word for "white," probably in reference to the white cliffs of Dover—which the Point Reyes coast resembles.)

Point Reyes Lighthouse

Sir Francis Drake Boulevard ends at the mountainous headland of Point Reyes itself. Many ships have run aground here. Point Reyes lighthouse, some 20 miles from the Bear Valley Visitor Center, was built in 1870 to warn ships off this most treacherous headland on the Pacific coast. The lighthouse sits 160 feet above the sea, and some 300 steps down an exposed spine of rock from the parking area. Waves crash and sea lions roar on the rocks below. From mid-December through March, you can watch migrating whales swim past Point Reyes. On clear days, you can see San Francisco, but when the fogs come in, they are thick enough to chew. *Lighthouse Visitor Center; 415-669-1534.*

WINE COUNTRY

The Sonoma and Napa Valleys make up the epicenter of the world-famous California Wine Country. The region is situated roughly between 40 and 90 miles to the northeast of San Francisco, making it an easy and well worthwhile excursion.

■ SONOMA VALLEY

The Sonoma Valley has the distinction of being the cradle of the California fine wine industry. Though the mission fathers were first to plant the grape, the Buena Vista Winery was founded in 1857 by a Hungarian count, Agoston Haraszthy. Haraszthy is often credited with being the first to plant imported European vine stock in the region, although it's now known that George Belden Crane, Sam Brannan, and other Napa vintners actually preceded Haraszthy in their European vinifera plantings. Nonetheless, Haraszthy gave the California Wine Country its first commercial push. We must also thank the count for two important breakthroughs. First, rather than follow the mission tradition in planting vines close to irrigation sources, Haraszthy planted his vines

Agoston Haraszthy, one of the first vintners to plant European grape varietals in California. (Courtesy Buena Vista Carneros Estate)

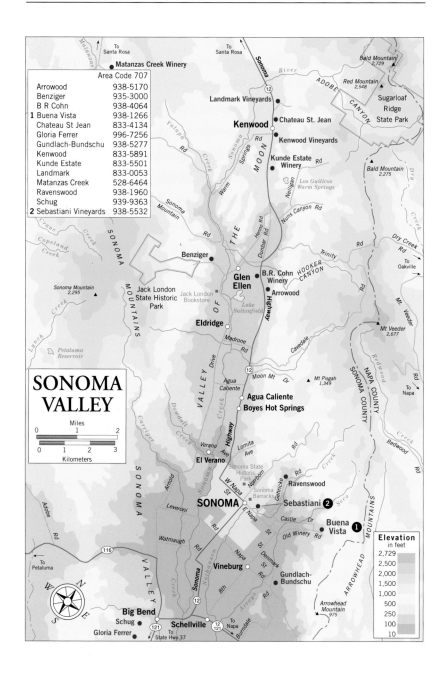

To
Santa Rosa

To
Santa Rosa

Matanzas Creek Winery

Bald Mountain
2,729

Red Mountain
2,548

Sugarloaf
Ridge
State Park

Area Code 707

Arrowood	938-5170
Benziger	935-3000
B R Cohn	938-4064
1 Buena Vista	938-1266
Chateau St Jean	833-4134
Gloria Ferrer	996-7256
Gundlach-Bundschu	938-5277
Kenwood	833-5891
Kunde Estate	833-5501
Landmark	833-0053
Matanzas Creek	528-6464
Ravenswood	938-1960
Schug	939-9363
2 Sebastiani Vineyards	938-5532

Landmark Vineyards

Chateau St. Jean

Kenwood

Kenwood Vineyards

Kunde Estate
Winery

Bald Mountain
2,275

Los Guilicos
Warm Springs

Nuns Canyon Rd

Dry Creek
Rd

To
Oakville

Benziger

B.R. Cohn
Winery

**Glen
Ellen**

Arrowood

Sonoma Mountain
2,295

Jack London
State Historic
Park

Jack London
Bookstore

Lake
Suttonfield

Mt Veeder
2,677

To
Napa

Eldridge

Madrone Rd

Cavedale

Petaluma
Reservoir

Moon Mt Dr

Mt Pisgah
1,349

Agua
Caliente

SONOMA
VALLEY

Miles
0   1   2

0   1   2   3
Kilometers

Agua Caliente

Boyes Hot Springs

El Verano

Verano Ave

Lomita
Ave

Sonoma State
Historic
Park

Northom

Ravenswood

SONOMA

Sonoma
Barracks

Gentricke Rd

Sebastiani 2

Castle Dr

**Buena
Vista 1**

Old Winery Rd

Watmaugh

Napa St

Denmark St

Vineburg

Gundlach-
Bundschu

To
Petaluma

8th

Arrowhead
Mountain
975

Elevation	
in feet	
2,729	
2,500	
2,000	
1,500	
1,000	
500	
250	
100	
10	

Big Bend

Schug

Schellville

To
Napa

Gloria Ferrer

To
State Hwy 37

on dry hillsides, proving that Sonoma's climate was moist enough to sustain viticulture without irrigation. He also was the first to use redwood barrels rather than oak ones to age his wines, a far less expensive storage method which vintners would use for the next 100 years.

Sonoma County's two main vineyard regions are the Sonoma Valley and the Russian River Valley, including the smaller independent appellations of the Alexander and Dry Creek Valleys near Healdsburg. Russian River wineries, of which more than 50 welcome tours, are listed in a free brochure called "The Russian River Wine Road" from the Healdsburg Chamber of Commerce. (*217 Healdsburg Avenue; 707-433-6935*). Many of the wineries have picnic grounds, encouraging you to buy a bottle and enjoy the lovely setting. (If you do picnic on the grounds, buy at least one of the winery's bottles: it's Wine Country etiquette.)

◆ Town of Sonoma

Sonoma was founded in 1823, over the hills east of Santa Rosa. General Mariano Vallejo, the richest and most powerful man in Mexican California, moved here to manage his huge rancho, and to lead occasional raids against hostile Indian tribes to the north. In Sonoma Plaza, Robert Semple and his American compatriots raised the Bear Flag and declared California a republic, after first seizing General Vallejo at his house across the street (where he calmly treated them to a glass of brandy). A heroic statue stands in the square, but historians disagree on the heroism of the rebels. Imprisoning the statesmanlike Vallejo as a prisoner of war was theatrical, but unjust. When Vallejo was set free, he found that his ranch had been ransacked by the state's "founding fathers," his livestock and tools carried off. Vallejo accepted the Yankee conquest philosophically, and even joined in the new government as one of California's first state senators.

The rich collection of vintage shops, cafes, hotels, and historic buildings surrounding the plaza make for a delightful stroll through history. **Mission San Francisco Solano de Sonoma**, last to be founded in California, occupies the corner northeast of the plaza. Especially impressive is the enormous cactus growing in the back. Across Spain Street, Vallejo built a hotel called The Blue Wing. Among his guests were the likes of Kit Carson, Ulysses S. Grant, William Tecumseh Sherman, and, by tradition, the bandits Joaquin Murietta and Three-Fingered Jack.

The barracks, the servants' wing of Vallejo's home, and the 1850-era Toscano Hotel, originally known as The Eureka, are on the north side of the plaza. The

two-story barracks is now a museum of early California history, with emphasis on the Bear Flag Revolt. Like the mission, all are administered as part of the **Sonoma State Historic Park**, covered by a single entrance fee also good for visiting General Vallejo's nearby home, Lachryma Montis, an elaborate gingerbread structure, furnished as it was when the general and his family (there were 16 kids) knew it. *Sonoma State Historic Park; 707-938-9559.*

◆ JACK LONDON HISTORIC STATE PARK

The town of Glen Ellen lies a few miles north of Sonoma. This section of the Sonoma Valley is also called Valley of the Moon, a name made famous by Jack London, who spent the last years of his life at the Beauty Ranch, in the hills above town. The ranch is preserved as Jack London State Historic Park. In his day, London sold more books than any other writer in the world, and he remains today probably the best-known American writer outside the country. He used his income to buy the Beauty Ranch, which he developed without heed to cost. His last big project was Wolf House, an immense mansion, which mysteriously burned on the eve of completion. You can see the magnificent ruins by taking a half-mile walk from the parking lot. London's ashes, placed in an urn and covered with a boulder, can be visited nearby.

The ranch house where London lived and died (of an apparently suicidal drug overdose in 1916) is also on the property, surrounded by barns and a distillery. Most interesting of all, however, is the House of Happy Walls, built by London's widow after the writer's death, and now a museum of London artifacts, photos, and books. *2400 London Ranch Road, Glen Ellen; 707-938-5216.*

■ NAPA VALLEY

The Napa Valley, America's most famous wine-producing region, draws so many tourists these days that local wine makers have taken measures to thwart them. Two and a half million visitors annually come to Napa not only to tour wineries, but to dine in excellent restaurants, shop in smart boutiques, and tootle through or over the valley by wine train, balloon, or glider. In response, Napa vintners have voted for zoning laws to restrict tourist-oriented "boutique wineries." Some wineries have even adopted the drastic measure of charging for tours and glasses of wine.

The glamour of the Napa grape is rooted firmly in the rare beauty of the Napa

Mustard blooms between dormant vines in Napa Valley.

Valley, especially the section north from Yountville. Here the valley closes in between high, forested ridges, sometimes sharpening to cliffs. The rolling vineyards are dotted with oak trees and old stone buildings, some the scale and shape of French chateaux, others of Rhineland estates. The wine mystique thrives in the old, musty cellars and wine caves in the hills, and the music and food that accompany it. And no doubt, too, it is bolstered by the romantic aura of exclusive quality that surrounds the mysterious art of making, and drinking, wine. Certainly, nobody makes much of a fuss over San Joaquin Valley vintages, which by far outweigh the Napa Valley's in volume. The beauty, the quality, the mystique of a Fresno wine grape just can't compete with one from Napa.

Visitors can savor the Napa Valley better if they go on a weekday to beat traffic jams and extra charges. They will enjoy tours and tastings more, too, if they read up on wineries and viticulture before they go. Many famous wineries are found on both Highway 29, on the west side of the valley, and the Silverado Trail, on the east side. The latter is the more bucolic, and usually less crowded, route.

◆ CALISTOGA

Calistoga is the town at the northern end of the Napa Valley, 27 miles from Napa. Sam Brannan founded it as a hot-spring resort, with hopes that it would become the California version of Saratoga; hence the name. The venture did not work out for Brannan, and indeed, Californians' enthusiasm for Calistoga has bounced up and down over the decades. Today, however, Calistoga is back in favor. The surging interest in health-oriented resorts, as well as the concomitant success of Napa wineries, has made Calistoga and its spas very fashionable indeed.

Calistoga retains its comfortable, Old West feel in the false-front buildings and bracing air of the surrounding mountains. Most businesses, spas, and restaurants are concentrated around Lincoln Avenue.

Calistoga's **hot baths** are today enjoying the business that Brannan hoped to reap. The little industry offers a whole gamut of treatments—saunas, mud baths, facials, herbal wraps, hot-spring soaks, Swedish and shiatsu massage, steam baths, mineral jacuzzi, body wraps, foot reflexology—with, and even more blissfully without, the 20th-century version of a snake-oil seller's claims. The volcanic mud feels great, but it sure looks ugly. *Call the Calistoga Chamber of Commerce for a detailed listing of spa facilities; 707-942-6333.*

	Area Code 707
1 Bale Grist Mill	942-4575
Beaulieu	963-2411
2 Beringer Brothers Winery	963-7115
Burgess Cellars	963-4766
Cakebread Cellers	963-5221
Carneros Alembics	253-9095
Carneros Creek	253-9463
Caymus	967-4204
Charles Krug	963-2761
Chateau Woltner	963-1744
Chimney Rock	257-2641
Clos du Val	259-2200
3 Clos Pegase	942-4981
4 Codorniu Napa	224-1668
5 Culinary Institute of America	967-1100
Cuvaison	942-6266
6 Domaine Chandon	944-7108
Freemark Abbey	963-9694
Frog's Leap	963-4704
Greystone	967-1100
Grgich Hills	963-2748
Heitz Wine Cellers	963-3542
7 The Hess Collection Winery	255-1144
Joseph Phelps	963-2745
Louis M Martini	963-2736
Mayacamas	224-4030
Mumm Napa Valley	942-3300
8 Niebaum-Coppola Winery	963-9099
Opus One	944-9442
Raymond	963-3141
9 Robert Mondavi	963-9611
Robert Sinskey	944-9090
Round Hill	963-5251
Rutherford Hill	963-1871
Saint Clement	963-7221
10 Saint Supery Winery	963-4507
Saintsbury	252-0592
11 Schramsberg Vineyards	942-4558
Silver Oak	944-8808
12 Silverado Museum & Library	963-3757
Stag's Leap Wine Cellars	944-2020
Stags' Leap Winery	944-1303
13 Sterling Vineyards	942-3344
Stonegate	942-6500
Stony Hill	963-2636
Trefethen	255-7700
Truchard	253-7153

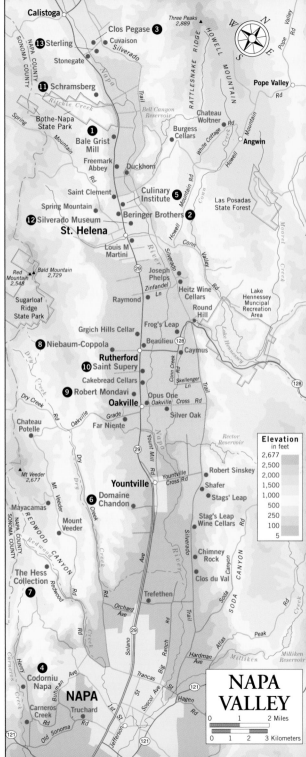

NAPA VALLEY

History buffs will enjoy browsing through the **Sharpsteen Museum** in the center of town. Aside from a lively diorama of the Calistoga of Brannan's dreams, you can see odds and ends of Brannan memorabilia, pioneer guns, and assorted displays on animation. The latter was the special interest of museum founder Ben Sharpsteen, an Oscar-winning animator with Walt Disney. *Pinocchio, Fantasia,* and *Dumbo* are among his movie credits. *1311 Washington Street; 707-842-5911.*

◆ WINERIES AND OTHER HIGHLIGHTS IN SONOMA & NAPA VALLEYS

Choosing which of the countless wineries to visit in the Napa and Sonoma Valleys is a task beyond the scope of this guidebook. Below are some selected wineries, along with other recommended sites, to visit in Wine Country. Detailed discussions of the towns and wineries can be found in Compass American Guides' *Wine Country: California's Napa & Sonoma Valleys* and the *Wine Spectator's Wine Country Guide to California.*

Bale Grist Mill

Just south of town on Highway 29 stands a reminder that Napa's wealth was once based on wheat, not grapes. Built in 1846, the old Bale Grist Mill ground the grain of Napa Valley farmers with a 36-foot-high waterwheel and two one-ton mill stones. Built and run by Edwin Bale, General Vallejo's English brother-in-law, the mill has been lovingly restored to working condition by the state of California. *3369 Highway 29, just north of St. Helena, Napa Valley; 707-224-1668.*

Beringer Brothers Winery

On the north side of charming St. Helena, this landmark winery is famous for its half-timbered mansion and its deep caves, dug in the 1870s by Chinese laborers. *2000 Highway 29, St. Helena, Napa Valley; 707-963-7115.*

Buena Vista Carneros Estate

The original Wine Country winery, founded in 1857 by Count Agoston Haraszathy, is still in full operation. Visitors can picnic on the tree-shaded grounds, and guide themselves through the foliage-covered stone buildings that front rough-hewn, cask-filled caves. *18000 Old Winery Rd., Sonoma; 707-938-1266.*

Clos Pegase

While powerfully evocative of Classical architecture, the earth-tone walls and angular courts and entryways of this new winery are at the same time unabashedly modern. Designed by Michael Graves in 1987, the winery buildings wed the fine and vintner's arts, with artists' works arranged extravagantly about the grounds, which themselves are a work of art accentuated with majestic, native oaks. What a great place to linger while you sample the elixir. *1060 Dunaweal Lane, between St. Helena and Calistoga, Napa Valley; 707-942-4981.*

Codorniu Napa

An unusual complex built on a hilltop behind an earthen berm designed to keep temperatures cool inside, this winery lies at the heart of the Carneros Region, the vineyard district closest to San Francisco Bay. *1345 Henry Rd., Carneros Valley, between Napa and Sonoma; 707-224-1668.*

Culinary Institute of America
at Greystone

This magnificent stone chateau once housed the Christian Brothers, and today

offers instructions in the culinary arts. Its graduates have won great honors and work their magic in renown kitchens around the globe. Casual cooking seminars are open to those with less lofty culinary ambitions, and the store is stuffed with excellent cookbooks and a huge selection of fine cooking gear. The 1,800 corkscrews collected by Brother Timothy of the Christian Brothers includes many a specimen as delightful and quirky as the man who collected them. *2555 Highway 29, St. Helena; 707-967-1100.*

·Domaine Chandon

Banish the workaday world with a glass of bubbly amid the oak-studded gardens of this French vintner of sparkling wines. And

Greystone being built in 1889. The massive structure became Christian Brothers Winery in 1950 and now accommodates the Culinary Institute of America's West Coast school.

if you really want to celebrate, reserve a table at the elegant restaurant. *1 California Dr., Yountville, Napa Valley; 707-944-8844.*

The Hess Collection Winery

Tucked away out of the main Napa Valley, this beautifully renovated 1903 stone winery building now serves as an art gallery as well as a winery. Self-guided tours start with a video describing the four seasons of the vintner in Napa Valley. One of the most impressive private collections in the country, the gallery displays works by 20th-century American and European artists, including Robert Motherwell and Francis Bacon. The wines are well-crafted too. *4411 Redwood Rd., Napa Valley; 707-255-1144.*

Niebaum-Coppola Winery

In the best of all possible worlds, we'd all be filmmakers, winemakers, or travel-guide writers. Francis Ford Coppola's got two out of three. Having been raised with wine, Coppola bought into the winery business in 1979, obtaining a historic property founded as Inglenook Wines in 1879 by a Finnish sea captain, Gustave Niebaum. Greeting visitors at the entrance is the Captain's Room, a tasting parlor furnished in the style of an elegant ship-board cabin. The grand staircase beckons you upstairs for a peak at some props from Coppola's movies, including some *Godfather* memorabilia. Though by no means overdone, and by every means a serious winery, Niebaum-Coppola is likelier than any other Napa

(above) Niebaum-Coppola Estate near Yountville in Napa Valley. (opposite) Lunch on the terrace at Auberge du Soleil affords diners a view of the Napa Valley. (both photos, Kerrick James)

winery to appeal to the whole family. *1991 Highway 29, Rutherford, Napa Valley; 707-944-9442.*

Robert Mondavi Winery

Mondavi is an old Napa name, but his venerable winery, the first to build in Napa after prohibition ended, continues to evolve with the times. In addition to its new tasting and visitors facilities, the winery sponsors a summer music festival. *7801 Highway 29, Oakville, Napa Valley; 707-226-1395.*

St. Supery

This modern winery should figure early on any novice wine-taster's list, thanks to its excellent **Wine Discovery Center**. In addition to tackling such arcane subjects as the effect of soil types and micro-climate on varietal characteristics, it also takes a stab at the mystery of bouquet by providing sample smells with descriptive labels—a godsend for the olfactory-challenged among us who can't tell an "amusing hint of raspberry" from a "full-bodied, fruity aroma." *8440 Highway 29, Rutherford, Napa Valley; 707-963-4507.*

Schramsberg Vineyards

In part because it is not open without appointment, this vintage 1862 winery retains the isolated feel that it had when Robert Louis Stevenson visited. As described in *The Silverado Squatters*, the amiable Scot met the original Mr. Schram, tasted every variety on the premises, and observed that the setting "made a pleasant music for the mind." In more specific terms, he praised the "stuffed birds in the veranda, cellars far

dug into the hillside, and resting on pillars like a bandit's cave: all trimness, varnish, flowers and sunshine, among the tangled wildwood." *1400 Schramsberg Lane, near Calistoga; 707-942-4558.*

Sebastiani Vineyards

Rows of enormous redwood tanks and oak barrels march with pungent gusto through the aging cellars, close to downtown Sonoma. Comprehensive tours guide visitors through the vast plant, which is noted for its decorative wood-carving. *Fourth St. East, Sonoma; 707-938-5532.*

Silverado Museum

Commemorating Robert Louis Stevenson, who honeymooned in the Napa Valley in 1880, this small museum next to the library houses some 8,000 pieces of memorabilia, including several first editions of his works. It's such a good collection that Scottish documentary film makers have shot footage here on more than one occasion. *Library Lane, St. Helena; 707-963-3757.*

Sterling Vineyards

Rising like a great, white, Greek monastery on a high knoll overlooking the vineyards, Sterling is accessible to the public only by cable car. Self-guided tours take visitors step-by-step on elevated platforms through the wine-making process, ending in an airy tasting room—a fascinating and elegant experience. (There's an extra fee for the cable car.) *1111 Dunaweal Lane, between St. Helena and Calistoga; 707-942-3300.*

EAST BAY

Alameda and Contra Costa Counties are together known as the East Bay, a region that embraces the bay-side cities of Oakland and Berkeley, as well as the ridges and valleys marching east from the bay to the Central Valley. BART (Bay Area Rapid Transit) provides good connections between San Francisco and the densely populated corridors of the East Bay, while ferries link the Embarcadero with Oakland's Jack London Square.

■ OAKLAND

The eastern end of the Bay Bridge drops down to Oakland, passing docks and train yards, and merges into one of the biggest, busiest freeway interchanges in the country. For old-time San Franciscans, Oakland was the perfect butt of many a joke. Herb Caen once pointed out that when you cross the Bay Bridge into San Francisco, you have to pay a toll; but to go to Oakland doesn't cost a plugged nickel. While Oakland has many problems—drug problems, high crime rates, ghettos, and poverty—it is also true that the city has much to offer, and visitors can easily make a full day of exploring its sites.

◆ JACK LONDON SQUARE

The San Francisco ferry and Amtrak trains meet at Jack London Square, named for Oakland's most famous writer, who spent much of his stalwart youth on these docks. The splendid plaza, with stores, hotels, harborside restaurants, and late-closing bookstores, is a delightful place to spend an evening. The passing ships on the estuary and the yachts tied up at the waterfront make a pretty enough picture from window-side seats at the seafood restaurants. Looking up the channel, past Oakland's hard-working container harbor, you can glimpse the distant towers of San Francisco. The Port of Oakland offers personal tours of President Roosevelt's (FDR's) yacht, the *Potomac,* docked at the western end of the public waterfront.

Although born in San Francisco, Jack London was raised in Oakland, where he was coached in his reading at the Oakland Free Library by the librarian, Ina Coolbrith. Several of the houses where London lived still stand in Oakland (which you can find with the help of Don Herron's aforementioned guide), but it is the waterfront that he is most powerfully associated with. It was along here that he docked his boat, the *Razzle Dazzle,* which carried him on night raids of rivals' oyster beds. So adept was he at this dangerous game that he earned the title "Prince of the Oyster Pirates." It was here, also, that he drank in the bars and met many of the characters who would later appear in his novels.

One authentic London hangout still stands by the wharf, a saloon called **Heinold's First and Last Chance** (so called because the ferry to the "dry" city of Alameda docked nearby). London supposedly bought the *Razzle Dazzle* here when he was 16 years old. Still open for business, Heinold's is a curious shack half sunken below present street level. Nearby stands part of the cabin where London lived during the Klondike Gold Rush of 1897–98. Rediscovered in Yukon Territory in 1960, it was spirited back to its present site overlooking the Oakland Estuary.

◆ OAKLAND MUSEUM OF CALIFORNIA

The Oakland Museum of California, devoted to the state's art and history, both natural and human, is one of the West's most exciting museums, rising in three meandering, landscaped terraces around a central garden court, handsome and intriguing. There's a decent cafe on the third floor, and the museum store, a good place for books on California, is on Level One. *1000 Oak St.; 510-238-2200.*

Hall of California Ecology

From this exhibit you'll get a sense of the state's complex geography and biology by taking an imaginary cross-country walk from the Pacific eastwards across the state, visiting complex dioramas showing the life and terrain of the Coast Ranges, Central Valley, the Sierra Nevada and, finally, the high deserts of the Great Basin. Packed with plants and animal, the displays illustrate the interdependency of species within an ecosystem.

Cowell Hall of California History

The museums second level maintains one of the largest and most eclectic collections of Californiana. Not only do you get a wonderful sense of the California myth—the images of Hollywood, Hell's Angels, oranges, and Mel's Drive-in—but you also glean a sense of how *real* people *really* lived, from prehistoric times to the present. It does this through an ingenious grouping of everyday objects, evoking a distinctive sense of our ancestors' times, and of our own.

Art Gallery

Level three focuses on painters and photographers with California connections, including Albert Bierstadt, Eadweard Muybridge, Dorothea Lange, and Imogen Cunningham. The museum is renowned for its early California paintings, especially its romantic oils of Yosemite and the Sierra, and the rivetingly detailed paintings of old San Francisco.

♦ PARAMOUNT THEATER

Restored to its original glory in 1973, this 1931 movie palace ranks as one of the supreme showcases of Art Deco in the entire country. It is the masterpiece work of architect Timothy Plueger, whose many other outstanding jobs include the Bay Bridge suspension towers and the nearby former I. Magnin building. The stunning lobby, where a glowing, amber Fountain of Light soars to the ceiling, is home to 16 life-size, metallic painted statues of Egyptian maidens, gracefully bending in a stylized contredanse from opposite walls. Although you can visit the theater on a twice-monthly tour, try to go for a live performance by some of the top-name acts being booked here, or for the occasional classic film screening. It is well worth it to behold the thundering Wurlitzer organ rising on a hydraulic lift from beneath the stage in full performance. *2025 Broadway, Oakland; 510-465-6400.*

♦ USS HORNET

Decommisioned in 1970 and made a National Historic Landmark in 1994, this famous aircraft carrier—a heroic veteran of World War II—was launched in 1943 and exacted a terrible toll in 18 months of fighting on the front, without once tying up at dockside. During that short period, it joined the battles of Iwo Jima, the invasion of Okinawa, and the island-hopping campaigns in between, destroying 1,420 aircraft, 42 cargo ships, 10 destroyers, one aircraft carrier, one cruiser, and the 72,000-ton battleship Yamato, largest of its day. It managed to rack up these numbers while deflecting 59 direct attacks without once being hit by a single bomb, torpedo, or Kamikaze pilot. Only when its flight deck was damaged by a 60-foot wave during a typhoon in June 1945 was it forced to retreat to the West Coast for repairs. The *Hornet* was also the retrieval ship that picked up the Apollo 11 astronauts returning from their first manned landing on the Moon in May 1969.

Your self-guided tour begins in the cavernous Hanger Deck, where you can experience the sensation of launching and landing a fighter plane on a carrier deck in the flight simulator, provided you can weather a cocktail-shaker ride while watching a dizzying film of cockpit aeronautics. A climb up to the vast flight deck reminds you of just how big this ship really is. (Its 894 feet stretch 11 feet longer than the ill-fated *Titanic.*) The tour highlight takes you up into the island—the control tower—where you can inspect the Navigation Bridge and the Flag Bridge. From a third bridge overlooking the flight deck runways, the "Air Boss" controlled the launching and landing of the fighter planes, two examples of which are on display below on the hanger deck. *Pier 3, Alameda Point; 510-521-8448.*

EXCURSIONS

■ BERKELEY

Berkeley—you either love it or hate it. There is no middle ground, save perhaps a love-hate relationship.

Intellectually, Berkeley is the most exciting city in the West, jammed with scholars from around the world, new ideas and discoveries, Nobel laureates, books, classic cinemas, and seekers of revolution, social freedom, or just a soapbox. There's also a wealthy, liberal Berkeley, crusaders in quest of a gastronomic Holy Grail, a new breed of Medici whose generous patronage has fueled a renaissance of bakers, paper-makers, organic farmers, espresso-pourers, micro-brewers, and other inspired artisans.

But ask anyone from outside the Bay Area what Berkeley is famous for, and they will say crackpots, revolutions, and protests. That's hardly a fair assessment, especially nowadays, when Berkeley's student population is going through a decidedly conservative stage. But the colorful history of Berkeley in the 1960s and '70s, when it was a socialistic town with its own foreign policy and a spectacular lunatic fringe, still lives on in the minds of Middle America—and in more than a few yet-lively characters and corners of the city.

◆ UNIVERSITY OF CALIFORNIA
AT BERKELEY

When the University of California at Berkeley was founded in 1868, it was called the Athens of the Pacific. The campus grew to be one of the largest and most beautiful anywhere, with a faculty and alumni who have, quite literally, changed the way the world thinks. To list all its contributions to science and the humanities is a task too daunting for these pages, but probably the two most momentous events in the popular imagination were the development of nuclear science, and the protest movements of the 1960s.

The Berkeley campus was planned along twin branches of Strawberry Creek by Frederick Law Olmsted. Although the hallmark Beaux-Arts buildings of John Galen Howard set the tone, a montage of architectural styles graces the campus, from log cabin to high-tech. Glens and garden-like settings abound between the buildings. The eucalyptus trees to the right of the West Entrance at the end of University Avenue are reputed to be the tallest in the world. The forks of Strawberry Creek meet in the grove before being swallowed up under the pavements of downtown Berkeley.

EXCURSIONS

Sather Gate (top) and an Egyptian motif from Berkeley's Valley Life Sciences Building. (following pages) The peerless view toward San Francisco from the Lawrence Hall of Science.

◆ U.C. BERKELEY HIGHLIGHTS

Valley Life Sciences Building

The gargantuan Valley Life Sciences Building, a Hollywood Egyptian monstrosity distinguished by bas-reliefs of bison skulls, saber-toothed tiger heads, and Babylonian scientists, houses the university's enormous collections of plant and animal specimens. Foremost among them is the **Paleontology Museum**, which contains an enormous Tyrannosaurus skeleton, a Triceratops skull, a frozen mammoth carcass (not on public display), and other prehistoric specimens. *510-642-1821.*

Doe Library

Doe Library is the central depository of books on campus, supplemented by several department libraries and the large Moffitt Undergraduate Library. The collected papers of Mark Twain are kept in the adjacent **Bancroft Library**, which maintains the university's rare book collection and a small museum of Californiana, including Gold Rush paintings and the brass plate supposedly left by Sir Francis Drake during his 16th-century visit to California. The consensus nowadays is that it's a fake. *510-642-3781.*

Sather Tower

Better known as **the Campanile** because of its likeness to the *campanile* (bell-tower) of St. Mark's Cathedral in Venice, this is Berkeley's most famous landmark. Visitors can ride the elevator 200 feet to the top for a superlative view of downtown Oakland,

Between students and street life, Berkeley is never dull.

EXCURSIONS

San Francisco, Marin County, and straight out the Golden Gate to the Farallon Islands. Though the tower strikes the hours automatically, a bell-ringer ascends to play the carillon three times a weekday during semester. You can hear it all over campus, and though it is interesting to watch the carillonneur at work, you'll have to cover your ears or suffer being (one hopes only temporarily) deafened. There is a small charge to ascend. *510-642-5215.*

Phoebe Apperson Hearst Museum of Anthropology

The Phoebe Apperson Hearst Museum of Anthropology occupies a ground-floor corner of Kroeber Hall. Exhibits change regularly, but the permanent collection features thousands of artifacts of Native American, European, Asian, African, and Pacific cultures, including the weapons and tools made by Ishi, the last California Indian to come into contact with whites. Ishi walked into Oroville, California, from his mountain home in 1911. Anthropologist A. L. Kroeber invited Ishi to live at the Museum of Anthropology in San Francisco, now the site of the U.C. Medical Center, where Ishi taught him firsthand about the Yana language, handicrafts, music, and customs. *103 Kroeber Hall; 510-643-7648.*

The University Art Museum

This museum consists of open galleries that dovetail into a central hall. It features works from Asian and Western artists, a sculpture gallery, and cafeteria. Unfortunately, as of press time, the building has been closed indefinitely because of concerns over its ability to withstand a major earthquake. *(Call 510-642-0808 for the latest information.)* The **Pacific Film Archive**, which is usually housed in the building as well, screens celluloid obscurities and classics nightly, and provides screening rooms for film researchers. It has moved to a temporary facility across the street from the museum, on the main campus. *510-642-1124.*

Sproul Plaza

The liveliest part of the university is Sproul Plaza, just outside Sather Gate. Activists and leafleteers are thick on the ground here, a Berkeley tradition since 1964. That was the year that students challenged university regulations controlling public speech on campus. The Free Speech Movement gained momentum, culminating in a sit-in at Sproul Hall and the largest mass arrest in California's history. The movement spread throughout the country and to campuses around the world. Throughout the Vietnam War, Sproul Plaza was a forum for anti-war protests, some of which were met with tear gas and the National Guard.

◆ BEYOND THE CAMPUS

Telegraph Avenue

Sproul Plaza feeds into Telegraph Avenue on the south side of campus, where the streams of humanity flow with almost Gangetic fecundity. Here, undergraduates rub karmas with anarchists, musicians, crafts-sellers, prophets, lunatics, booksellers, revolutionaries, artists, missionaries, runaways, pushers, professors, and assorted riffraff. For big-city people accustomed to running a gauntlet of street people, Telegraph Avenue holds no terrors. For more timid souls, it is a chance to turn one's thoughts to the woof and warp of the human condition.

Bookstores

Nirvana of book lovers, the south side packs in more booksellers per acre than any other corner of the Bay Area—and probably the country, west of the Appalachians. Among the book emporia on Bancroft, **University Press Books** stocks publications of university presses from around the world, while the tiny **Map Center** sells travel and wilderness handbooks from the back of an alley. Three blocks up Telegraph, beyond Haste Street, Berkeley opens up its big guns. **Cody's** not only sells books; it fosters literacy with coffee and regular readings by local and visiting authors. **Moe's** is reputed to be the largest used book store in the Bay Area. **Shambhala** deals in metaphysics, Eastern religions, and Asian medicine. **Shakespeare**

and Company anchors down the corner across the street. And if book-hunting makes you a bit peckish, or if you want a cozy place to read your latest purchases, hunker down in one of the many **coffeehouses** that thrive in this neighborhood.

People's Park

Berkeley's most infamous symbol of radicalism is People's Park, which sits a half block up from Telegraph, on a rectangle of land bounded by Haste, Bowditch, and Dwight. Although owned by the university, the land was seized for a park in 1969 by a coalition of hippies, activists, and radical students. Attempts by the university to retake the land sparked rioting, in which one man was killed, another blinded, and scores injured by county sheriff buckshot. The property has sat in limbo ever since, and though it is a vibrant symbol to radicals and conservatives, in reality today it is almost anti-climactically park-like.

Botanical Gardens

The Botanical Gardens are reached by ascending Centennial Road, above the stadium. You can walk, but it's so long and steep that you're better off riding the shuttle from Mining Circle, in front of Hearst Mining Building. The gardens shelter more than 7,500 plant species from around the world, arranged in thematic gardens linked by paths. Californian, Asian, African, European, South American, and other sections are used for scientific research, but are also beautiful just for walking. A small botanical bookstore and information center stands at the gate. *510-642-3343.*

Lawrence Hall of Science

Further up Centennial Road, the Lawrence Hall of Science, like the Exploratorium in San Francisco, inspires people, especially kids, with the wonder and excitement of science. Using holograms, computers, lasers, telescopes, a planetarium, laboratories, and other resources, visitors can reach an understanding of such difficult concepts as evolution, prehistoric human migration, atomic theory, random selection, biological engineering, and the history of science, while having fun. Traveling exhibits and science fairs are set up regularly, including the ever-popular displays of enormous (though not quite life-size) mechanical dinosaurs, called Dynomation. A magnificent array of books, experiments, and scientific toys is sold in the lobby store. By night the view of the city lights from the parking lot is astounding. *510 642-5132.*

◄○►

SOUTH BAY

■ SILICON VALLEY

Once held firmly in the hands of San Franciscans, the economic reins of power that drove the city through its first brilliant century have slipped, and been taken up by other cities around the Bay. San Francisco yet remains the cultural hub of the Bay Area; but the South Bay, and specifically Silicon Valley, now controls the manufacturing base which, more than any other single element, drives the regional economy of the San Francisco Bay Area.

Less than 50 years ago, the South Bay was a fertile land of orchards. Now San Jose is the most populous city in the Bay Area—yes, larger than San Francisco. Santa Clara, Sunnyvale, Cupertino, and other towns have joined in a massive and complex grid of freeways, sprawling city blocks, parking lots, and malls that remind San Franciscans somewhat disconcertingly of Los Angeles. The metropolis is loosely linked under the name of Silicon Valley, in reference to the semiconductor and computer-chip industries that were largely pioneered here in the 1960s, when the likes of Steve Jobs and Steve Wozniak (the duo behind Apple Computers), Bill Hewlett, and Dave Packard worked out of garages, while John Warnock and Chuck Geschke created the first program for what was to become Adobe Systems in a bedroom office. Hewlett-Packard, Apple, Lockheed, and many other high-tech corporations are headquartered here, making Silicon Valley the epicenter of the digital revolution.

EXCURSIONS

◆ STANFORD UNIVERSITY

One of the prettiest and most intellectually stimulating cities of the Bay Area, Palo Alto is best known as the home of Stanford University. In marked contrast to the manic streets of Stanford's nemesis, Berkeley, the main commercial district of Palo Alto gathers handsomely along a clean, prosperous, charming, and eminently walkable thoroughfare, University Avenue. At its head, beyond the Caltrain railroad station, sprawls the Stanford campus—likewise a markedly different scene from Berkeley's, though each is consistently one of the highest-ranked universities in the nation.

The entrance to the campus always surprises first-time visitors with its natural vegetation of sparse native oak and wild weeds. Within these dry Elysian fields stands a lonely white **mausoleum**, guarded by sphinxes, encompassed by trees. Leland Stanford Jr., the namesake of the university, lies entombed therein with his parents. After you pass through this strangely deserted landscape, the Main Quadrangle and Hoover Tower jump up with sudden, refreshing vigor. You can obtain a map of the grounds from the information desks to the left of the entrance to the Main Quad (as it's called) and at Tressider Union.

The **Main Quad** is the focus of the university, surrounded by symmetrical cloisters and buildings made of peach-colored sandstone, heavy, almost monastic, in feel. In the seat of honor basks **Stanford Memorial Church**, a Romanesque affair with brilliant murals and mosaics.

The grounds are dominated by the 285-foot-square **Hoover Tower**, named after Herbert Hoover, Stanford's most famous graduate. Visitors ride to the top for an overview of the South Bay area. The **Stanford University Art Gallery**, exhibiting contemporary work, stands in front. Not far behind is White Plaza, home of the Stanford Bookstore, a huge and lively emporium.

Iris & B. Gerald Cantor Center for Visual Arts

The newest major art museum in the Bay Area is this swan-like reincarnation of a very old institution, the Leland Stanford Jr. Museum. First opened in 1894 as a memorial to its namesake, it reopened in 1999 as the Cantor Center, and is now regarded as one of the nation's premier teaching museums for art history. The collection spans six continents and thousands of years, but in breadth, setting, and display the collection appears fresh and dynamic, dazzling and magnificent. Some of the artifacts from the original Stanford family collection—including the actual Golden Spike—are still on display. *Lomita Drive at Museum Way; 650-723-4177.*

◆ FILOLI

The supposed resemblance of Crystal Springs reservoirs to Ireland's Lakes of Killarney inspired one William Bourn II, in 1915, to build a fabulous 654-acre estate on its southernmost shore. (The fact that he was president of the water company no doubt provided further inspiration.) Bourn, who made a big hunk of his fortune from his Empire gold mine in Grass Valley, California, named his mansion Filoli, an acronym of his motto: Fight, Love, Life. Television viewers familiar with the Carington estate on "Dynasty" already know some of its exquisite gardens and buildings.

Designed by Willis Polk, the mansion is a great pseudo-Georgian manor house set amidst ancient California oaks and unobstructed views of the distant hills. Tours visit the house, but dawdle longest in the gardens. These are a virtual Eden of blooms, trees, lawns, formal alleys, fountains, arbors, courts, and special gardens, such as the English knot garden, the Dutch garden, the Chartres garden (planted to resemble the cathedral window pattern), a sunken garden, and an extensive rose garden. Among the special trees are dawn redwoods, pomegranate, and avenues of Irish yew. Every season brings new blooms, but peak season for color is probably March.

Filoli feels more like a house than a museum. Busy gardeners in their slouch hats, helpers in the kitchen, the tea shop on the patio, and the gift shop in the carriage house fill the estate with life and purpose. *Canada Rd., Woodside; 650-304-2880.*

(above) Filoli's gardens are among the most ornate and sophisticated in the West.
(opposite) Stanford Memorial Church reflects both Californian and Byzantine influences.

◆ PENINSULA AND SILICON VALLEY HIGHLIGHTS

NASA **Ames Research Center**

The hottest tour in Mountain View is this NASA (National Aeronautics and Space Administration) facility at Moffett Field, where scientists test new aircraft design with a score of wind tunnels (including the world's largest) and computers. Visitors are welcome on free, escorted tours, but reservations are mandatory and should be made two to three weeks in advance. *Moffett Field, Mountain View; 650-604-5000.*

Tech Museum of Innovation

This dynamic new monument to the creative genius of Silicon Valley uses cutting-edge, hands-on exhibits to show how utterly pervasive technology is in our world today. The style and setting make it a totally engaging and entertaining endeavor.

The **Hackworth IMAX Dome Theater's** seats are on a steep embankment before an eight-story-high screen that bends overhead, drawing viewers in to the picture. The **Digital Studio** lets you create and star in your own multi-media exhibit, video, or cartoon. You can also pilot a robotic submarine, build an earthquake-proof building, learn how to protect yourself from computer hackers, let it rip on a virtual Olympic bobsled run, make a 3-D hologram self-portrait, or design a rollercoaster. *201 Market St., San Jose; 408-294-8324.*

Winchester Mystery House

Sarah Winchester, superstitious heiress of the Winchester Repeating Rifle fortune, commenced building the house in response to a fortune teller's prophecy that she would live only while the house remained unfinished. The bottom line is that Mrs. Winchester made sure her carpenters kept busy 24 hours a day for 38 years, until she died. The result is something really weird: a 160-room monstrosity with some 2,000 doors and 10,000 windows, stairs that lead nowhere, secret passages, and sealed doorways. The tour guides milk the story for all it's worth—and who can blame them? The house is intriguing and, naturally, is said to be haunted. *525 S. Winchester Blvd.; 408-247-2101.*

Rosicrucian Egyptian Museum

This museum features the largest collection of Egyptian antiquities in the western United States, including a large collection of mummies, dioramas of pyramids and ancient cities, displays of Egyptian, Sumerian, Babylonian, Assyrian, and Persian artifacts, and the only full-sized reproduction of an Egyptian rock tomb in the Western Hemisphere. Winding your way down the dark, narrow passages to a ransacked burial chamber is exciting and a little creepy. *Park Ave. at Naglee, San Jose; 408-947-3600.*

The rugged San Mateo coast, on the western side of the South Bay peninsula, is but a short drive from the high-tech electronics plants of Silicon Valley.

HOTELS & INNS

SAN FRANCISCO'S MAIN HOTEL DISTRICT lies north and west of Union Square, a good location for shopping, theater, and restaurants. Cheaper hotels can be found in the neighboring Tenderloin, and though the hotels themselves may be quite good, the neighborhood usually is not. Nob Hill is famed for grand and historic hotels, while the large hotels in the Financial District cater to executives on large business accounts. A few family-style motels congregate on Lombard Street, along Van Ness, and around Fisherman's Wharf. San Francisco and environs have some of the most charming bed-and-breakfasts, many occupying older Victorian buildings in interesting neighborhoods. Budget-minded travelers might search out a Spartan, European-style pensione in areas like North Beach and Chinatown.

The East Bay offers B&Bs, while in the South Bay, larger corporate-style hotels are the norm. The North Bay and Wine Country offer many lovely resorts, historic inns, and charming country bed & breakfasts.

Room Rates:
Per night, double occupancy, before tax:
$ = under $85; $$ = $85 - 130; $$$; $130 - 180; $$$$ = over $180

Hotel and Motel Chains

Best Western 800-528-1234	Marriott Hotel 800-228-9290
Comfort Inn 800-228-5150	Radisson 800-333-3333
Days Inn 800-329-7466	Ramada Inn 800-2RAMADA
Holiday Inn 800-465-4329	Double Tree 800-547-8010
ITT Sheraton 800-325-3535	Super 8 800-800-8000

Helpful Websites for San Francisco Hotel Information and Reservations

www.citysearch.com
www.stayinsanfrancisco.com
www.sidewalk.com

Archbishops Mansion

Once the official home of local Catholic prelates, this opulent B&B on Alamo Square is decorated in Belle Epoque style and is topped with a 16-foot-wide leaded glass dome. The staff is genuinely helpful and attentive without being smothering. Some rooms with fireplaces and Jacuzzis.

$$$
Neighborhood: *Western Addition*
Address: 1000 Fulton St. (Steiner)
Phone: (415) 563-7872 or (800) 543-5820
Fax: (415) 885-3193
Website: www.sftrips.com

Number of Rooms: 10; Suites: 5
Gym/Spa Facilities: No
Parking: Free for guests
Pets allowed: No
Business Services: In-room dataport, voice mail

✗ No restaurants in-house
🍸 No bars or lounges in-house

The Argent Hotel

This 36-story high-rise hotel is centrally located next to Yerba Buena Center for the Arts, Moscone Center, and the Museum of Modern Art. The air-conditioned and sound-proof guestrooms are lavishly done with a smooth blend of rich custom furniture and original paintings.

$$$
Neighborhood: *South of Market*
Address: 50 Third Street (Market)
Phone: (415) 974-6400
Reservations: (800) 505-9039
Fax: (415) 543-8268
Website: www.destinationtravel.com

Number of Rooms: 641; Suites: 26
Gym/Spa Facilities: Full gym facilities
Parking: Valet, $26 per night
Pets allowed: No
Business Services: In-room dataport, voice mail; business center on premises

✗ **Cafe 53:** *Classic French Cuisine*
🍸 Jester's

Campton Place

Excellent personal service and lavish decor make this one of the city's most highly rated hotels. Rooms from the ninth floor up overlook an atrium. Close proximity to the Financial District and Union Square make this a good choice for business or pleasure.

$$$$

Neighborhood: *Union Square*
Address: 340 Stockton St. (Post)
Phone: (415) 781-5555
Reservations: (800) 235-4300
Fax: (415) 955-5536
Website: www.camptonplace.com

Number of Rooms: 107; Suites: 10
Gym/Spa Facilities: No
Parking: Valet, $17 per night
Pets allowed: Yes
Business Services: In-room dataport, voice mail; business center on premises

✕ **Campton Place:** *California Cuisine*
🍸 **Lobby Bar**

Clift Hotel

First choice for many seasoned travelers; known for its exceptional personal service. Patrons admire the subdued urban contemporary style of the guest rooms, and swoon over the beautiful Art Deco Redwood Room lounge.

$$$$

Neighborhood: *Theater District*
Address: 495 Geary St. (Taylor)
Phone: (415) 775-4700
Reservations: (800) 65-CLIFT
Fax: (415) 441-4621
Website: www.travelbase.com

Number of Rooms: 302; Suites: 24
Gym/Spa Facilities: Full fitness center
Parking: Valet, $20 per night
Pets Allowed: No
Business Services: In-room dataports, fax, voice mail; business center on premises

✕ **Redwood Room:** *New American*
🍸 **Redwood Room Bar**

Commodore Hotel

The designers of this ultra-hip boutique hotel have artfully fused the sleek lines and sharp angles of a 1920s luxury liner with a crisp Neo-Deco decor. Colorful and dramatic mosaics and murals liven up the walls, and the warm, custom furnished rooms are simple yet elegant.

$$

Neighborhood: *Union Square*
Address: 825 Sutter St. (Leavenworth)
Phone: (415) 923-6800
Reservations: (800) 338-6848
Fax: (415) 923-6804
Website: www.sftrips.com

Number of Rooms: 113; Suites: 1
Gym/Spa Facilities: No
Parking: Off-site, self park, $16 per night
Pets Allowed: No
Business Services: In-room dataports, fax, voice mail

✗ **Titanic Cafe:** *Upscale diner-style*
🍸 **Red Room**

Donatello

A recent renovation has given this high-rise hotel an Old World European flair. Modern amenities include in-room modem links, meeting rooms, exercise room, and sauna, but the antique decor helps this hotel maintain a classic, elegant feel. Guest appreciate little extras such as thick bathrobes left on the bed.

$$ - $$$

Neighborhood: *Theater District*
Address: 501 Post St. (Mason)
Phone: (415) 441-7100
Reservations: (800) 227-3184
Fax: (415) 775-0987
Website: www.donatellohotel.com

Number of Rooms: 110; Suites: 12
Gym/Spa Facilities: Exercise room; sauna
Parking: Valet, $25 per night
Pets Allowed: No
Business Services: In-room dataports, voice mail

✗ **Zingari:** *Italian*
🍸 **Zingari Bar**

Fairmont Hotel

The grand Nob Hill classic, with a huge red-carpeted, faux-marbled lobby replete with chandeliers, as well as the (in)famous Tonga Room, known for its waterfall and tropical drinks. Corporate travelers like the large meeting rooms (once ballrooms), transport to downtown, and health club.

$$$ - $$$$
Neighborhood: *Nob Hill*
Address: 950 Mason St. (California)
Phone: (415) 772-5000
Reservations: (800) 527-4727
Fax: (415) 837-0587
Website: www.fairmont.com

Number of Rooms: 600; Suites: 60
Gym/Spa Facilities: Full gym; sauna
Parking: Valet, $26 per night
Pets Allowed: Yes
Business Services: In-room dataports, fax; business center on premises.

✗ **Crown Room:** *California Cuisine*
  Mason's: *Classic French*
🍸 **Tonga Room; New Orleans Lounge**

Handlery Union Square

Business travelers often prefer the relatively personal feel of this well-appointed, family-owned and run hotel. Large comfortable rooms are done in a straightforward yet tasteful style.

$$$
Neighborhood: *Union Square*
Address: 351 Geary St. (Powell)
Phone: (415) 781-7800
Reservations: (800) 843-4343
Fax: (415) 781-7800
Website: www.handlery.com

Number of Rooms: 322; Suites: 42
Gym/Spa Facilities: Pool; sauna
Parking: Valet, $21 per night
Pets Allowed: No
Business Services: In-room dataports, voice mail; business center on premises

✗ **New Joe's:** *Traditional Italian*
🍸 **New Joe's Lounge**

Hotel Bijou

This economically priced "gourmet" hotel beckons to film lovers with its design theme centered around San Francisco's rich cinematic history. Black and white photos of stars, an Art-Deco-style mini-theater in the lobby, and even contact numbers for those who want to land a walk-on part in a current TV or film production. Guestrooms are themed after films shot in the city.

$$$
Neighborhood: *Union Square*
Address: 111 Mason St. (Eddy)
Phone: (415) 771-1200
Reservations: (800) 771-1022
Fax: (415) 346-3196
Website: www.sftrips.com

Number of Rooms: 65; Suites: 0
Gym/Spa Facilities: No
Parking: Valet, $19 per night
Pets Allowed: No
Business Services: In-room voice mail

✗ No restaurants in-house
🍸 No bars or lounges in-house

Hotel del Sol

This colorfully converted 50s-style motor lodge exudes a shorts-and-sandals feel reminiscent of a California beachhouse. With a great pool and free kites for the kids to fly at the nearby Marina Green, the del Sol is perfect for families, and there's even a kids' suite equipped with bunk beds and board games and other toys; close to the Exploratorium and Golden Gate Bridge.

$$
Neighborhood: *Marina* District
Address: 3100 Webster (Lombard)
Phone: (415) 921-5520
Reservations: (800) 738-7477
Fax: (415) 931-4137
Website: www.sftrips.com

Number of Rooms: 47; Suites: 11
Gym/Spa Facilities: Pool; sauna
Parking: Free to guests
Pets Allowed: No
Business Services : In-room voice mail

✗ No restaurants in-house
🍸 No bars or lounges in-house

Hotel Diva

This stylish boutique hotel got a $2 million renovation in 1999, and innovative design is found around every corner. The guestrooms are modern and funky, accentuated with sculptured-steel details and deep, rich colors, yet they manage to retain a warm and enveloping feel. Located directly across the street from the Curran and Geary Theaters.

$$
Neighborhood: *Theater District*
Address: 440 Geary (Mason)
Phone: (415) 885-0200
Reservations: (800) 553-1900
Fax: (415) 346-6613
Website: www.hoteldiva.com

Number of Rooms: 110; Suites: 40
Gym/Spa Facilities: Exercise room
Parking: Valet, $22 per night
Pets Allowed: No
Business Services: In-room dataports, modems, voice mail; business center on premises

✕ **California Pizza Kitchen:** *New American*
🍸 No bars or lounges

Hotel Griffon

Situated on the newly refurbished Embarcadero walkway and close to Embarcadero Center and the Ferry Building, this 1906 building features whitewashed brick walls, lofty ceilings, inviting window seats looking out over the bay, and stylish, comfortable rooms.

$$
Neighborhood: *Downtown/Embarcadero*
Address: 155 Steuart (Howard)
Phone: (415) 495-2100
Reservations: (800) 321-2201
Fax: (415) 495-3522
Website: www.hotelgriffon.com

Number of Rooms: 62; Suites: 5
Gym/Spa Facilities: Off-site gym
Parking: Self park, $18 per night
Pets Allowed: No
Business Services: In-room dataports, voice mail; business center on premises

✕ **Red Herring:** *Seafood*
🍸 Red Herring Bar

Hotel Majestic

Old World elegance melds with modern services and warm, knowledgeable hospitality in this restored Edwardian inn. Original built in 1902 as one of the city's earliest grand hotels, the romantic rooms feature French Empire and English antiques, and many have fireplaces, clawfoot tubs, four-poster beds, and restored woodwork.

$$

Neighborhood: *Cathedral Hill*
Address: 1500 Sutter St. (Gough)
Phone: (415) 441-1100
Reservations: (800) 869-8966
Fax: (415) 673-7331
Website: www.hotelres.com

Number of Rooms: 57; Suites: 9
Gym/Spa Facilities: Full gym; pool; sauna
Parking: Valet, $20 per night
Pets Allowed: No
Business Services: In-room dataports, voice mail; business center on premises

✕ **Cafe Majestic:** *Continental Cuisine*
🍸 **Majestic Bar**

Hotel Metropolis

This swank boutique hotel boasts an "Earth, Wind, Water, and Fire" theme, with guestrooms decorated in natural color schemes designed to reflect "forces of nature." Vivid colors such as tangerine, icy-blue, and "acid green," liven up the comfortable rooms. The highly inviting Mezzanine Library is the perfect spot to hole-up and prepare for a presentation or dive deep into a good book.

$$

Neighborhood: *Union Square*
Address: 25 Mason St. (Turk)
Phone: (415) 775-4600
Reservations: (800) 553-1900
Fax: (415) 775-4606
Website: www.hotelmetropolis.com

Number of Rooms: 105; Suites: 5
Gym/Spa Facilities: Exercise room
Parking: Valet, $19 per night
Pets Allowed: No
Business Services: In-room dataports, voice mail; business center on premises

✕ No restaurants in-house
🍸 No bars or lounges in-house

Hotel Nikko

This elegant hotel offers a harmonious blend of Western and Japanese-styles, evident in the clean lines of the two-story lobby, complete with marble columns and the soothing sounds of cascading waters; efficient service, Japanese garden atrium, and an exquisite indoor pool and gym facilities.

$$$$

Neighborhood: *Union Square*
Address: 222 Mason St. (O'Farrell)
Phone: (415) 394-1111
Reservations: (800) nikko-us
Fax: (415) 394-1106
Website: www.nikkohotels.com

Number of Rooms: 524; Suites: 22
Gym/Spa Facilities: Full gym; pool; sauna; full spa
Parking: Valet, $30 per night
Pets Allowed: No
Business Services: In-room fax, dataports; business center on premises

✗ **Anzu-Nikko:** *Steaks and sushi*
🍸 **Z-Bar**

Hotel Monaco

With its playful, technicolor decor and chic atmosphere, this suave and slick hotel attracts stylish out-of-towners; meanwhile, locals frequent the hyper Art Nouveau–style Grand Cafe restaurant and bar. Impressive sauna and gym; in-room fax and modem.

$$$

Neighborhood: *Theater District*
Address: 501 Geary St. (Taylor)
Phone: (415) 292-0100
Reservations: (800) 214-4220
Fax: (415) 292-0111
Website: www.hotelmonaco.com

Number of Rooms: 201; Suites: 28
Gym/Spa Facilities: Exercise room; sauna; Jaccuzi
Parking: Valet, $24 per night
Pets Allowed: Yes
Business Services: In-room dataports, fax, voice mail

✗ **Grand Cafe:** *French-California Cuisine*
🍸 **Grand Cafe Bar**

Hotel Rex

The atmosphere at the Rex is inspired by the literary salons that thrived in San Francisco in the 1930s. Wall length bookshelves filled with antiquarian books, original portraits, and Art-Deco period pieces fill the lobby, giving it the feel of a swank parlor in an art patron's home. Sophisticated, sumptuous guestrooms are equipped with writing desks if the ambience stirs up your muse.

$$

Neighborhood: *Union Square*
Address: 562 Sutter St. (Powell)
Phone: (415) 433-4434
Reservations: (800) 738-7477
Fax: (415) 433-3695
Website: www.sftrips.com

Number of Rooms: 86; Suites: 8
Gym/Spa Facilities: No
Parking: Valet, $25 per night; self park, $18 per night
Pets Allowed: No
Business Services: In-room dataports, voice mail

✕ No restaurants in-house
🍸 Hotel Rex Bar

Hotel Triton

The whimsically decorated lobby of this hotel might have been inspired by Dr. Seuss. There's a suite designed by and named after Jerry Garcia, as well as more affordable "Zen Den" rooms, which are small, but extremely comfortable and stylishly decorated. A favorite among art directors, designers, and other like-minded types.

$$

Neighborhood: *Union Square*
Address: 342 Grant Ave. (Bush)
Phone: (415) 394-0500
Reservations: (800) 433-6611
Fax: (415) 394-0555
Website: www.hotel-tritonsf.com

Number of Rooms: 140; Suites: 7
Gym/Spa Facilities: Exercise room; sauna
Parking: Valet, $24 per night
Pets Allowed: Yes (Deposit required)
Business Services: In-room dataports, fax, voice mail

✕ **Cafe de la Presse:** *French Cuisine*
🍸 Cafe de la Presse Bar

Hotel Vintage Court

This 100-room hotel offers reasonably priced yet lovely rooms furnished in a Wine Country theme with a European style and flair. The warm and inviting lobby features a cozy fireplace and comfortable sofa and chairs to lounge in. Home of the renowned Masa's restaurant (see "RESTAURANTS").

$$$

Neighborhood: *Union Square*
Address: 650 Bush St. (Powell)
Phone: (415) 392-4666
Reservations: (800) 654-1100
Fax: (415) 433-4065
Website: www.vintagecourt.com

Number of Rooms: 107; Suites: 1
Gym/Spa Facilities: No
Parking: Valet, $24 per night
Pets Allowed: No
Business Services: In-room dataport, voice mail; business center on premises

X   **Masa's:** *New French/California*
Y   **Masa's Bar**

Hotel Union Square

This boutique hotel successfully blends the lively history of its 1913 building with modern lines laid out in beautiful cherry wood cabinets and rich colors such as eggplant, golden yellows, and deep greens, and topped off with original artworks, including newly commissioned works by Gladys Perint Palmer.

$$$

Neighborhood: *Union Square*
Address: 114 Powell St. (Ellis)
Phone: (415) 397-3000
Reservations: (800) 553-1900
Fax: (415) 399-1874
Website: www.hotelunionsquare.com

Number of Rooms: 130; Suites: 7
Gym/Spa Facilities: No
Parking: Self park, $19 per night
Pets Allowed: No
Business Services: In-room dataports, voice mail

X   No restaurants in-house
Y   No bars or lounges in-house

Huntington Hotel

Perched atop prestigious Nob Hill, just across the street from Grace Cathedral, Huntington Park, and the Flood Mansion, this brick-and-ivy hotel is renowned for highly attentive service and exclusive clientele. Plush guestrooms are done in inviting leather and velvet and are stylish and understatedly elegant.

$$$$

Neighborhood: *Nob Hill*
Address: 1075 California St. (Taylor)
Phone: (415) 474-5400
Reservations: (800) 227-4683
Fax: (415) 474-6227
Website: www.slh.com/huntingt/

Number of Rooms: 140; Suites: 21
Gym/Spa Facilities: Full gym
Parking: Valet, $19.50 per night
Pets Allowed: No
Business Services: In-room dataports, fax, voice mail; business center on premises

✕ **The Big Four:** *New American Cuisine*
🍸 **The Big Four Bar**

Hyatt Regency

The 800 large, stylishly appointed rooms here are arranged around a dramatic sunlit atrium lobby. Amenities and location make it ideal for business travelers.

$$$

Neighborhood: *Financial District*
Address: 5 Embarcadero Center (Market at Drumm)
Phone: (415) 788-1234
Reservations: (800) 233-1234
Fax: (415) 398-2567
Website: www.hyatt.com

Number of Rooms: 760; Suites: 45
Gym/Spa Facilities: Exercise room
Parking: Valet, $30 per night
Pets Allowed: No
Business Services: In-room voice mail, fax, dataports; business center on premises

✕ **Equinox:** *California Cuisine*
🍸 **13 Views Bar**

Inn at the Opera

This small, elegant hotel frequently hosts divas, primas, and jazz musicians. The well-connected staff can often provide its other guests with access to seats at the opera, ballet, and symphony. Rooms are furnished with half-canopy beds, antiques, and lots of pillows.

$$$
Neighborhood: *Civic Center*
Address: 333 Fulton St. (Franklin)
Phone: (415) 863-8400
Reservations: (800) 325-2708
Fax: (415) 861-0821
Website: www.shellvacations.com

Number of Rooms: 48; Suites: 3
Gym/Spa Facilities: No
Parking: Valet, $22 per night
Pets Allowed: No
Business Services: In-room dataports, voice mail

✗ **Ovation:** *French*
🍸 **Ovation Bar**

Inn at Union Square

An alternative to the large downtown hotels, this small inn offers guestrooms furnished in Chippendale reproductions and floral printed upholstery, as well as shared sitting rooms with woodburning fireplaces on each floor; 24-hour concierge.

$$ - $$$
Neighborhood: *Union Square*
Address: 440 Post St. (Mason)
Phone: (415) 397-3510
Reservations: (800) 288-4346
Fax: (415) 989-0529
Website: www.unionsquare.com

Number of Rooms: 30; Suites: 6
Gym/Spa Facilities: Full gym
Parking: Valet, $24 per night
Pets Allowed: No
Business Services: In-room dataports; business center on premises

✗ No restaurant in-house
🍸 No bars or lounges in-house

Jackson Court B & B Inn

This magnificent turn-of-the-century brownstone is located in the prestigious Pacific Heights neighborhood and features rooms tastefully furnished with a blend of contemporary and antique pieces; a sunny library; wood-beamed ceilings; and a private garden.

$$
Neighborhood: *Pacific Heights*
Address: 2198 Jackson St. (Buchanan)
Phone: (415) 929-7670
Reservations: (800) 738-7477
Fax: (415) 929-1405
Website: www.sftrips.com
Number of Rooms: 10; Suites: 2
Gym/Spa Facilities: No
Parking: Valet, $22 per night
Pets Allowed: No
Business Services: In-room voice mail
✕ No restaurants in-house
🍸 No bars or lounges in-house

Mandarin Oriental

Occupying the top 11 floors in one of downtown's tallest and most recognizable buildings, this luxury hotel boasts terrific views of the bay. The guestrooms are opulent and comfortable, and the efforts of the congenial staff continue to keep the Mandarin Oriental rolling in the awards for being one of the city's top hotels.

$$$$
Neighborhood: *Financial District*
Address: 222 Sansome St. (California)
Phone: (415) 885-0999
Reservations: (800) 622-0404
Fax: (415) 433-0289
Website: www.mandarin-oriental.com
Number of Rooms: 158; Suites: 4
Gym/Spa Facilities: Full fitness center
Parking: Valet, $27 per night
Pets Allowed: Yes
Business Services: In-room dataports, voice mail; business center on premises
✕ **Silks:** *California-Asian Fusion*
🍸 **Mandarin Lounge**

Mansions Hotel

At this lovely Victorian—built in 1887 and supposedly haunted—quirky theme rooms are named after famous San Franciscans: there's a "Huntington Room" and a "Tom Thumb Room." The flamboyant innkeeper hosts weekend "magic extravaganzas."

$$$
Neighborhood: *Pacific Heights*
Address: 2220 Sacramento St. (Laguna)
Phone: (415) 929-9444 or
Toll Free: (800) 826-9398
Fax: (415) 567-9391
Website: www.themansions.com

Number of Rooms: 16; Suites: 5
Gym/Spa Facilities: No
Parking: Valet, $25 per night
Pets Allowed: No
Business Services: In-room voice mail

✕ **The Mansions:** *Continental Cuisine*
🍸 No bars or lounges in-house

Mark Hopkins Inter-Continental

Capped by the famous Top of the Mark bar, this Nob Hill landmark features a sun-filled grand lobby, resplendent with crystal chandeliers and marble floors. Rooms are sleekly and comfortably decorated.

$$$
Neighborhood: *Nob Hill*
Address: One Nob Hill (Mason)
Phone: (415) 392-3434
Reservations: (800) 327-0200
Fax: (415) 392-0822
Website: www.interconti.com

Number of Rooms: 365; Suites: 28
Gym/Spa Facilities: Exercise room
Parking: Valet, $27 per night
Pets Allowed: Yes
Business Services: In-room voice mail, dataports; business rooms available; full business center on premises

✕ **Nob Hill Restaurant:** *California Cuisine*
🍸 Top of the Mark; Nob Hill Terrace

Maxwell Hotel

This 1908 building—formerly home of the Raphael Hotel—underwent a major renovation in 1997 when the Joie de Vivre hotel group bought it and restored it with a harmonious melding of Theater Deco and Victorian decor. The warm, luscious rooms tempt even the earliest of early birds to sleep in.

$$
Neighborhood: *Union Square*
Address: 386 Geary (Mason)
Phone: (415) 986-2000
Reservations: (888) 734-6299
Fax: (415) 397-2447
Website: www.sftrips.com

Number of Rooms: 122; Suites: 31
Gym/Spa Facilities: No
Parking: Off site, self park, $17 per night
Pets Allowed: No
Business Services: In-room voice mail, dataports

✕ **Max's on the Square:** *New American*
🍸 **Max's Bar**

Miyako Hotel

The East-West fusion of the Miyako equates to both the comfort and convenience of Western-style rooms and the tranquility and graciousness of traditional Japanese suites with tatamis and furo tubs. After taking care of work concerns in the 24-hour business center, stroll through the authentic Japanese garden and sit by the Koi pond to wind down.

$$ - $$$
Neighborhood: *Japantown*
Address: 1625 Post St. (Laguna)
Phone: (415) 922-3200
Reservations: (800) 333-3333
Fax: (415) 921-0417
Website: www.radisson.com

Number of Rooms: 205; Suites: 13
Gym/Spa Facilities: Full fitness center
Parking: Off-site, self-park, $15 per night
Pets Allowed: No
Business Services: In-room voice mail, dataports; full business center on premises

✕ **Yoyo Bistro:** *French and Japanese*
🍸 **Yoyo Lounge**

Monticello Inn

Standing amid the downtown giant hotels, this intimate inn is decorated in American-Colonial style, with warm and inviting sitting areas in the library and lobby. The guestrooms are comfortable and homey, but unless you're particularly fond of a frilly atmosphere, the excessive use of floral patterns on bedspreads, curtains, and pillows gets a little tired.

$$

Neighborhood: *Financial District*
Address: 127 Ellis St. (Powell)
Phone: (415) 392-8800
Reservations: (800) 669-7777
Fax: (415) 398-2650
Website: www.monticelloinn.com

Number of Rooms: 71; Suites: 20
Gym/Spa Facilities: Off-site facility
Parking: Valet, $16 per night
Pets Allowed: No
Business Services: In-room voice mail, dataports

✕ **Puccini & Pinetti:** *Italian-American*
🍸 Puccini & Pinetti Bar

Pan Pacific Hotel

This luxurious hotel, designed by John C. Portman in a soaring atrium style, pampers its guests with lovely rooms and a highly attentive staff. A perfect hotel for business executives, with extensive business services, limousine drop off, and a central location.

$$$

Neighborhood: *Theater District*
Address: 500 Post St. (Mason)
Phone: (415) 771-8600
Reservations: (800) 533-6465
Fax: (415) 398-0267
Website: www.panpac.com

Number of Rooms: 285; Suites: 45
Gym/Spa Facilities: Full fitness center
Parking: Valet, $18 per night
Pets Allowed: No
Business Services: In-room voice mail, dataports, fax; business center on premises

✕ **Pacific:** *Asian-California Cuisine*
🍸 Pacific Bar; Atrium Court

Park Hyatt

This landmark hotel features a stunning 17-story atrium lobby. Plush rooms, excellent service, and little extras like gourmet chocolates and imported soaps appeal to both pleasure and business travelers. Best are the rooms with balconies and bay views.

$$$
Neighborhood: *Financial District*
Address: 333 Battery St. (Sacramento)
Phone: (415) 392-1234
Reservations: (800) 323-7275
Fax: (415) 421-2433
Website: www.hyatt.com

Number of Rooms: 313; Suites: 47
Gym/Spa Facilities: Full fitness center
Parking: Valet, $30 per night
Pets Allowed: No
Business Services: In-room dataports, voice mail; full business center on premises

✗ **Park Grill:** *Continental Cuisine*
🍸 **Park Grill Bar**

Phoenix Hotel

This funky, revitalized motel has a 1950s Hollywood-bungalow-hotel feel, and indeed it has become the trendy first choice for touring rock musicians and starlets donning sunglasses. Rooms are tropically flavored with bamboo furniture and vibrant original works by local artists. The ultra-hip Backflip Lounge overlooks a colorfully painted swimming pool, where complimentary breakfast is served to guests.

$$
Neighborhood: *Van Ness/Civic Center*
Address: 601 Eddy St. (Larkin)
Phone: (415) 776-1380
Reservations: (800) 248-9466
Fax: (415) 885-3109
Website: www.sftrips.com

Number of Rooms: 41; Suites: 3
Gym/Spa Facilities: Pool
Parking: Free for guests
Pets Allowed: No
Business Services: In-room voice mail

✗ **Backflip:** *"Cocktail" Cuisine*
🍸 **Backflip Lounge**

Prescott Hotel

Perhaps best known as the site of Wolfgang Puck's Postrio restaurant (see "Restaurants"), this renovated old hotel has plush, handsome guest rooms decorated in rich colors and cherry wood. The capable staff provides personal service.

$$$

Neighborhood: *Union Square*
Address: 545 Post St. (Taylor)
Phone: (415) 563-0303
Reservations: (800) 283-7322
Fax: (415) 563-6831
Website: www.prescotthotel.com

Number of Rooms: 164; Suites: 30
Gym/Spa Facilities: No
Parking: Valet, $25 per night
Pets Allowed: No
Business Services: In-room dataports, voice mail

✗ **Postrio:** *California/Eclectic*
🍸 Postrio Bar

Queen Anne Hotel

Originally a posh girls' school, this lovely "painted lady" on Cathedral Hill offers 49 rooms, all differently decorated; many have fireplaces. The breakfast buffet is served in the large lobby, which is replete with gorgeous cedar and oak woodwork. Service can be somewhat less than perfect at times.

$$

Neighborhood: *Cathedral Hill*
Address: 1590 Sutter St. (Octavia)
Phone: (415) 441-2828
Reservations: (800) 227-3970
Fax: (415) 775-5212
Website: www.queenanne.com

Number of Rooms: 40; Suites: 8
Gym/Spa Facilities: No
Parking: Off-site, self park, $12 per night
Pets Allowed: No
Business Services: In-room dataports

✗ No restaurants in-house
🍸 No bars or lounges in-house

Red Victorian

Situated on a bustling block of the Upper Haight, this very popular and affordable spot is perfect for young hipsters or 60s throwbacks. Famous for theme rooms like the "Japanese Tea Garden," the "Flower Child," and the "Summer of Love." There's also a meditation room, library, and Peace Center gift store on the premises as well. Breakfast is included and the staff is friendly, helpful, and entertaining.

$$

Neighborhood: *Upper Haight/Golden Gate Park*
Address: 1665 Haight St. (Cole)
Phone: (415) 864-1978
Fax: (415) 863-3293
Website: www.linex.com/~redvic/

Number of Rooms: 18; Suites: 1
Gym/Spa Facilities: No
Parking: No
Pets Allowed: No
Business Services: No

✗ No restaurants in-house
🍸 No bars or lounges in-house

Renaissance Stanford Court

This Nob Hill grandee features a beautiful stained glass dome over its central court, and the generously sized rooms are decorated with 19th-century reproductions.

$$$$

Neighborhood: *Nob Hill*
Address: 905 California St. (Powell)
Phone: (415) 989-3500
Reservations: (800) 227-4736
Fax: (415) 391-0513
Website: www.stanfordcourt.com

Number of Rooms: 393; Suites: 8
Gym/Spa Facilities: Exercise room
Parking: Valet, $27 per night
Pets Allowed: No
Business Services: In-room dataports, fax, voice mail; business center on premises

✗ **Fournou's Ovens:** *Italian*
🍸 **Fournou's Bar**

HOTELS & INNS

Ritz-Carlton

Actually a renovation of the neoclassical Metropolitan Life building, this superb hotel impresses visitors with a splendid lobby replete with crystal chandeliers and museum-quality oil paintings. Legendary afternoon teas, and excellent sports facilities to boot.

$$$

Neighborhood: *Nob Hill*
Address: 600 Stockton St. (California)
Phone: (415) 296-7465
Reservations: (800) 241-3333
Fax: (415) 291-02888
Website: www.theritzcarlton.com

Number of Rooms: 336; Suites: 22
Gym/Spa Facilities: Full gym; pool
Parking: Valet, $30 per night
Pets Allowed: No
Business Services: In-room dataports, voice mail; business center on premises

✕ **The Dining Room:** *New French*
    Terrace Cafe: *California*
Y **Lobby Lounge; Terrace Bar**

San Francisco Marriott

The huge, arched windows at the top of this hotel near SoMa's Moscone Center have earned it the sobriquet of the Jukebox Hotel among San Franciscans. The 1,500 rooms are large and nicely decorated, and the View Lounge on the 39th floor is vertiginously spectacular.

$$$

Neighborhood: *Financial District*
Address: 55 Fourth St. (Market)
Phone: (415) 896-1600
Reservations: (800) 228-9290
Fax: (415) 777-2799
Website: www.marriott.com

Number of Rooms: 1500; Suites: 90
Gym/Spa Facilities: Full gym; sauna
Parking: Valet, $27 per night
Pets Allowed: Yes
Business Services: In-room dataports, voice mail; business center on the premises

✕ **Garden Terrace:** *Continental Cuisine*
Y **View Lounge; Terrace Lounge**

Sheraton Palace Hotel

Built on the site of the old Palace Hotel, this elegantly renovated version features the spectacular, glass-ceilinged Garden Court restaurant, a pool with a skylight, a health club, and Maxfield's Grill, home of Maxfield Parrish's Pied Piper painting.

$$$

Neighborhood: *Financial District*
Address: 2 New Montgomery (Market)
Phone: (415) 512-1111
Reservations: (800) 325-3535
Fax: (415) 543-0671
Website: www.travelweb.com

Number of Rooms: 520; Suites: 32
Gym/Spa Facilities: Full gym; pool; sauna
Parking: Valet, $26 per night
Pets Allowed: No
Business Services: In-room dataport, fax, voice mail; business center on premises

✕ **Garden Court:** *California Cuisine*
 Kyoya: *Japanese*
🍸 **Pied Piper Lounge**

Sherman House

This French-Italianate mansion is one of the city's most opulent accommodations, providing an oasis of luxury with personalized and attentive service. It was built in 1876 for the founder of the Sherman Clay Music Company, and it still retains the soaring, three-story music hall, now used as a salon for guests. The rooms are elegant, and the suites in the carriage house, which is set in the middle of intoxicating gardens, are the ultimate in comfort and luxury.

$$$$

Neighborhood: *Cow Hollow*
Address: 2160 Green St. (Fillmore)
Phone: (415) 563-3600
Reservations: (800) 424-5777
Fax: (415) 563-1882
Website: No

Number of Rooms: 11; Suites: 3
Gym/Spa Facilities: No
Parking: Free to guests
Pets Allowed: No
Business Services: In-room voice mail

✕ **Sherman House:** *French*, guests only
🍸 No bars or lounges in-house

Sir Francis Drake

Beefeater-costumed doorman usher you into to the regal lobby, decorated with wrought-iron balustrades, chandeliers, and Italian marble. The guestrooms are done in a more simple decor, with California-style furnishings and frilly floral-print fabrics. The swank Harry Denton's Starlite Room is always in full swing, but even more so when the Starlite Orchestra is in full effect at this 21st-floor lounge with a dance floor.

$$$
Neighborhood: *Union Square*
Address: 450 Powell St. (Post)
Phone: (415) 392-7755
Reservations: (800) 268-7245
Fax: (415) 395-8599
Website: www.sirfrancisdrake.com

Number of Rooms: 411; Suites: 6
Gym/Spa Facilities: Exercise room
Parking: Valet, $24 per night
Pets Allowed: No
Business Services: In-room dataports, voice mail; business center on premises

✕ **Scala's Bistro:** *Italian/Seafood*
🍸 **Starlite Ballroom**

Spencer House

The hospitable proprietors of this B&B across from Buena Vista Park—near the shops of bustling Haight Street—have lavishly appointed their 1885 Queen Anne Victorian with silk wall-covering, Oriental rugs, and Louis XVI antiques. The exquisite rooms feature thick, plush feather beds, and down duvets.

$$$
Neighborhood: *Middle Haight*
Address: 1080 Haight St. (Baker)
Phone: (415) 626-9205
Fax: (415) 626-9205
Website: www.spencerhouse.com

Number of Rooms: 6; Suites: 0
Gym/Spa Facilities: No
Parking: Free for guests
Pets Allowed: No
Business Services: No

✕ No restaurants in-house
🍸 No bars or lounges in-house

Tuscan Inn

The condolike exterior of the Tuscan Inn—reddish brick with white concrete—gives little indication of the charm of the smallish, Italian-influenced guestrooms. The staff is exceptionally friendly and attentive, and they provide such services as complimentary limousine service to the Financial District and Union Square.

$$$

Neighborhood: *Fisherman's Wharf*
Address: 425 Northpoint St. (Mason)
Phone: (415) 561-1100
Reservations: (800) 648-4626
Fax: (415) 561-1199
Website: www.tuscaninn.com

Number of Rooms: 220; Suites: 6
Gym/Spa Facilities: Off-site facility
Parking: Valet, $17 per night
Pets Allowed: No
Business Services: In-room dataports, voice mail

✗ **Cafe Pescatore:** *Italian/Seafood*
🍸 **Cafe Pescatore Bar**

Union Street Inn

Run by a former schoolteacher, this quaint Edwardian-era B&B—conveniently located along the toney shopping lane of Union Street—has a redwood patio in the back that overlooks a fragrant and colorful English garden. Rooms are furnished with antiques and original artworks. For extra privacy, book the carriage house with its whirlpool bathtub.

$$ - $$$

Neighborhood: *Cow Hollow*
Address: 2229 Union St. (Fillmore)
Phone: (415) 346-0424
Fax: (415) 922-8046
Website: www.unionstreetinn.com

Number of Rooms: 6; Suites: 0
Gym/Spa Facilities: No
Parking: Off-site, self park, $12 per night
Pets Allowed: No
Business Services: Fax available

✗ No restaurants in-house
🍸 No bars or lounges in-house

Victorian Inn on the Park

This lovingly restored 1890s Victorian B&B is situated along the peaceful swath of greenbelt of Golden Gate Park's Panhandle. The Historic Landmark home is splendidly decorated with period furnishings, lots of pillows, and William Morris reproductions. Breakfast is a sumptuous affair.

$$ - $$$
Neighborhood: *Middle Haight*
Address: 301 Lyon St. (Fell)
Phone: (415) 931-1830
Reservations: (800) 435-1967
Fax: (415) 931-1830
Website: www.citysearch.com/sfo

Number of Rooms: 10; Suites: 2
Gym/Spa Facilities: No
Parking: Self park, $15 per night
Pets allowed: No
Business Services: Fax available

✕ No restaurants in-house
🍸 No bars or lounges in-house

Villa Florence Hotel

A multi-million dollar renovation completed in 1998 spruced things up at the Villa Florence. Rooms here are warm and quiet, despite the bustling locale right in the heart of Union Square. Overstuffed chairs in the rooms beckon the wary shopper for a well-deserved nap. The marble-appointed lobby contains Kuleto's (see "RESTAURANTS").

$$$
Neighborhood: *Union Square*
Address: 225 Powell St. (Geary)
Phone: (415) 397-7700
Reservations: (800) 553-4411
Fax: (415) 397-1006
Website: www.villaflorence.com

Number of Rooms: 150; Suites: 33
Gym/Spa Facilities: No
Parking: Valet, $23 per night
Pets Allowed: No
Business Services: In-room dataports, voice mail; business center on premises

✕ Kuleto's: *Italian*
🍸 Kuleto's Bar

Washington Square Inn

This beautifully appointed B&B on Washington Square—smack-dab in the heart of North Beach—recalls a fine country home and offers personalized service in the European tradition. Thick robes and down comforters in the guestrooms and the complimentary wine, high tea, and hors d'oeuvres served in the afternoon add to an air of relaxed luxury.

W Hotel

The W manages to put forth a sleek and hip style without the hard edge that often accompanies modernist design. There's a meticulous attention to detail in the guestrooms, which artfully meld the finer comforts of home with hyper-fast internet access, full-size writing desks, and other business amenities.

$$

Neighborhood: *South of Market*
Address: 181 Third St. (Howard)
Phone: (415) 777-5300
Reservations: (877) 946-8357
Fax: (415) 812-7800
Website: www.whotels.com

Number of Rooms: 418; Suites: 5
Gym/Spa Facilities: Full gym; pool
Parking: Valet, $30 per night
Pets Allowed: Yes
Business Services: In-room dataports, fax, voice mail; business center on premises

✗ XYZ: *California/French*
🍸 XYZ Bar; The W Bar

$$

Neighborhood: *North Beach*
Address: 1660 Stockton St. (Filbert)
Phone: (415) 981-4220 or
Toll Free: (800) 388-0220
Fax: (415) 397-7242
Website: www.wsisf.com

Number of Rooms: 15; Suites: 1
Gym/Spa Facilities: No
Parking: Valet, $20 per day
Pets Allowed: No
Business Services: In-room voice mail

✗ No restaurants in-house
🍸 No bars or lounges in-house

Westin St. Francis

This grand dame first opened its doors in 1904, and from the get-go it has been lauded for its innovations and opulence. A $60 million renovated began in 1994, when three giant trompe l'oeil murals were added to the lobby; followed by overhalls to the grand ballroom as well as the addition of a private party venue and a state-of-the-art fitness and spa center. Many guestrooms retain their original 1904 woodwork.

$$ - $$$
Neighborhood: *Union Square*
Address: 335 Powell St. (Geary)
Phone: (415) 397-7000
Reservations: (800) 228-3000
Fax: (415) 774-0124
Website: www.westin.com

Number of Rooms: 1200; Suites: 65
Gym/Spa Facilities: Full gym and spa
Parking: Valet, $30 per night
Pets Allowed: Yes
Business Services: In-room dataports, voice mail; business center on premises

✗ **St. Francis Cafe:** *California Cuisine*
🍸 **Compass Rose Lounge; Dewey's**

White Swan Inn

The White Swan has all the comforts of home—personal front-door keys, complimentary newspapers, and free soft drinks and bottled water. In addition to the fireplaces, Laura Ashley-style decor, and four-poster beds which grace every guest room are conveniences such as hair dryers and TVs. Homemade breakfast dishes and afternoon refreshments are so delightful that the proprietors have published their own cookbook.

$$$
Neighborhood: *Union Square*
Address: 845 Bush St. (Mason)
Phone: (415) 775-1755 or
Toll Free: (800) 999-9570
Fax: (415) 775-5717
Website: www.foursistersinn.com

Number of Rooms: 23; Suites: 3
Gym/Spa Facilities: No
Parking: Valet, $19 per night
Pets Allowed: No
Business Services: In-room voice mail

✗ No restaurants in-house
🍸 No bars or lounges in-house

The San Francisco Marriott—a.k.a. the Jukebox Hotel—appears to rise above Grant Avenue.

East Bay Hotels & Inns

Claremont Resort and Spa *Berkeley* $$$$
41 Tunnel Rd. (Ashby); (510) 843-3000
Covering 22 acres, this historic resort hotel
(ca. 1915) offers uniquely decorated rooms,
two pools, a workout center, 10 tennis
courts, and restaurants offering standard as
well as spa cuisine. The vast chateau-like
structure, with its surrounding woodland,
is visible even from the city.

French Hotel *Berkeley* $ 1538 Shattuck
Ave. (Cedar); (510) 548-9930
This narrow, red-brick hotel faces Berkeley's
well-known Chez Panisse. The reasonably
priced rooms are decorated in high-tech
style. Cafe downstairs.

Gramma's Rose Garden Inn *Berkeley*
$$ - $$$ 2740 Telegraph Ave. (Ward);
(510) 549-2145
This B&B comprises a beautiful Tudor-
style mansion (ca. 1900) and three smaller
houses behind it. Rooms are furnished with
antiques; some have fireplaces and balconies. Sunny courtyard in back.

Hotel Durant *Berkeley* $$ 2600 Durant
Ave. (Bowditch); (510) 845-8981

A small European-style hotel close to U.C.
Berkeley; lovely restaurant and bar.

Marriott Inn *Berkeley* $$$ Berkeley Marina
(510) 548-7920/(800) 228-9290
Modern and attractively decorated, Berkeley's largest hostelry has waterfront views,
but is just two miles from downtown
Berkeley. Two indoor pools; fitness room.

Oakland Marriott *Oakland* $$ 1001
Broadway (10th St.); (510) 451-4000
This full-service luxury hotel caters to exec-
utives and professionals doing business in
downtown Oakland.

Washington Inn *Oakland* $$ 495 10th St.
(Broadway); (510) 452-1776
Turn-of-the-century charm and elegance,
convenient to downtown Oakland.

Waterfront Plaza Hotel *Oakland* $$ - $$$
10 Washington St. (Embarcadero);
(510) 836-3800
Situated on Jack London Square, this large
hotel offers 144 luxury guest rooms, fireplaces, and health facilities including a pool
and indoor sauna.

South Bay Hotels & Inns

Garden Court Hotel *Palo Alto* $$$$
520 Cowper St. (University); (650) 322-
9000/(800) 824-9028
Situated downtown, this elegant hotel offers 62 lovely, comfortable rooms—some
with whirlpools and fireplaces. There's also
the appeal of ordering room service from Il
Fornaio Cucina (see "RESTAURANTS").

Hyatt St. Claire *San Jose* $ - $$$
302 S. Market St. (San Carlos); (408)
295-2000/(800) 824-6835
With its original Spanish tile courtyard,
fountain, and wood-beamed ceiling re-
stored in 1992, this impressive downtown
hotel (ca. 1926) is today a national historic
landmark. Business travelers can expect the
full range of amenities.

Mill Rose Inn *Half Moon Bay* $$$ - $$$$
615 Mill St. (Church); (650) 726-9794
or (800) 900-ROSE
This small, charming bed-and-breakfast inn features six plush guestrooms, each with a private entrance and a garden view. Half Moon Bay's stunning coastline beckons just a few yards outside of your door. Breakfast is a sumptuous affair.

Stanford Park Hotel *Menlo Park* $$$
100 El Camino Real (Cambridge);
(650) 322-1234 or (800) 368-2468
A short walk from Stanford University and the Stanford Shopping Center is this cedar-shingled and red-brick hotel. Nicely furnished rooms come in varying shapes and sizes, some with fireplaces and sitting rooms. Pool, sauna, and fitness room.

North Bay Hotels & Inns

Marin County

Casa Madrona *Sausalito* $$ - $$$
8015 Bridgeway ; (415) 332-0502
With the warmth of a B&B, this small hotel offers 39 rooms—some with contemporary and some with Victorian decor—most of which have stunning views of the Sausalito harbor and San Francisco. Hot tub and stylish restaurant.

Manka's Inverness Lodge *Inverness*
$$ - $$$$ Callendar Way (Argyle);
(415) 669-1034
Just uphill from the tiny hamlet of Inverness is this former hunting lodge, with eight rooms and four cottages, as well as an enchantingly rustic dining room where fresh-caught fish and wild game dishes are served. Perfect for an idyllic weekend.

Pelican Inn *Muir Beach* $$$
Hwy. 1 (Pacific Way); (415) 383-6000
A little bit of Old England in Marin, this whitewashed Tudor features seven rooms with leaded windows, hanging tapestries, and Oriental rugs. Sample any number of stouts, ales, ports, and sherries in the hotel pub, and the hearty breakfast is included.

Ten Inverness Way *Inverness* $$ - $$$
10 Inverness Way; (415) 669-1648
The redwood living room of this homey B&B features a large stone hearth and lots of bookshelves, and the simple but pretty guest rooms have hand-sewn quilts. Delicious breakfast items.

Napa County

Ambrose Bierce House *St. Helena* $$
1515 Main St. (Pine); (707) 963-3003
Yes, America's favorite literary curmudgeon did indeed live here—until 1913, when he became bored with the peaceful wine valley and vanished into tumultuous wilds of Pancho Villa's Mexico. The two suites have private baths.

Auberge du Soleil *Rutherford* $$$$
180 Rutherford Hill Rd. ; (707) 963-1211
This deluxe French country inn is the valley's most famous lodging. Set in an old olive grove and overlooking the valley, the Auberge has stunning views. Guest rooms have French doors, terra-cotta tiles, and a private terrace. The more deluxe rooms have fireplaces and whirlpool baths.

North Bay Hotels & Inns *(con't)*

Brannan Cottage Inn *Calistoga* $$ - $$$
109 Wapoo Ave. (Lincoln);
(707) 942-4200
The last cottage remaining from Sam Brannan's 1860 Calistoga Hot Springs Resort which is still on its original site. Six rooms with private entrances and baths.

Fanny's *Calistoga* $
1206 Spring St.; (707) 942-9491
This simple, quiet, Craftsman-style cottage (ca. 1915) is a relaxing retreat just off Calistoga's busy main street. Private baths and window seats, with spacious living room and dining room. Sumptuous breakfast are the perfect way to start the day.

La Residence *Napa* $$-$$$
4066 St. Helena Hwy.; (707) 253-0337
This ultra-comfortable hotel is comprised of an ornate mansion built in 1870 and Cabernet Hall, which is supposed to resemble a French barn. Heated swimming pool and rose gardens separate the two buildings. Excellent wine and cheese repasts and delicious breakfasts. Rates are about two thirds of what they are at lesser lodgings up-valley.

Meadowood Resort *St. Helena* $$$$
900 Meadowood Ln., ; (707) 963-3646
A truly great resort and a cozy place to hide out in. The spacious, well-insulated, and perfectly quiet guest rooms are spaced over the property in small clusters, touching the nine-hole golf course on one side and the oak woods on the other. Croquet grounds, tennis courts, pool, and spa.

Silverado Country Club & Resort *Napa*
$$$ 1600 Atlas Peak Rd. (Hwy. 121);
(707) 257-0200
With two 18-hole golf courses, 9 swimming pools, 20 tennis courts, and hundreds of condos, this 1,200-acre resort may not be intimate, but it's perfect for weekend athletes. The two- to three-room condos also work well for families.

White Sulphur Springs Resort & Spa
St. Helena $ -$$$ 3100 White Sulphur Springs Rd.; (707) 963-8588
The oldest hot springs resort, established in 1852, is still going strong.

Sonoma County

Applewood–An Estate Inn *Guerneville* $$$
13555 Hwy. 116; (707) 869-9093
This pink Mediterranean-style villa somehow fits right into the redwoods and apple trees. A truly great place, with comfortable rooms, inviolate privacy, and some of the best breakfasts in the Wine Country—all within walking distance of Guerneville.

Camellia Inn *Healdsburg* $$ - $$$
211 North St. (East); (707) 433-8182
This quiet, very homey old building dates to 1869, and the more than 50 varieties of camellias on the property go all the way back to horticulturist Luther Burbank, who was a family friend. Innkeeper Ray Lewand is an accomplished amateur winemaker—happy hour on the swimming pool is an education. Huge breakfast and private baths. Just a few blocks from the Healdsburg Plaza.

El Dorado Hotel *Sonoma* $$ 405 First St. W. (Spain); (707) 996-3030
Built as the home of Gen. Mariano Vallejo's never-quite-respectable brother Salvador, the El Dorado has been extensively restored, and the newer ground-level suites beyond the patio and pool are luxurious. Enjoy breakfast under the courtyard fig tree. Since it faces the Plaza, the El Dorado is convenient to everything in town.

Gaige House Inn *Glen Ellen* $$ - $$$
13540 Arnold Dr.; (707) 935-0237
A very quiet, though very lively, B&B housed in an 1890 Queen Anne and run by Ardath Rouas, founder of Auberge du Soleil. The hammock hanging from the trees just invites you to snooze under the stars. Breakfasts are outrageously good.

Kenwood Inn & Spa *Kenwood* $$$$
10400 Sonoma Hwy.; (707) 833-1293
A Mediterranean feel pervades this compound of yellow buildings, which surround the quiet, flowery courtyard. Oak woods rise to one side of the road, vineyards to the other. A substantial breakfast is served from the large dining room's open kitchen.

Raford House *Healdsburg* $$
10630 Wohler Rd. (River);
(707) 887-9573
Built in the 1880s in Russian River Wine Country, the Raford House is surrounded by vines as well as tall palms that were planted as status symbols in the 19th century. Very comfortable and down-to-earth. Delicious breakfast, and generous afternoon wine and appetizers.

Sonoma Hotel *Sonoma* $$$
110 W. Spain St. (First St. W.);
(707) 996-2996
Conveniently located on the Sonoma Plaza, this beautiful historic 17-room hotel—a former dry goods store and meeting hall—is accented with old oak and stained glass. The hotel bar is usually hopping.

Sonoma Mission Inn *Boyes Hot Springs* $$$ 18149 Hwy. 12 (Boyes Blvd.);
(707) 938-9000 or (800) 862-4945
Established as a health spa in the mid-1800s, the 170-room Sonoma Mission Inn offers packages structured around your choice of physical regimen: there are tennis courts, an Olympic-sized pool—and two restaurants (see "RESTAURANTS").

Timberhill Ranch *Cazadero* $$$$
35755 Hauser Bridge Rd.;
(707) 847-3258
Truly an incredible retreat, just a short drive from the Russian River: it's like a summer camp for adults. The ultra-plush cabins stand on extensive grounds which lie at the edge of wilderness. A private chef offers delicious multi-course dinners every night in the grand dining room; the wine list is laudable, too.

San Francisco Hotels by District

Refer to pages 259 - 284 for alphabetically listed reviews of the hotels below.

Civic Center
Inn at the Opera $$$
Phoenix Inn $$

Cow Hollow/Marina
Union Street Inn $$ - $$$
Hotel del Sol $$
Sherman House $$$ - $$$$

Financial District
Argent Hotel $$$
Hotel Griffon $$ - $$$
Hyatt Regency *Financial District* $$$
Mandarin Oriental $$$$
Monticello Inn $$
Park Hyatt $$$
San Francisco Marriott $$$
Sheraton Palace Hotel $$$
W Hotel $$$ - $$$$

Fisherman's Wharf
Tuscan Inn $$$

Haight
Red Victorian $$
Spencer House $$$
Victorian Inn on the Park $$ - $$$

Japantown/Cathedral Hill
Hotel Majestic $$
Miyako Hotel $$ - $$$
Queen Anne Hotel $$

Marina/Pacific Heights
Hotel del Sol $$
Jackson Court Bed & Breakfast Inn $$
Mansions Hotel $$

Nob Hill
Fairmont Hotel $$$ - $$$$
Huntington Hotel *Nob Hill* $$$$
Mark Hopkins Inter-Continental $$$
Renaissance Stanford Court $$$$
Ritz-Carlton $$$

North Beach
Washington Square Inn $$

Union Square/Theater District
Campton Place $$$$
Commodore Hotel $$
Donatello $$$
Four Seasons Clift Hotel $$$$
Handlery Union Square $$$
Hotel Bijou $$
Hotel Diva $$
Hotel Metropolis $$
Hotel Monaco $$$
Hotel Nikko $$$$
Hotel Rex $$$
Hotel Triton $$
Hotel Union Square $$ - $$$
Hotel Vintage Court $$
Inn at Union Square $$ - $$$
Maxwell Hotel $$ - $$$
Pan Pacific Hotel $$$
Prescott Hotel $$$
Sir Francis Drake $$$
Villa Florence $$$
Westin St. Francis $$ - $$$
White Swan Inn $$$

Western Addition
Archbishops Mansion $$$
Queen Anne Hotel $$

East Bay Hotels by Town*

Berkeley
Claremont Resort and Spa $$$$
French Hotel $
Gramma's Rose Garden Inn $$ - $$$
Hotel Durant $$

Marriott Inn $$$

Oakland
Oakland Marriott $$
Washington Inn $$
Waterfront Plaza Hotel $$ - $$$

South Bay Hotels by Town*

Half Moon Bay
Mill Rose Inn $$$ - $$$$

Menlo Park
Stanford Park Hotel $$$

Palo Alto
Garden Court Hotel

San Jose
Hyatt St. Claire $ - $$$

North Bay Hotels by Town*

Boyes Hot Springs
Sonoma Mission Inn $$$

Calistoga
Brannan Cottage Inn $$ - $$$
Fanny's *Calistoga* $

Cazadero
Timberhill Ranch $$$$

Glen Ellen
Gaige House Inn $$ - $$$

Guerneville
Applewood–An Estate Inn $$$

Healdsburg
Camellia Inn $$ - $$$
Raford House $$

Inverness
Manka's Inverness Lodge $$ - $$$$
Ten Inverness Way *Inverness* $$ - $$$

Kenwood
Kenwood Inn & Spa $$$$

Muir Beach
Pelican Inn $$$

Napa
La Residence $$-$$$
Silverado Country Club & Resort $$$

Rutherford
Auberge du Soleil $$$$

Sausalito
Casa Madrona $$ - $$$

St. Helena
Ambrose Bierce House $$
Meadowood Resort $$$$
White Sulphur Springs Resort $ -$$$

Sonoma
El Dorado Hotel $$
Sonoma Hotel $$$

* Refer to pages 286 - 289 for alphabetically listed reviews of the Bay Area hotels above.
***East Bay Hotels:** 286; **South Bay Hotels:** 286 - 287; **North Bay Hotels:** 287 - 289.*

RESTAURANTS

DINING OUT IS SAN FRANCISCO'S MOST CONSUMING PASSION. Finicky critics may quibble about the city's place in the culinary firmament, but people who simply *enjoy* eating know that San Francisco is tops. In a recent Condé Nast *Traveler* poll, readers rated the city first in the *world* for restaurants. Certainly those of us who live here appreciate what we've got: we eat out more often than any other citizenry in the nation.

San Francisco Bay Area residents know food and have little patience for a place that's all style and no substance, or one that's mediocre value for the money. As a result, the Bay Area is full of restaurants in every price range that uphold high standards of freshness, innovation, and presentation. While you can expect to be served exquisite food at a pricy spot like Masa's, you might not anticipate relishing the smoky, full flavor of a three-dollar grilled chicken burrito; the baby artichokes on foccacia available at a corner deli; brilliant green water spinach from a Chinese take-out; or red pepper and sweet potatoes sauteed into the hash browns at a sidewalk cafe. Such thoughtful preparations of the region's excellent produce and meats exemplify the operating principle of "California cuisine:" creative yet unpretentious presentation of the finest and freshest ingredients. California cuisine is not just a trend, but an invitation to explore new cuisines, techniques, and ingredients.

California is a hodgepodge of immigrant and transplant cultures, and in San Francisco we enjoy countless traditional cuisines, especially from Italy, various American regions, Latin America, and a whole panoply of Asian nations and provinces. A little borrowing back and forth was inevitable. Granted, chefs at many ethnic and traditional American eateries preserve their specific cuisines (the Tadich Grill is not likely to start serving pad thai anytime soon, and most of us probably prefer it that way), but today many Bay Area chefs, especially those in the vanguard, mix and match ingredients and techniques to create their own eclectic styles. We've seen the impact of French and, more recently, Latin cuisine on local restaurants; currently, the influence of Asian cooking continues to grow. Some restaurants offer "Asian" or "Pacific Rim fusion" menus, on which dishes from Japan, Thailand, India, and China, are mixed wholesale. More common are restaurants which serve East-West hybrids like polenta with shiitake mushrooms, or tuna carpaccio—sashimi in Italian clothing. Chefs draw upon Far Eastern spices and techniques to accent Mediterranean, say, or classic American dishes. Lemongrass, cumin, and ginger are used to accent Maine lobster, risotto, roast duck, even ice cream. ("Continental cuisine"? What's that?)

Another culinary trend is "regional" cooking (inspired by "country-style" cuisines in rural regions, usually of America, France, and Italy). This means you'll find homey comfort foods like polenta, white beans, potatoes, risotto, braised lamb, and roast chicken even in very formal establishments. A growing trend in dining *style* is the sharing of several dishes at one table. Taking their cue from Chinese and European country-style restaurants, places like LuLu and Mecca encourage family-style service, where patrons share a few platters and serve themselves as they please. At tapas and antipasti bars, as well as at restaurants like Fog City Diner, customers order from a list of small plates. This way, even a party of two can try the asparagus *and* the mussels *and* the portabello fritters.

Any room for dessert? Currently, polished versions of American sweets—sundaes and parfaits, brownies and devil's food cake, blackberry and apple crumbles—seem to be preferred at eateries of every stripe. Usually a silky crème brulée (Meyer lemon, perhaps, or vanilla bean) and a refreshing granita, sorbet, or cold fruit soup are thrown in for good measure. Small plates of cookies and/or candy are often options as well.

Food fashion aside, every taqueria and trattoria, every bistro and sushi bar is aiming to distinguish itself from the pack and to please its patrons. Ultimately, experimentation with cuisines and ingredients can be considered successful only if it tastes good.

—Julia Dillon

Prices:
Per person, excluding tax, tip, and drinks:
$ = under $12; $$ = $12 - 25; $$$; $25 - 45; $$$$ = over $45

RESTAURANTS

Absinthe

Hayes Valley 398 Hayes St. (Gough);
415-551-1590 **$$$**

A bustling spot on weekend evenings—
especially during the symphony's season—
Absinthe is a good rendez-vous point for
people who work (or party) late. Modeled
on a Left Bank cafe, Absinthe offers a con-
genial atmosphere, pretty wicker chairs in
the windowside bar area, warm red walls,
and plenty of vintage absinthe posters, too.
Best to stick with the roast chicken (though
it's a bit overpriced) or a cocktail and a few
of the salty bar snacks. But those glittery
vests the bartenders wear have *got* to go.

Acquerello

Polk Gulch 1722 Sacramento St. (Polk);
415-567-5432 **$$$$**

At this highly regarded restaurant, the tal-
ented chef and knowledgeable maitre d'
present exceptional dishes covering a range
of regional Italian cuisines. You might start
with tortiglioni with foie gras and black
truffles, or a more rustic wild boar sausage
with greens.

Angkor Wat

Richmond 4217 Geary (Sixth Ave.);
415-221-7887 **$$**

The French-trained chef at this serene
Cambodian restaurant impresses diners
with specialties like lemongrass-charbroiled
rabbit and banana blossoms in lime.

Antica Trattoria

Polk Gulch 2400 Polk (Union);
415-928-5797 **$$**

Wonderfully simple and inexpensive Italian
food is served in this crowded, underdeco-
rated but nonetheless appealing trattoria.

Be forewarned that Antica can get noisy, a
few of the servers have accents thicker than
a manicotti, and you're almost sure to wait
even with a reservation, but the friendly
staff will win you over when they serve you
that free glass of wine for waiting. And if
that doesn't work, the seasonal appetizers
and soul-satisfying pastas and entrees will.

Aqua

Financial District 252 California St.
(Front); 415-956-9662 **$$$ - $$$$**

With its airy, mirrored dining room and so-
phisticated menu, this stylish restaurant has
earned many kudos for highly original
seafood dishes made from the freshest fish
—some local and some flown in specially.
Your starter might be black mussel soufflé,
and your entrée an Idaho trout with foie
gras and chanterelles. Maine lobster is usu-
ally available, too; at Aqua it might come
with smoked sturgeon ravioli. Heavenly
desserts are arranged with a Bauhaus flair.

Avenue 9

Inner Sunset 1243 Ninth Ave. (Lincoln);
415-664-6999 **$$**

This narrow storefront is perfect for a casual, yet high-end and hearty dinner. A ban-
quette bench with closely placed tables
lines one wall, a bar and exhibition kitchen
the other. Look for New American dishes
such as hanger steak, warm prawn and
spinach salad, and duck confit. Brunch is
served daily, as well.

Betelnut Peiju Wu

Marina 2030 Union St. (Buchanan);
415-929-8855 **$$**

Lines of "Friends" types stretch out the
door of this boisterous eatery. The small

plates of various Asian specialties can be wonderful (such as the spicy house-curied anchovies) but the kitchen, though admirably flexible, can be inconsistent, and the decor verges on fast-foodish. Nonetheless, the prices are good, and the housemade ale and rice lager are better. Go late at night for a nosh and brew.

Bix

Financial District 56 Gold St.
(Montgomery); 415-433-6300 $$$
Housed in a historic building on a side street sandwiched by Jackson and Pacific, this 1940s-style supper club offers classic American dishes like steak tartare and grilled pork chops with greens. Service is truly Old School: waiters toss salads, assemble various appetizers, and shake martinis tableside on a tableclothed cart. Comfortable banquettes line the second floor mezzanine, allowing diners to watch the clubby shenanigans of the management-consultant types at the bar.

Bizou

South of Market 598 Fourth St.
(Brannan); 415-543-2222 $$
Hard to miss the huge, square lettering painted on the yellow corner building which stands but a hundred feet from a freeway entrance. But step inside and you enter another world. This warm (if often noisy) bistro features the robust food of Provence, and sometimes beyond. The varied menu is always appealing and reasonably priced. Batter-fried green beans with fig sauce are the way to kick off a meal here; follow with the signature braised beef cheek. Chef Loretta Keller knows what she's doing.

Boulevard

Embarcadero South 1 Mission St.
(Steuart); 415-543-6084 $$ - $$$
With a sumptuous Art Nouveau interior (by San Francisco restaurant designer Pat Kuleto) and sweeping views, this lively restaurant features Nancy Oakes's impressive brand of seasonal American cuisine. Recent dishes have included foie gras with cider and black peppercorn sauce; scallops with potato-lobster-shrimp strudel; and spit-roasted, cider-cured pork loin with figs. If anyone has ever had a bad dinner here, I don't know about it. Housed in the 1889 Audiffred Building, the velvety, hyper-stylized dining room contains a colorful mosaic floor in the bar area, cushy chairs, dark wood trim, flowery 1920s-style metal work, and ornate ceiling light fixtures which emanate a warm glow.

BOULEVARD

Bruno's

Mission 2389 Mission St. (21st St.);
415-550-7455 $$ - $$$
One of the first groovy nightspots on what is now a solidly hippified stretch of Mission

Street. The richly flavored menu offered in the dining room manages to compete with the bar one room over and the band playing two rooms over: roasted sea bass comes with fennel risotto and spring artichokes, braised oxtails with parsnip mashed potatoes. Once a 1950s family-style Italian restaurant, the decor of Bruno's was left largely unchanged when it reopened. The red leather banquettes, glass brick, dark paneling, and huge sign outdoors are straight off a Scorsese movie set.

Café Bastille

Financial District 22 Belden Pl. (Pine); 415-986-5673 $

Situated on a quiet street in the middle of downtown is this French bistro, which offers delicious niçoise salads and pizzas. Office workers enjoy the outside tables at lunch. Live jazz some nights.

Café Claude

Union Square 7 Claude Ln. (Bush); 415-392-3505 $ - $$

Like Café Bastille, this Parisian sidewalk cafe is tucked away on a narrow street in the Financial District, and attracts the office crowd for lunch. A younger set shows up on nights when jazz musicians perform. The owner brought the zinc-topped bar (along with the rest of the interior) from Paris.

Cafe Jacqueline

North Beach 1454 Grant Ave. (Green); 415-981-5565 $$

All soufflés, all the time. In the back of this small, romantic storefront eatery, Jacqueline whips up the eggs for the soufflés du jour, then whips up more for the dessert soufflés du jour. These are temperamental

treats—and so is the service at times—so if you need to leave the table, be sure to hurry back. Cause your server to wait, pancetta-and-asparagus soufflé in hand, and he will greet your return to the table with a contemptuous glare.

Caffe Delle Stelle

Civic Center/Hayes Valley 395 Hayes St. (Gough); 415-252-1110 $ - $$

Almost always crowded, this Italian corner bistro in Hayes Valley features inventive pasta dishes with a Tuscan accent. The room is bright and upbeat, and closely packed tables add to the sense that you're at a lively party. And although the kitchen uses deluxe ingredients such as truffle oil and chanterelles, a meal here is surprisingly affordable.

Caffe Macaroni

North Beach 59 Columbus (Jackson); 415-956-9737 $$

The lively atmosphere and enthusiastic service here guarantee a delightful lunch or dinner. The jovial brothers who own this *tiny* Southern Italian spot serve up fabulous antipasti and tasty homemade pastas in record time. You won't leave hungry. But if you're claustrophobic and taller than four foot three, don't let them seat you upstairs.

Campton Place

Union Square 340 Stockton St. (Post); 415-781-5555 $$$$

At this serene, elegant hotel restaurant, chef Todd Humphries conjures savory, flawless entrées such as grilled rouget and turbot with celery root puree in artichoke broth. Try the sumptuous Sunday brunch, or indulge in a quiet dinner for two. The tables are well spaced, the atmosphere quiet, the service perfect.

CAMPTON PLACE

Cha Cha Cha

Upper Haight 1801 Haight St. (Shrader).;
415-386-5758 $ - $$

The music's always going and the crowd is always hopping at this crazily colorful Central American tropical restaurant, where plates of tapas please the palate. Try the Cajun shrimp, plantains, or spicy calamari. And sangria. Plenty of it. After all, everyone else is having it—but remember that what goes down like Hawaiian punch tonight packs a different punch tomorrow.

CHA CHA CHA

Cypress Club

Financial District 500 Jackson St.
(Montgomery); 415-296-8555 $$$

In this spacious and festive Jackson Square bar/brasserie, the stylized murals and unusual furnishings form a kind of Cubist hallucination of women and, well, chickens. Plates look eccentric too, but the food itself relies on fresh ingredients, prepared simply. "San Francisco brasserie" entrées include dishes like venison chop with winter potatoes, black trumpet mushrooms, and huckleberries. Some folks come here to drink a glass of wine with gossipy friends.

CYPRESS CLUB

Delancey Street

Embarcadero South 600 Embarcadero
(Brannan); 415-512-5179 $$ - $$$

This waterfront restaurant is part of a highly successful halfway house rehabilitation program and a source of pride and strength for the Delancey Street residents who staff the kitchen. The varied ethnic and regional backgrounds of the cooks are revealed in the wide range of specialties on offer here — from barbecued ribs to grilled ahi to Thai stir-fry to salmon mousse.

Ebisu

Inner Sunset 1283 Ninth Ave. (Irving);
415-566-1770 $$
Sushi-lovers in the know come here, order a sake, and wait (you *will* wait) outside for fresh and reasonably priced house maki specialties like the "Tootsie Roll." Try a "Pink Cadillac"—raw scallops wrapped in saba (salmon). A huge draw here is the boisterous sushi team: by evening's end, they've downed several glasses of Kirin each, and joked, toasted, and/or flirted with everyone at the sushi bar.

Ecco

South of Market 101 South Park
(2nd St.); 415-495-3291 $$
Set in the charming South Park neighborhood, this refined Italian eatery lets diners select interesting variations on classic dishes, say a carpaccio of salmon served with marscapone and red caviar. Order the antipasto platter and a ravioli dish to share. In addition to being very reasonably priced, Ecco is quiet enough to allow for proper conversation—a somewhat unusual feature in this town.

Enrico's

North Beach 504 Broadway (Kearny);
415-982-6223 $$
Although this open air cafe (kept warm with floor and space heaters) is better known for its history and jazz, the flavorful salads, pizzas, and cockles and mussels are great, too. Don't miss the Aviation cocktail, born in Havana in the 1930s.

Eos

Cole Valley 901 Cole St. (Carl);
415-566-3063 $$$

With a spare, airy interior and lots of windows, this corner restaurant offers Asian-accented, flavorful, and extremely *colorful* food. Unlike most San Francisco chefs, Alfred Wong likes garnish—that's an understatement—and portions tend to be large. Wong might marinate pork in soy and ginger, or duck in tea, then roast it to a perfect, succulent rareness. If venison's available, order it. The adjacent wine bar shares the kitchen, and the hip but unassuming servers know their stuff and enjoy their job, too. An impressive list of wines is sold by the glass, making this a favorite haunt for Cole Valley wine buffs.

FARALLON

Farallon

Union Square 450 Post St. (Mason);
415-956-6969 $$$ - $$$$
Pat Kuleto designed this aquatic wonderland of a restaurant inside an old mosaic-ceilinged swimming pool. He built another floor above the pool, and then decorated or accented every square inch of the place with oceanic-themed objects—sea urchin and jellyfish lamps, a kelp lighting column, shell-like ceiling, octopus bar stools, you name it. But the seafood-dominated menu

(surprise!) can be just as spectacular. One recent appetizer was a sea urchin shell filled with crab, truffled mashed potatoes, and orange salmon caviar; one entree, seared scallops with lobster, fennel nage, and celery root. Oysters, house-made caviars, and house-smoked fish are always available.

Firefly
Noe Valley 4288 24th St. (Douglass); 415-821-7652 $$$

An instant hit among locals, this neighborhood prize strikes a perfect balance: intriguing, wide-ranging, and well-executed dishes like Thai-spiced salmon cakes, and gumbo with duck breast. The country-style decor makes patrons feel welcome and relaxed.

Fleur de Lys *French* $$$$
Union Square 777 Sutter St. (Jones); 415-673-7779

Fleur de Lys has a solid reputation as one of the city's very best French restaurants. Underneath a ceiling dramatically draped in richly colored, hand-painted fabric, diners relish starters like cold cucumber soup with vodka sorbet and caviar. The tasting menus (one for omnivores, one for vegetarians) offer bite-sized treasures. Servers are eager to please, but can be disorganized.

Flying Saucer
Mission 1000 Guerrero St. (22nd St.); 415-641-9955 $$$ - $$$$

Inventive combinations of feisty flavors come almost bizarrely arranged on every plate. Chef Albert Tordjman may be part Escoffier and part Dali, but he is *very* contemporary and *very* much his own person, culinarily and otherwise. This groovy restaurant, with its quirky decor—you can

picture Ming the Merciless living here—is extremely popular, so make a reservation.

Flytrap
South of Market 606 Folsom (Second St.); 415-243-0580 $$ - $$$

Looking for San Francisco's olden golden days? Hankering for hangtown fry, celery Victor, calf's brains? Flytrap is hopping at lunch; your grandfather would have loved it. Should you prefer something a little more current, the fresh fish and pastas are good, too.

Fog City Diner
Embarcadero North 1300 Battery St.; 415-982-2000 $$$

At this always crowded (and often noisy) restaurant at the foot of Telegraph Hill, the chrome and paneling recall a 1940s train diner car, not a highway burger joint—but you *can* order a chili dog. The kitchen puts a spin on a range of American regional fare: try the Maryland crabcakes with sherry-cayenne mayonnaise, along with Southwest-inspired cornsticks with red pepper.

42 Degrees
Outer Mission/China Basin 235 16th St. (Third St.); 415-777-5558 $$$

Chef-owner James Moffat's restaurant on the bay feels industrial but personable — concrete floors, yes, but giant, curvy banquettes too. Moffat draws from cuisines practiced at Western Europe's 42-degree latitude (Provençal, Southern Italian, et al.) for hearty dishes like grilled salmon with white beans and chanterelles. Live jazz at night and a chic atmosphere draw in the evening crowd; the eatery's large patio is the preferred spot for weekday lunch.

42 DEGREES

Fringale

South of Market 570 Fourth St. (Bryant); 415-543-0573 **$$$**

At this comfortable, cheerful eatery, Basque chef Gerald Hirigoyen showcases the savory dishes of southwestern France, emphasizing their warming Gallic appeal: duck confit comes with toasted walnuts and mashed potatoes, and Roquefort ravioli is spiked with basil and pine nuts. Though some find this bistro too crowded with tables, the yellow and pale-wood decor make most patrons feel they're miles from the very busy SoMa boulevard outside. Fringale manages to balance sophisticated food, excellent service, moderate prices, and a warm, upbeat atmosphere.

Globe

Jackson Square 290 Pacific Ave. (Battery); 415-391-4132 **$$**

Joseph Manzaro runs the kitchen at this insider favorite. Exposed brick walls, wood banquettes, and grey and black paintings.

You may recognize employees from other local restaurants: the kitchen's late hours—12 on weekdays, 1 on weekends—attracts people from the food biz. The menu usually features classic salads (served in thick ceramic bowls) such as salad Lyonnais; there's often delicious smoked salmon, tasty pastas, and a homey pork or beef entree.

Gordon's House of Fine Eats

Potrero Hill 500 Florida (Mariposa); 415-861-8900 **$$-$$$**

Set in an up-and-coming quarter of the Mission District/Potrero Hill area, this spacious supper club offers a playful range of options: the menu is divided into "Comfort," "Luxury," "Healthful," "Local Showcase," and "Continental." Fried chicken, caviar, and asparagus spring rooms could easily crowd the same table. While this sounds gimmicky (OK, maybe it is), the kitchen's great attention and creativity is evident in every dish. The largely industrial-looking dining room is accented with exposed chromey pipes; brightly colored, non-functional—um—"wall-fins;" and dark wood beams and tables.

Greens

Marina Fort Mason, Building A; 415-771-6222 **$$ - $$$**

Affiliated with the Green Gulch Zen Center, this airy converted warehouse right on the water is the city's most established vegetarian restaurant: Greens has changed many a food-snobby San Franciscan's negative opinion on meat-free dining. (Vegans note: dairy and eggs are used liberally.) Have a brunch of asparagus omelette with roasted potatoes and enjoy the lovely room with its view; you'll enjoy the view for a little while, as service can be very slow. On weeknights, an a la carte dinner is offered; prix-fixe dinners on weekends.

Harris's Steak House
Russian Hill 2100 Van Ness (Pacific); 415-673-1888 $$$

The leather upholstery and wood paneling in this steakhouse resonate with masculine vibes, even though it's run by a woman— Texan Ann Harris, the widow of Harris Ranch's Jack Harris. The aged beef, available in 26-ounce size, is incomparable.

HAWTHORNE LANE

Hawthorne Lane
South of Market 22 Hawthorne St. (Howard); 415-777-9779 $$$$

David and Anne Gingrass turned the ground floor of the Crown Point Press building into a highly acclaimed eatery. In the main dining room, Asian- and French-influenced American dishes—like seared yellowfin with hummus, maque choux, and frisée salad—are served. The smaller room features a central oval bar of satiny cherry in the center, where casual satays, pizzas, and other small plates are featured. In addition to stunning metalwork outside, warm light-

ing, and cushiony banquettes and chairs, both dining rooms boast gorgeous Crown Point prints by the likes of Sol LeWitt, Frank Stella, and Robert Kushner.

Hayes Street Grill
Civic Center 320 Hayes St. (Gough); 415-863-5545 $$ - $$$

This Hayes Valley standby has been a reliable choice for seafood for years. The concept is simple: your choice of fish (of the dozen or so listed on the blackboard) grilled and served with your choice of sauce (from tomatillo salsa to Szechuan peanut sauce).

Hong Kong Flower Lounge
Richmond 5322 Geary (18th Ave.); 415-668-8998 $$

This highly acclaimed San Francisco outpost of Alice Wong's Hong Kong restaurant features excellent Cantonese soups and seafood—ask the waiter if there's any fresh rock cod. Order pea shoots if they're available; and if you've ever had Beijing-style roast duck, see if the one served here isn't better. It will be.

Jardinière
Civic Center 300 Grove St. (Franklin); 415-861-5555 $$$$

Traci des Jardins opened this sparkly two-story restaurant near the symphony and opera to rave reviews. The two-level dining room centers around a circular marble and mahogany bar; the ceiling above centers around a gold dome with tiny stars—like an upside down glass of champagne. Expect luxurious and extremely flavorful food here: des Jardins reveals her French sensibility in dishes such as a terrine of foie gras and a roast chicken with chanterelles and sweet

RESTAURANTS

corn. Jardinière also boasts a cheese-aging room, sumptuous desserts, extensive list of wines by the glass, and a lively yet elegant atmosphere.

JARDINIERE

Kuleto's
Union Square 221 Powell St. (Geary); 415-397-7720 $$ - $$$
Chef Bob Helstrom cures the prosciutto and makes the mozzarella, vinegar, and bread served in this lively Italian restaurant, beautifully designed by Pat Kuleto and housed in the Villa Florence Hotel. You might enjoy snacking on an antipasta of grilled radicchio and pancetta while sitting at the inviting mahogany bar, which graced the old Palace Hotel before the 1906 quake.

La Folie
Russian Hill 2316 Polk St. (Union); 415-776-5577 $$$$
Beneath the clouds painted on the ceiling at this lovely yet light-hearted French restaurant, Roland Passot and his wife present plates arranged fancifully into swirls and towers. The food may look eccentric, but Passot's contemporary cooking makes perfect sense on the tongue: a salad of porcini

mushrooms, slivers of yellowfin potatoes, frisee, and black truffle; an entree of roast quail with foie gras and wild fall mushrooms; and a Meyer lemon and cranberry terrine in raspberry coulis to finish. Reserve ahead.

LA FOLIE

Liberty Cafe
Bernal Heights 410 Cortland (Bennington); 415-695-8777 $$
Cathi Guntli (formerly of Zuni Cafe) combined a yellow and wedgewood blue decor and high-end all-American fare to make this neighborhood storefront a perfect place to meet your sister and her two-year-old. A pile of lightly steamed asparagus comes with buttery crumbs and quail eggs; the chicken pot pie is organic comfort food extraordinaire. No reservations are taken, and you're likely to wait—most Bernal residents love this place.

LuLu
South of Market 816 Folsom St. (Fourth St.) 415-495-5775 $$
Under the impressive barrel-vaulted ceiling of this converted warehouse, waiters in neckties and blue jeans sprint back and

forth bearing platters of chicken cooked on the open rotisserie, hot skillets full of mussels, and generous salads. Portion size may make up for the sometimes less-than-perfect food; you might choose to join the sleek San Franciscans sipping cosmopolitans at the bar, where the cocktails are reliably perfect. Bookending LuLu are the more intimate **LuLu Bis** ($$$) a long narrow room where patrons often order from the prix-fixe menu (try the artichoke and fava bean salad), and the informal **LuLu Cafe** ($$), which is open all day and offers oysters and light meals such as pizzettas.

CHEFS REED HEARON (LEFT) AND
JODY DENTON (RIGHT) AT LULU

Masa's

Union Square 648 Bush St. (Powell);
415-989-7154 $$$$

Invariably listed among the Bay Area's top restaurants, Masa's oozes indulgence. Each artfully presented course is complex and richly flavored—without making you feel the chef is screaming to be noticed. All of San Francisco cried when Las Vegas stole chef Julian Serrano away, but regulars say the current staff has lived up to Masa's legendary reputation. Service is attentive in the extreme: one diner claims that when

she dropped her salad fork, a waiter caught it in mid-air with his left hand while placing a fresh utensil on the table with his right. A fantastic dining experience is guaranteed.

Mecca

Castro 2029 Market St. (Dolores);
415-621-7000 $$ - $$$

Smack dab in bustling Duboce Triangle is the industrial exterior of this ultra-hip, velvety supper club. Dim, plush alcoves surround the central circular bar; a dj spins soul at a raised booth; and flirtatious patrons and bartenders go at it. Dishes tend to be on the rich side, and prices, especially for drinks, may be a tad high—but you might think of the extra cash as a cover charge. The food here is robust enough to compete with the atmosphere. Do go to Mecca prepared for sensory overload.

The Meetinghouse

Pacific Heights 1701 Octavia St. (Bush);
415-922-6733 $$$

Husband and wife chef-owners John Bryant Snell and Joanna Karlinsky emphasize unpretentious, but complex American regional cuisine in this lovely 40-seat restaurant, sparely furnished with cherry wood in Shaker style. One recent menu featured hominy-crusted catfish with black-eyed peas and smoked tomato stew, as well as roasted duck breast with wild rice and apple fritters.

Millennium

Civic Center 246 McAllister St. (Hyde);
415-487-9800 $$

If you're a vegan looking for a night out, a vegetarian who's eaten over a dozen times at Greens, or an omnivore looking for a change of pace, try this upmarket restaurant near the new library. Sophisticated vegan food like portobello mushrooms with Moroccan spice, as well as macrobiotic stews. Dairy items (parmesan for your Caesar) are provided on request.

Moose's

North Beach 1652 Stockton St. (Union); 415-989-7800 $$

Frisco socialite/restaurateur Ed Moose has proved able to attract the famous and powerful to the white tablecloths of his Washington Square Italian/Mediterranean brasserie, where items like gnocchi and risotti are consistently good.

One Market

Financial District 1 Market St. (Steuart); 415-777-5577 $$$

Bradley Ogden at this huge, often noisy, two-tiered brasserie, where the accent is on updated American classics: from grilled boneless quail with warm potato salad and white truffle to Ogden's signature Yankee pot roast with roasted winter vegetables.

Osome

Cow Hollow 3145 Fillmore St. (Greenwich); 415-931-8898 $$ - $$$

Come here for impeccably fresh sushi, but you'll have to select from over 40 choices. These sushi chefs take pride in their creations. An unusual beef roll of sliced sirloin wrapped around Asian chives nicely complements sashimi.

Pacific

Union Square 500 Post St. (Mason); 415-771-8600 $$$

At the Pan Pacific Hotel's attractive restaurant, the chef emphasizes local produce with his classically French, yet unpretentious cooking style. Perhaps because it's hidden away on the third floor, not many residents have discovered this place. Reasonable prix-fixe dinners.

Palio D'Asti

Financial District 640 Sacramento St. (Battery); 415-395-9800 $$$

At lunchtime, this restaurant fills up with downtown professionals who come for the Italian regional cuisine of Gianni Fassio (former chef at the landmark Blue Fox). Try an antipasti of salmon cured in grappa, then Piedmontese braised duck. But no dinner is served, to the chagrin of many.

PASTIS

Pastis

Embarcadero North 1015 Battery St. (Green); 415-391-2555 $$ - $$$

When Fringale's chef-owner Gerald Hirigoyen opened this bright bistro near Levi Plaza, he met with instant success for his signature Basque-influenced French dishes, this time executed with a simpler and more summery touch. A starter of roasted piquillos (the red peppers native to Navarre, near Hirigoyen's birthplace) might come with chèvre, zucchini, and basil; crispy striped bass could sit atop shredded cucumber with lemon and coriander.

PlumpJack Cafe

Marina 3127 Fillmore St. (Filbert);
415-563-4755 **$$ - $$$**

A warm, romantic atmosphere and fantastic food for the price make this bistro a local favorite. Adding to its popularity is the fact that it's owned by a few Getty boys and Gavin Newsom, a city supervisor and eligible socialite bachelor. Mussels in lemongrass broth are subtle perfection; you'll also appreciate the very reasonable wine prices (bottles come from the affiliated shop next door).

Postrio

Union Square 545 Post St. (Taylor);
415-776-7825 **$$$$**

Wolfgang Puck opened this San Francisco venue—a three-level number frequented by local and visiting glitterati. You really can't go wrong with the food here... Asian-Mediterranean hybrids never misfire, and a classic seared foie gras will be perfect, too. Although the large, modern dining room is extremely comfortable, and there are some impressive paintings, it does feel a bit L.A.-ish; still, Postrio's service and cuisine suit San Franciscans *just fine.* The bar serves pizzas and other appetizers past midnight.

Red Herring

Embarcadero South 155 Steuart St. (Mission); 415-495-6500 **$$**

Seafood, seafood, and more seafood... This inviting waterfront eatery. Floor-to-ceiling windows allow views of the Bay Bridge and Embarcadero; another more intimate room is decorated in mahogany and soft browns. The "Raw and Not" Bait Bar menu lists fresh cold seafood, shucked or very simply prepared. The internationally eclectic (and moderately priced) entrees range from a salmon tagine to a tandoori snapper to a tuna "steak au poivre."

Ritz-Carlton

Nob Hill 600 Stockton St. (Pine);
415-296-7465

The exquisite **Dining Room ($$$$)** rates high for its opulent decor and superior service (it is the Ritz, after all), but especially for the complex, memorable food served here. The kitchen, headed by former Le Cirque chef Sylvain Portay, transforms perfect ingredients into intriguing dishes redolent with flavor. Formulate your own prix-fixe meal from the seasonal menu. A little more casual is the **Terrace ($$ - $$$)** which offers one of the best brunches in town: on fair days you can sit on the patio and listen to live jazz while enjoying a salad of, say, warm scallops and prawns with spinach and avocado in a ginger-sesame dressing; or check out the buffet. Dinner is also served here.

Rose Pistola

North Beach 532 Columbus (Stockton);
415-399-0499 **$$ - $$$**

At this popular trattoria, chef Reed Hearon serves what's best described as North Beach cuisine. Like the cooking of early North Beach immigrants, the cuisine here is Ligurian—which means that plenty of garlic, lemon, and olives are used. The menu also offers neighborhood classics such as a wonderful cioppino—the hearty seafood stew. Don't miss the cured fish (anchovies will never taste the same) or the rabbit. Other dishes can be a little haphazard, and the servers indifferent to their customers. One plus is that the bright dining room, done in wood and colorful tile, is open past 12 on weekends.

Rubicon
Financial District 558 Sacramento St. (Sansome); 415-434-4100 $$$$
Because it's owned by Robin Williams, Robert DeNiro, and Francis Ford Coppola (who named this spot for the red wine blend produced at his winery) some might think Rubicon might be an elitist Planet Hollywood. But chef Scott Newman's the star here. Dishes like roast duck are out of this world. (Prices are, too, but you pay to rub elbows with stars.)

Rumpus
Union Square 1 Tillman Pl. (Grant); 415-421-2300 $$ - $$$
Excellent New American dishes like veal chops, lamb shanks, and roast chicken, presented with unintimidating sophistication. Great wine list and reasonable prices, especially for this neighborhood.

The Slanted Door $
Mission 584 Valencia (17th St.); 415-861-8032
The high-ceilinged dining room here is spare but warm, thanks to color-stained wood, strategically placed crushed velvet cushioning, and a neo-French Colonial cast-iron balcony. The Vietnamese cuisine,

executed with a California sensibility, is nothing less than delightful. All of the curries, full of sweet potatoes and other vegetables, and eggplant simmered in coconut are amazing, especially at these prices and in this setting. Roast duck is not to be missed.

THE SLANTED DOOR

Slow Club
Potrero Hill 2501 Mariposa St. (Hampshire); 415-241-9390 $ - $$
While this dimly lit, industrial-style restaurant on the corner attracts mostly the neighborhood, it's increasingly drawing crowds from further afield. On those rare warm evenings, this is the perfect spot to sit outisde for a drink and yummy antipasto.

South Park Café
South of Market 108 South Park; 415-495-7275 $$ - $$$
In the green oasis of South Park, this bistro serves simple French country food in a casual, comfortable setting. On nice days, the rather hip clientele sits outside to eat onion soup or sweetbreads with baby greens.

Suppenküche
Hayes Valley 601 Hayes St. (Buchanan); 415-252-9289 $$

Who'd expect German food to be so cool? This corner spot in fashiony Hayes Valley, with its boarding-house tables, wooden benches, and nearly art-free white walls, is like a Calvinist clubhouse. Except the pared-down German food is authentic and thoroughly modern at the same time, and the crowd is nothing less than way hip. Gravlax, sauerbraten, spaetzle are all delicious, but you might go just to sample a few of the many German beers on tap.

Tadich Grill

Financial District 240 California St. (Battery); 415-391-2373 $$$

To many second- or third-generation natives (and some tourists), this near 150-year-old restaurant, with its wooden booths and veteran waiters, defines old-time San Francisco. Straightforward, high-quality seafood, along with sourdough bread and a heavy dose of Gilded Age nostalgia.

Thanh Long

Sunset 4101 Judah St. (46th Ave.); 415-665-1146 $ - $$

Local word-of-mouth recommendations for Vietnamese restaurants always include this family-run outpost (the An family also own Crustacean restaurant) not far from Ocean Beach. Dungeness crab, cooked with garlic and ginger, is the specialty here.

Thep Phanom

Lower Haight 400 Waller St. (Fillmore); 415-431-2526 $ - $$

Those in the know come here for "Weeping Lady," a fantastic eggplant and chicken dish, or anything based on roast duck. The soups are also delicious; most locals name it as their favorite Thai eatery. Not many reasonably priced, non-fusion Asian restaurants have been praised in *Gourmet,* but Thep Phanom has.

Tommy Toy's Haute Cuisine Chinoise

Financial District 655 Montgomery St. (Washington); 415-397-4888 $$$$

This extremely upmarket Chinese restaurant is famous for entrées like whole lobster with peppercorn sauce on angel-hair pasta. The elegantly presented but rather straightforward food may not justify these prices, but the gleaming surfaces and attentive service exude luxury. Well-spaced tables allow plenty of privacy when you want to make a call from your mobile phone.

RESTAURANT AT 2223 MARKET

2223 Market

Castro 2223 Market St. (Sanchez); 415-431-0692 $$ - $$$

Also known as "No Name," this elegantly spare but comfortable eatery draws many Castro residents, who wait, Stoli martini in hand, to get seated in the rather loud dining area. Entrees like roast pork are wonderful, and salads—Thai shrimp salad, or a classic Caesar—are paid equal attention, a plus for those eating light. You *might* be

RESTAURANTS

able to find someone who doesn't look like he reads *Details*—but I'll bet he gets *Architectural Digest.*

Universal Cafe
Potrero Hill 2814 19th St. (Florida); 415-821-4608 $$ - $$$

Another in the dimly lit, industrial decor category, but this one's quieter and more intimate than its colleagues. Chef Julia McClaskey has made this bistro a major magnet for the slick-and-foodie crowd. Snack on the flat bread appetizer with caramelized onions, but definitely save room for large portions of smoked trout salad, filet mignon, grilled halibut, or pretty much anything coming out of the kitchen.

Woods
Financial District 600 Montgomery St. (Clay); 415-433-7250 $$$ - $$$$

This toney yet welcoming two-level restaurant at the base of the Transamerica Pyramid affords views of the redwood grove outside (hence the name) and, straight up, of the striking skyscraper itself. Locals and the occasional celeb come here for upscale regional American fare, or sit in the nouveau-clubby tavern upstairs for more casual versions of same—say, grilled salmon on house-baked bread.

Waterfront Restaurant & Cafe
Embarcadero Pier 7, The Embarcadero; 415-391-2696 $$$

Chef Bruce Hill, one of the city's fusion cuisine innovators, transformed this old standby on the Embarcadero into a destination seafood restaurant. A recent dinner entree was roast Atlantic salmon roulade with sweet corn, black-eyed peas, and shiitake mushrooms served with Chinese celery. In the more casual, less expensive cafe downstairs, wood-fired pizzas and grilled rib-eye are available, but so are dishes such as felafel-crusted seabass in sumac yogurt sauce.

Woodward's Gardens
Mission 1700 Mission St. (Duboce); 415-621-7122 $$$

Despite an urban no-man's-land location, foodies and locals in-the-know flock to this intimate and rather chic eatery, the creation of veteran chefs Dana Tomassino and Margie Conrad. In the shadow of the freeway at a busy intersection, Woodward's Gardens is named for the formal garden that was planted here in the 19th century (note archival images on wall). Dishes like broiled tangerine with gorgonzola and almost any fresh fish are beautifully presented, and less expensive than they'd be elsewhere in town. Make reservations: nine tables and four seatings per night.

CHEF MARGIE CONRAD AT WOODWARD'S GARDENS

XYZ
South of Market 181 Third St.
(Howard); 415-777-5300 $$$
Housed in the chic W Hotel is this plush, smallish dining room, where French California cuisine is given a little Asian twist. The seared scallops are to die for, and other seafood entrees are wonderful. Save room for dessert, as there are too many consistently delicious ones for your table to order just one or two. Get at least three.

Yank Sing
Financial District 427 Battery St.; 415-362-1640
South of Market 49 Stevenson St.; 415-495-4510 $ - $$
Both locations of this relatively upscale teahouse fill quickly at lunchtime with fans of this restaurant's house specialty, dim sum.

YoYo Bistro
Japantown 1611 Post St. (Laguna); 415-922-7788 $$$
This nouvelle bistro features entrées such as crisp-skinned salmon with wild mushrooms and gingered parsnip puree, but the staff is most proud of its menu of "tsumami" (snacks to accompany cocktails): oysters come with wasabi vinaigrette or tomato lemongrass gelee.

Zarzuela
Russian Hill 2000 Hyde St. (Union); 415-436-0800 $$
More authentic (if pricier) than the city's other tapaterias, this attractive, popular storefront offers plates of octopus (thankfully less oily than you'd find in Madrid),

marinated mushrooms, and Spanish tortilla. Plus a seafood-stocked paella.

Zax
North Beach 2330 Taylor St.
(Columbus); 415-563-6266 $$$
Zax has many a fan across San Francisco. The small, casual room allows for good conversation, and the kitchen's light California/Mediterranean cuisine never seems to miss. The goat-cheese soufflé is a specialty that patrons swear by.

Zuni Café
Civic Center 1658 Market St. (Rose); 415-552-2522 $$ - $$$
Excellent service, moderate prices, terrific cocktails, and an informal yet tony atmosphere make this a favorite spot for San Franciscans. The expertly prepared food is never precious. Choose from an impressive list of oysters, then order Caesar salad or roast chicken with Tuscan bread salad.

ZUNI CAFE

RESTAURANTS

WORTH THE TRIP
RESTAURANTS AROUND THE BAY

Bay Wolf

Oakland 3853 Piedmont (Rio Vista)
(510) 655-6004 $$$

The talented kitchen staff at this quiet, unpretentious restaurant do outstanding interpretations of various Mediterranean and regional American cuisines, changing their menu every few weeks to highlight a different cooking tradition. They might serve a duck liver flan with green peppercorns and marsala; another day, crabcakes with peanut slaw and black-eyed peas.

Bistro Ralph *California/French* $$

Healdsburg 109 Plaza St. (Healdsburg);
(707) 433-1380

Friendly and fun, with a winemaker clientele, Ralph Tingle's place pleases with an array of well-executed tony bistro dishes: try Dungeness crab ravioli, Szechuan calamari, or lamb meatloaf. Great wine list, with unusual varieties like cinsault listed.

Brava Terrace

St. Helena 3010 Hwy. 29 (Lodi Ln.);
(707) 963-9300 $$ - $$$

At this pretty bistro, diners relish flavorful French provincial cassoulets and Italian risotti while seated in the maple-floored dining room or on the lovely back terrace overlooking a creek. Great service.

Cafe Rouge

Berkeley 1782 Fourth St. (University);
510-525-1440 $$$

This airy converted warehouse is always convivial; sitting at the long bar to the left with oysters and a martini is a wonderful way to pass an hour. Meat (*red* meat) is the draw here; chef Marsha McBride works wonders with beef, pork, lamb—and with salads, fish, and poultry, too. While starters may be petite, main courses certainly are not. Accompanying California/Mediterranean vegetables are delicious as well.

Chez Panisse

Berkeley 1517 Shattuck Ave. (Cedar);
(510) 548-5525 $$$$

Chez Panisse is no less than mecca to a generation of chefs. In 1971, Alice Waters and a clowder of like-minded chefs re-invented American cuisine when they opened the doors of this Craftsman-style former home. Using only the finest organic produce and free-range meats and poultry—Waters cultivates personal relationships with free-range and organic farmers and producers in the region—the kitchen staff presents new dishes every day in their prix-fixe, preset seasonal menus. You don't have any choices (except for wine) once you sit down, but who would turn down green asparagus and spring onion risotto with black trumpet mushrooms, or grilled striped bass with black olives, white bean puree, escarole, and spinach? The dining room has a hominess to it that many prefer to glitzier, more citified establishments. Upstairs is the more affordable **Cafe at Chez Panisse** (548-5049 $$ - $$$), a simple but warm Mission oak-trimmed room where the pizzettas, pastas, salads, and grilled entrées are impeccable.

Domaine Chandon

Yountville 1 California Dr. (Hwy. 29); (707) 944-2892 $$$$

Since its arrival 20 years ago as the region's first fine restaurant, chef Philippe Jeanty has maintained impeccable standards at this sparkling-wine house. A California accent is used in French dishes such as roasted squab with wild mushrooms, fava beans, foie gras, and black Mission fig sauce.

French Laundry

Yountville 6640 Washington St. (Creek); (707) 944-2380 $$$$

Chef Thomas Keller showcases high-profile ingredients such as caviar, duck confit, and foie gras in award-winning haute cuisine. Tasteful country French decor and soft lighting are inviting; service, flawless. French Laundry has won national kudos—so make a reservation *way* ahead.

Lark Creek Inn

Larkspur 234 Magnolia St. (William) 415-924-7766 $$$

Bradley Ogden's "rural sophisticate" cooking style is featured in this attractive clapboard house, nestled in a redwood grove. Best is brunch, when you can sit on the patio or in the skylit dining room and feast on eggs with smoked salmon or wild berry flapjacks with lemon butter.

Mustard's Grill

Yountville 7399 Hwy. 29 (Yountville Cross); (707) 944-2424 $$$

The black-and-white tile floor here has been much trod upon: Cindy Pawlcyn's Mustard's is noisy and lively. Food is American country fare with a California twist: grilled rabbit, mesquite-grilled seafood, and excellent salads and soups.

Rivoli $$

Berkeley 1539 Solano Ave. (Peralta) (510) 526-2542

Superb creative Mediterranean and Italian regional cuisine is offered by chef-owners (and husband and wife) Roscoe Skipper and Wendy Brucker; and this incredibly personable pair have a very loyal following in the East Bay. Try portobello fritters with lemon aioli and arugula. Desserts are fabulous, too. Sit in the elegant back room, with its glass wall overlooking the garden and its resident raccoons and other critters.

Terra

St. Helena 1345 Railroad (Hunt) (707) 963-8931 $$$

Critics and patrons rave about this place. Chef-owner Hiro Sone combines French, Italian, and Asian cuisines in dishes like duck liver wontons with wild mushroom sauce or salmon in miso. Sone's wife, Lissa Doumani, handles the service, as well as the fantastic desserts. The dining rooms' exposed wood beams and fieldstone walls create a casual, unpretentious atmosphere.

Tra Vigne *Italian* $$$

St. Helena 1050 Charter Oak Ave. (Hwy. 29); (707) 967-4444

Inside this fieldstone former wine cellar, you'll feel warmed by the sun; at night, by the gilt trim, wood floor, and Italian tiles. After considering the house-cured pancetta and homemade mozzarella, breads, vinegars, sauces, and pastas, you might order several antipasti and pastas, then share.

P R A C T I C A L I T I E S

■ TOURIST INFORMATION

Compass American Guides makes every effort to ensure the accuracy of its information; however, as conditions and prices change frequently, we recommend that readers also contact the local visitors bureaus listed. In San Francisco, contact:

San Francisco Convention & Visitors Bureau. (415) 974-6900. Daily Events Line: (415) 391-2001. Visit the lower level of Hallidie Plaza at Powell and Market.

For information outside the city, contact:

Oakland Convention & Visitors Bureau. (510) 839-9000.

Napa Valley Conference & Visitors Bureau. (707) 226-7459.

San Jose Convention & Visitors Bureau. (800) SAN JOSE.

Sonoma County Convention & Visitors Bureau. (707) 524-7589.

■ PUBLIC TRANSPORTATION

T O   &   F R O M   A I R P O R T S

San Francisco International Airport (SFO) is just east of U.S. 101 about 14 miles south of downtown San Francisco, in San Mateo County. The terminals are built in a partial circle around a parking garage, making it easy to find your way around once you understand the layout. For the benefit of travelers caught between flights, SFO maintains a hall in the north terminal for art and museum exhibits. Call (415) 761-0800 for airport information.

For general information regarding ground transportation to and from the airport, call the **Transportation Hotline** at (800) SFO-2008. Buses run frequently to the city from dawn until midnight. The downtown airport bus terminal is located in the Tenderloin (one of the rougher sections of town, but close to Union Square); the bus also stops at the Transbay Terminal, Stonestown, and Daly City BART. Every 20 minutes from 5 A.M. to 10 P.M., the SFO Airporter bus service makes the round of downtown hotels to take passengers to the airport. Taxis and door-to-door shuttle service are also available. Check the telephone book yellow pages under "Airport Transport" for companies.

Oakland International (OAK) and San Jose International (SJC) airports offer less stressful alternatives. Oakland is handy for passengers using BART to San Francisco. San Jose is convenient for visiting Silicon Valley. Train connections from SJC to San Francisco's railroad depot are available on CalTrain. For airport information, call Oakland International at (510) 577-4000, and San Jose International at (408) 277-4759.

A R O U N D   T O W N

San Francisco's public bus and streetcar system is called MUNI. It's cheap, convenient, and relatively safe (relative to New York, for example). Exact fares are required, and passes are available. Call (415) 673-MUNI for information.

BART (Bay Area Rapid Transit) is San Francisco's small and tidy subway system, whisking commuters from downtown San Francisco to Colma along the city's southern border, and under the bay to North Concord, Richmond, and Fremont in the East Bay. You are better off riding BART than driving if your destination lies near a BART station and you're not traveling between midnight and 4 A.M. (or 6 A.M. on Saturdays, 8 A.M. on Sundays). All stations have neighborhood street maps posted. Call (415) 788-BART for information.

MUNI streetcars share four downtown stations with BART, making Embarcadero, Montgomery, Powell, and Civic Center stations the four key transfer points between intra-city and inter-city transport systems. The streetcar is a particularly interesting and easy way to ride to Golden Gate Park (the N-Judah to 9th Ave.) or the San Francisco Zoo (the L-Taraval to the end of the line). MUNI sells "Passports" to ride all streetcars, buses, and cable cars for one, three, or seven days. Passports also entitle you to discounts at the zoo and city museums. Buy them from cable car terminals at Fisherman's Wharf, Ghirardelli Square, and Hallidie Plaza; or from the Cable Car Barn or the visitors center at Hallidie Plaza.

The commercial coach terminal is south of Market in the Transbay Terminal, on Mission between First and Fremont. **CalTrain,** a commuter rail line, connects San Francisco's Townsend Street station (at Fourth) with San Jose and points between; call (800) 228-4661. **Amtrak** pulls into Oakland Station (corner of 17th and Wood streets), and runs passengers across the bay by bus; call (800) 872-7245.

F E R R I E S

Ferries, a most civilized means of transport, are limited to a few commuter routes. Golden Gate Transit ferries run to Larkspur and Sausalito in Marin County from the downtown Ferry Building. Red and White Ferries go to Angel Island, Sausalito, and Vallejo from Fisherman's Wharf. Ferry service also connects Oakland's Jack London Square and Alameda with the Ferry Building. For schedules and information, call **Golden Gate Transit** at (415) 332-6600, **Red and White** at (415) 546-2815, and the **Oakland-Alameda** ferry at (510) 522-3300.

PRACTICALITIES

CABLE CARS

The three operational lines are as follows: the **Powell-Mason Line** between Hallidie Plaza and Bay Street, near Fisherman's Wharf; the **Powell-Hyde Line** runs from Hallidie Plaza to Ghirardelli Square, via the thrilling 21.3 percent Hyde Street grade; and the **California Street Line** runs 17 blocks in a straight line along California Street from Embarcadero Center (Frost Plaza) to Van Ness Avenue. To avoid long lines boarding at any terminus, catch a car somewhere along its route, if there's room.

For a coordinated, comprehensive explanation of all the transport systems of the Bay Area, buy a copy of the San Francisco Bay Area Regional Transit Guide, published by the Metropolitan Transportation Commission. The book is available in downtown BART stations, among other places.

■ FESTIVALS & EVENTS

Late January to March (depending on lunar calendar): Chinese New Year. Firecrackers, the Miss Chinatown pageant, and the famous Chinatown parade; (415) 982-3000.

March 17: Saint Patrick's Day. Be Irish for a day: join the big parade (call 415-661-2700 for date), or hoist a few with the merrymakers at the bars.

April: Cherry Blossom Festival. Japantown celebrates the new blooms with a fair featuring traditional arts and crafts; (415) 922-6776.

Late April to May: San Francisco International Film Festival. The city's biggest cinematic event, based at the Kabuki Theater and Berkeley's Pacific Archive; (415) 931-FILM.

Easter: Easter Sunday. Sunrise service is held at dawn on Mount Davidson. Russian Orthodox Easter is colorfully celebrated at the Cathedral of the Holy Virgin, in the Richmond District.

May: Cinco de Mayo. Anniversary of the Mexican defeat of the French army at Puebla, celebrated in the Mission District around May 5 with a colorful parade and festivities; (415) 826-1401.

Late May: *San Francisco Examiner* **Bay to Breakers.** Over 100,000 runners (from international athletes to costumed joggers) participate in a $7^1/_2$-mile road race that begins at the Embarcadero and ends at Ocean Beach; (415) 777-7770.

Late May: Carnaval. Over Memorial Day weekend, the Mission District hosts San Francisco's version of Brazil's Carnaval; (415) 826-1401.

June: Ethnic Dance Festival. At the Palace of Fine Arts; (415) 474-3916.

June: Street Fairs. Neighborhood celebrations with food and arts and crafts. Haight Street's hosts big-name music acts. **Haight Street,** (415) 661-8025; **North Beach,** (415) 403-0666; **Union Street,** (415) 346-4561.

Late June: Lesbian and Gay Freedom Day. Marked by a parade down Market from Civic Center to Justin Herman Plaza, where a huge street party takes place; (415) 864-3733.

June - August: Stern Grove Midsummer Music Festival. Outdoor concerts at Sigmund Stern Grove; (415) 252-6252.

Fourth of July. Fireworks over the bay (fired from San Francisco's Aquatic Park), though the fog layer is often too low for viewers to see much.

July: San Francisco Marathon. (800) 722-3466.

July through September: San Francisco Shakespeare Festival. One play showing weekends at Golden Gate Park, San Jose's St. James Park, and Oakland's Duck Pond Meadow; (415) 666-2221.

August: Nihonmachi Street Fair. Japantown festival, with taiko drummers, arts, and crafts; (415) 922-8700.

Labor Day Weekend: À la Carte, À la Park. Fine restaurants sell samples of their wares to benefit the Shakespeare Festival; live music; (415) 383-9378.

September: Opera Season Opening. The city's premier gala event, with the opera glitterati; (415) 864-3330.

Late September: San Francisco Blues Festival. Concerts at Justin Herman Plaza and Fort Mason; (415) 979-5588.

October: Castro Street Fair. Neighborhood celebration with booths, arts, and crafts; (415) 467-3354.

October: Columbus Day. A city holiday, especially honored in the Italian community. Festivities include the blessing of the fleet, Columbus landing pageant, and parade; (415) 434-1492.

Late October to November: San Francisco Jazz Festival. Concerts throughout the city; (415) 864-5449.

November 2: Dia de los Muertos (Day of the Dead). Latino festival honoring dead ancestors, marked by dances, ethnic foods, costumes, and a parade in the Mission District; (415) 647-0224.

■ PROFESSIONAL SPORTS

San Francisco sports fans cheer the 49ers (the "Niners") in football and the Giants in baseball. Both teams play at 3Com Park (Candlestick Park). The Oakland Athletics (the "A's") and the Raiders play in the Oakland Coliseum across the bay. The Golden State Warriors basketball team bangs the boards in Oakland, but draws support from both sides of the bay.

Golden State Warriors: (510) 638-6300
Oakland Athletics: (510) 638-0500
Oakland Raiders: (800) 949-2626
San Francisco 49ers: (415) 486-2249
San Francisco Giants: (415) 467-8000
San Jose Sharks: (408) 287-7070

PRACTICALITIES

■ TOURS

BUS TOURS

Gray Line Tours. Bay Area tours; (415) 558-9400.

MUNI Tours. Public transport tours available on request; (415) 673-MUNI.

Near Escapes. Behind-the-scenes tour of San Francisco Zoo, shopping tours of SoMa, backstage theater tours, cemetery tours, etc.; (415) 386-8687.

WATER TOURS

Blue & Gold Fleet. Bay cruises; (415) 781-7890.

Golden Gate Ferry Service. Ferry service to Sausalito, Larkspur; (415) 332-6600.

Oceanic Society Expeditions. Boats leave the city and Half Moon Bay for whale watches (several hours long) during migration season (January to April); (415) 474-3385.

Red & White Fleet. Bay tours and scheduled service to Sausalito, Alcatraz, Wine Country, Tiburon, Angel Island; (415) 546-2896.

WALKING TOURS

Chinatown Adventure Tours with the Wok Wiz. Culinary and historical strolls with cookbook author and television chef Shirley Fong-Torres, with lunch or dinner. (415) 355-9657.

Chinese Culture Foundation. Culinary tour and heritage walk; (415) 986-1822.

City Guides. Architectural, cultural, and historical walking tours of City Hall, Civic Center, Coit Tower, Market Street, North Beach, Pacific Heights, fire houses, Mission District murals, Cathedral Hill, Japantown, Presidio, Jackson Square, Golden Gate Bridge, etc.; (415) 557-4266.

East Bay Regional Parks. (510) 635-0135. Ranger-led tours and activities in the parks are geared for all ages.

Frisco Tours. Film, fiction, and witty crime tours by bus or on foot with author Mark Gordon; (415) 681-5555.

Golden Gate National Recreation Area. Ranger-led interpretive walks through the parks, including Sutro Baths, Marin Headlands, Muir Woods, Tennessee Valley; tours of the Maritime Museum ships, gun batteries, tide pools; Indian folklore walks, photography walks, sunset walks, etc.; (415) 556-0560.

Helen's Walk Tours. (510) 524-4544. San Francisco neighborhood tours in English, French, Spanish, or Arabic.

Heritage Walks. (415) 441-3000. Architectural tours of Pacific Heights on Sunday afternoons.

Literary Tours. Don Herron leads a tour of Dashiell Hammett's haunts in the city, sometimes in period costume; other literary tours (e.g., Russian Hill) can be arranged (707) 939-1214.

Oakland Heritage Alliance. (510) 763-9218. Architectural and historical tours of Oakland's neighborhoods and Mountain View Cemetery.

■ PERFORMING ARTS

The Bay Area is a big center of the performing arts. Some, like the San Francisco Opera (415-864-3330), ACT (American Conservatory Theater; 415-749-2228), and the Berkeley Repertory (510-845-4700), have national reputations, but there are scores of innovative smaller companies, like the Eureka Theater, the Magic Theater, the Asian American Theater, Theater Rhinoceros, George Coates Performance Works, and the San Francisco Mime Troupe, scattered throughout the city and beyond. *Beach Blanket Babylon*, a campy, long-running musical revue, continues to play to packed houses at **Club Fugazi** in North Beach, call (415) 421-4222. If you're in the mood for a laugh, San Francisco is also famed for its comedy clubs, which nursed such national figures as Lenny Bruce, Bill Cosby, the Smothers Brothers, and Robin Williams. **Josie's Cabaret & Juice Joint** is well known for its gay-oriented comedians and performers.

San Francisco's dance aficionados like to follow the **San Francisco Ballet,** which performs at the War Memorial Opera House (415-703-9400). (While the War Memorial undergoes renovation, the ballet performs at the Yerba Buena Center for the Arts, 415-978-2787.) Other companies to follow include ODC Dance Company, Lines Contemporary Ballet, Margaret Jenkins Dance Company, Zaccho, and the Joe Goode Performance Group. These and other local companies perform at Theater Artaud, the Yerba Buena Center for the Arts, the Cowell Theater, ODC Performance Gallery, and Oakland's Laney College. Every summer, San Francisco State University hosts the **Ethnic Dance Festival,** where audiences are treated to a taste of capoeira, Balinese dance, traditional Scots folk dance, and In Berkeley, prominent national names in dance as well as music can be found at the University of California's **Zellerbach Hall;** call Cal Performances (510) 642-9988.

The **San Francisco Symphony** (415-431-5400) season runs from September through May. The **California Palace of the Legion of Honor** arranges regular concerts of classical music, including demonstrations of antique forms and instruments, as well as lectures. In the fall, **Jazz in the City** asks jazz musicians of every stripe—bebop, Latin, fusion—to play at venues throughout San Francisco. The Asian Art Museum hosts an annual **Asian American Jazz Festival.** Blues, jazz, folk, country and ethnic music, including Irish bands and Beijing opera, spice the mix.

New releases play nightly in the city's cinemas, and seldom-seen classic films and independent releases can be found at theaters including the Castro, Embarcadero, Lumiere, Gateway, Roxie, Vogue, and Clay theaters. Film lovers should keep an eye on the universities, especially Berkeley, where the **Pacific Film Archive** serves as the Bay Area's film gallery. The **San Francisco International Film Festival,** based in Japantown's Kabuki Theatre, brings works from around the world to San Francisco every spring. Call (415) 931-FILM.

PRACTICALITIES

In October, **Artists' Open Studios** offers a peek into artists' studios around San Francisco; call (415) 861-9838. In the East Bay, Artists' Open Studios takes place in June; call (510) 763-4361. You can pick up a free quarterly pamphlet called "Bay Area Gallery Guide" at many galleries around town, with a map and artist listings.

Complete listings of cinema, dance, music, clubs, and other happenings appear weekly in the *Sunday Chronicle* "Datebook" section, also called the "Pink Sheet." For the current word on concerts, festivals, and clubs, check out the *Bay Guardian* or *SF Weekly.*

■ MUSEUMS, AMUSEMENTS & CULTURAL CENTERS

The four big fine arts museums of San Francisco are the Museum of Modern Art, the M. H. de Young Museum, the Asian Art Museum, and the California Palace of the Legion of Honor. The city also has two large science museums: the Exploratorium and the California Academy of Sciences. (The latter houses an aquarium and a planetarium.) In addition, San Francisco supports a zoo, botanical gardens, the National Maritime Museum, and a surprising number of small, sometimes eccentric museums. Most large museums in San Francisco grant free entry on the first Wednesday of every month.

Beyond San Francisco are the Oakland Museum, the Lawrence Hall of Science and the University Art Museum in Berkeley, and the Egyptian Museum, the San Jose Museum of Art, and the Technical Museum of Innovation in San Jose.

The following institutions are described in the text; check the index.

San Francisco

African-American Museum. Building C, Fort Mason; (415) 441-0640.

Alcatraz. Ferry leaves from Pier 41, near Fisherman's Wharf; (415) 705--5555.

American Indian Contemporary Arts. 23 Grant Ave.; (415) 989-7003.

Ansel Adams Center. 250 Fourth St.; (415) 495-7000.

Asian Art Museum. Music Concourse, Golden Gate Park; (415) 668-8921.

Cable Car Barn. Mason and Washington; (415) 474-1887.

California Academy of Sciences. Music Concourse, Golden Gate Park; (415) 750-7145.

California Palace of the Legion of Honor. Lincoln Park; (415) 750-3600.

Cartoon Art Museum. 814 Mission St.; (415) 227-8666.

Chevron Oil Museum. 555 Market St.; (415) 894-7700.

Chinese Historical Society. 644 Broadway; (415) 391-1188.

Coit Tower. Telegraph Hill; (415) 362-0808.

Craft and Folk Art Museum. Building A, Fort Mason; (415) 775-0990.

Diego Rivera Gallery, San Francisco Art Institute. 800 Chestnut St.; (415) 771-7020.

Exploratorium. 3601 Lyon St.; (415) 561-0360.

Federal Reserve Bank. 101 Market St.; (415) 974-2000

Fort Point. End of Marine Dr., under the Golden Gate Bridge; (415) 556-1693.

Haas-Lilienthal House. 2007 Franklin St.; (415) 441-3004.

Jewish Community Museum. 121 Steuart St.; (415) 543-8880.

Josephine Randall Junior Museum. 199 Museum Way (near Corona Heights Park); (415) 554-9600.

Laserium. In Morrison Planetarium at the California Academy of Sciences, Golden Gate Park; (415) 750-7138.

M. H. de Young Museum. Music Concourse, Golden Gate Park; (415) 750-3600.

Mexican Museum. Building D, Fort Mason; (415) 441-0404.

Mission Dolores. Dolores (16th St.); (415) 621-8203.

Morrison Planetarium. California Academy of Sciences, Golden Gate Park; (415) 750-7141

Museo Italo Americano. Building C, Fort Mason; (415) 673-2200.

Museum of the Money of the American West. Basement, Bank of California, 400 California St.; (415) 765-0400.

National Maritime Museum. Beach St. at Polk; (415) 556-8177.

North Beach Museum. 1435 Stockton St.; (415) 626-7070.

Octagon House. 2645 Gough St.; (415) 441-7512.

Old U.S. Mint. Fifth St. (Mission); (415) 575-8000.

Pacific Heritage Museum. 608 Commercial St.; (415) 399-1124

Presidio Army Museum. Funston at Lincoln Blvd. in Presidio; (415) 561-4331

SS *Jeremiah O'Brien.* Pier 32, foot of Brannan St.; (415) 441-3101

San Francisco Craft and Folk Art Museum. Building A, Fort Mason; (415) 775-0990.

San Francisco Fire Department Museum. 655 Presidio Ave.; (415) 861-8000.

San Francisco Museum of Modern Art. 151 Third St.; (415) 357-4000.

San Francisco Performing Arts Library and Museum. 399 Grove St. (Gough); (415) 255-4800.

San Francisco Zoo. Sloat Blvd. at 45th Ave.; (415) 753-7080

Steinhart Aquarium. California Academy of Sciences, Golden Gate Park; (415) 750-7145.

Pacific Bell Museum. 140 New Montgomery; (415) 542-0182.

USS *Pampanito. See National Maritime Museum.*

Wax Museum at Fisherman's Wharf. 145 Jefferson St.; (415) 885-4975.

Wells Fargo History Room. 420 Montgomery St.; (415) 396-2619.

PRACTICALITIES

East Bay

Jack London Museum. Jack London Square, Oakland; (510) 451-8218.

John Muir House. 4202 Alhambra Ave., Martinez; (510) 228-8860.

Lawrence Hall of Science. Centennial Dr. (Grizzly Peak Blvd.); U.C. Berkeley; (510) 642-5133.

Oakland Museum. 1000 Oak St., Oakland; (510) 238-2200.

P. A. Hearst Museum of Anthropology. Kroeber Hall, U.C. Berkeley, Bancroft Way; (510) 643-7648.

Paleontology Museum. Earth Sciences Bldg., U.C. Berkeley; (510) 642-1821.

University Art Museum. 2626 Bancroft Way, Berkeley; (510) 642-1207.

University Botanical Gardens. Centennial Dr., U.C. Berkeley; (510) 642-3343.

Peninsula/Silicon Valley

Filoli Estate. Canada Rd. off US280, near Woodside; (650) 364-2880.

NASA/Ames Research Center. Moffett Field, near Mountain View; (650) 604-5000.

Rosicrucian Egyptian Museum. Park Ave. (Naglee); San Jose; (408) 287-9171.

Technical Museum of Innovation. 201 S. Market St., San Jose; (408) 294-8324.

Winchester Mystery House. 525 South Winchester Blvd. (near US 280 and CA 17), San Jose; (408) 247-2101.

North Bay

Bay Area Discovery Museum. 557 McReynolds Rd., Sausalito; (415) 487-4398.

Bay Model. 2100 Bridgeway, Sausalito. (415) 332-3870.

Jack London State Park. 24000 London Ranch Rd., Glen Ellen; (707) 938-5216.

Lachryma Montis. Spain and Third St. West, Sonoma; (707) 938-1519.

Napa Valley Wine Train. 1275 McKinstry St., Napa; (800) 427-4124 or (707) 253-2111.

Point Reyes Visitors' Center. Bear Valley, Point Reyes National Seashore; (415) 663-1092.

San Francisco Bay Model. See Bay Model.

Sharpsteen Museum. 1311 Washington St., Calistoga; (707) 942-5911.

Silverado Museum. 1490 Library Ln., St. Helena; (707) 963-3757.

Sonoma State Historical Park. 20 E. Spain St., Sonoma Plaza, Sonoma; (707) 938-1519.

RECOMMENDED READING

■ HISTORY

Ashbury, Herbert. *The Barbary Coast.* New York: Alfred A. Knopf, Inc., 1933. An entertaining jaunt through some of San Francisco's shadier byways.

Bronson, William. *The Earth Shook, the Sky Burned.* New York: Doubleday, 1959. Pictures and reporting from the 1906 earthquake.

Chinn, Thomas Wo. *Bridging the Pacific.* San Francisco: Chinese Historical Society, 1989. The most complete history of Chinatown.

Cole, Tom. *A Short History of San Francisco.* San Francisco: Lexikos, 1981. A succinct and entertaining account, widely available in museums and bookstores.

Dillon, Richard H. *The Hatchet Men.* New York: Ballantine, 1972. A somewhat lurid, if entertaining, account of the tong wars.

Hansen, Jim. *The Other Guide to San Francisco.* San Francisco; Chronicle Books, 1980. Written with humor, this guide is particularly informative for persons tracking down such fading memories as Haight-Ashbury hippie haunts and North Beach beatnik rendezvous.

Margolin, Malcolm. *The Ohlone Way.* Berkeley: Heyday Books, 1978. History of the major Bay Area tribe. The history and culture of other pre-European Bay Area residents are treated in *The Way We Lived: California Indian Reminiscences, Stories, and Songs* (Berkeley: Heyday Books, 1993).

Muir, John. *The Mountains of California.* 1977. Berkeley: Ten Speed Press, 1977. World-renowned conservationist's earliest book about the Sierras, cradle of the conservation movement. *The Yosemite* (New York: The Century Co., 1912) is a description of the Sierra's most famous scenery.

Russack, Benjamin, Ed. *Wine Country, a Literary Companion.* Berkeley: Heyday Books, 1998. A medley of wine-related essays, stories, and observations by Ambrose Bierce, M.F.K. Fisher, Ursula K. LeGuin, Jack London, John McPhee, and others.

■ GUIDEBOOKS

Bakalinsky, Adah. *Stairway Walks in San Francisco.* San Francisco: Lexikos, 1995. Illustrated. Pokes around some of the city's most enchanting stairways and obscure neighborhoods, territory unknown even to most natives.

Delehanty, Randolph. *The Ultimate Guide: San Francisco.* San Francisco: Chronicle Books, 1989. Delehanty's pleasant style, excellent maps, and rich observation of architecture, history, and city planning makes this a self-contained education in the humanities.

Ferlinghetti, Lawrence, and Nancy J. Peters. *Literary San Francisco.* San Francisco: City Lights, 1980. The literary sites of the city, with terrific portraits and group photos.

Fodor's San Francisco. New York: Fodor's Travel Publications, Inc., 1999. Practical info for the whole Bay Area, with coverage of the Wine Country.

Fong-Torres, Shirley. *San Francisco Chinatown—A Walking Tour.* San Francisco: China Books & Periodicals, 1991. An intimate guide to the city's most populous quarter.

Graham, Jerry and Catherine. *Bay Area Backroads.* New York: Harper & Row, 1997. Discover out-of-the-way destinations with the hosts of the popular television show.

Herron, Don. *The Literary World of San Francisco & Environs.* San Francisco: City Lights Books, 1985. Geared for literary tours of specific neighborhoods, and written by the man who gives the Dashiell Hammett walking tours.

Kingman, Henry. *Short Bike Rides: San Francisco.* Old Saybrook, CT: Globe Pequot, 1998. Scenic bike routes for those whose cycling aspirations fall very short of the Tour de France.

Selvin, Joel. *The Musical History Tour.* San Francisco: Chronicle Books, 1997. The guide for music freaks will lead you to, among other things, the guitar shop where the Grateful Dead first met and the hotel-room shrine to Billie Holliday, who was popped for opium will staying there.

Thollander, Earl. *Earl Thollander's San Francisco, 30 Walking Tours from the Embarcadero to the Golden Gate.* New York: Clarkson N. Potter, 1987. Charmingly illustrated.

Wach, Bonnie. *San Francisco As You Like It: 20 Tailor-Made Tour for Culture Vultures, Shopaholics, Neo-Bohemians, Fitness Freaks, Savvy Natives, and Everyone Else.* San Francisco: Chronicle Books, 1998. A witty, irreverent guide that, as the title implies, has something for just about every taste.

Wayburn, Peggy *Adventuring in San Francisco Bay Area.* San Francisco: Sierra Club Books, 1999. A thorough guide to the best things to see and do for the active outdoor enthusiast. Kayaking, mountain biking, hiking, windsurfing, and more.

Woodbridge, Sally and John. *San Francisco—the Guide.* San Francisco: American Institute of Architects, 1982. A serious guide to city architecture.

■ FICTION

Bierce, Ambrose. *The Devil's Dictionary.* Owings Mills, MD: Slemmer House, 1978. A devilishly clever list of bitingly cynical definitions. Arguably the most vitriolic book ever written. Published in part in 1906 under the title *The Cynic's Word Book.*

Coolbrith, Ina. *California.* San Francisco: Book Club of California, 1918. First poet laureate of California, longtime resident of San Francisco, and inspiring friend to many other literary lights.

Duane, Daniel. *Lighting Out, A Vision of California and the Mountains.* St. Paul, MN: Graywolf Press, 1994. A spiritual exploration of California landscape in the late twentieth century by the Berkeley-raised author and mountain climber.

Ferlinghetti, Lawrence. *These Are My Rivers: New & Selected Poems, 1955–1993.* New York: New Directions, 1993. The city's resident poet of the Beat generation.

Ginsberg, Allen. *Howl and Other Poems.* San Francisco: City Lights, 1959. The harbinger of the Beat movement in San Francisco.

Hammett, Dashiell. *Continental Op. Stories.* New York: Random House, 1974. Stories of the San Francisco-based detective with many colorful episode and characters around town. *The Maltese Falcon.* S. Yarmouth, MA: J. Curley, 1929. The most famous mystery story set in San Francisco, made into the classic film starring Humphrey Bogart.

Harte, Bret. *The Luck of Roaring Camp.* Oakland: Star Rover House, 1983. Written in San Francisco's Golden Era Building.

Kerouac, Jack. *On the Road.* New York: Viking Press, 1957. The book that defined the Beat Generation.

Kingston, Maxine Hong. *The Monkey King.* New York: Alfred A. Knopf, 1989. Novel with a Bay Area setting by the author of *China Men* (New York: Alfred A. Knopf, 1980) and *Woman Warrior* (S. Yarmouth, MA: J. Curley, 1978).

London, Jack. *Martin Eden.* New York: Macmillan, 1957. This semi-autobiographical novel describes the life of a struggling writer, and includes fictionalized characters of Bay Area literary figures like George Sterling.

Maupin, Armistead. *Tales of the City.* New York: Harper & Row, 1989. The serialized tales of contemporary city life collected in several volumes. Catch the television adaptation if you can.

Miller, Joaquin. *Selected Writings.* Eugene, OR: Orion Press, 1977. Poetry and "history" by the colorful frontiersman who lived in Oakland.

Norris, Frank. *The Octopus.* Cambridge, MA: R. Bentley, 1971. A scathing indictment of powerful 19th-century railroad corporations in California's Central Valley.

Seth, Vikram. *The Golden Gate.* New York, Random House: 1986. A contemporary novel of San Francisco life and manners in rhymed verse.

Sterling, George. *A Wine of Wizardry and Other Poems.* A. M. Robertson, San Francisco: 1909. Weird and wonderful, the poet at his best. *The Testimony of the Suns.* A. M. Robertson, San Francisco: 1907. Intensely beautiful language.

Stevenson, Robert Louis. *The Silverado Squatters.* Cutchogue, NY: Buccaneer Books, 1989. A pleasant jaunt with charming companions (Stevenson and bride Fanny on their honeymoon) through 19th-century Napa Valley.

Twain, Mark. *Roughing It.* Chicago: Gilman & Co., 1872. The funniest description of the 19th-century American West includes the author's colorful pictures of early San Francisco.

Wolfe, Tom. *The Electric Kool-Aid Acid Test.* New York: Farrar, Straus & Giroux, 1969. Recounting some of the local lore of the Merry Pranksters and the hippie years.

The voice of the Beat generation lives on at City Lights bookstore in North Beach.
(Kerrick James)

I N D E X

COMPASS AMERICAN GUIDES

Critics, booksellers, and travelers all agree: you're lost without a Compass.

"This splendid series provides exactly the sort of historical and cultural detail about North American destinations that curious-minded travelers need."
— *Washington Post*

"This is a series that constantly stuns us; our whole past book reviewer experience says no guide with photos this good should have writing this good. But it does."
— *New York Daily News*

"Of the many guidebooks on the market, few are as visually stimulating, as thoroughly researched, or as lively written as the Compass American Guides series."
— *Chicago Tribune*

"Good to read ahead of time, then take along so you don't miss anything."
— *San Diego Magazine*

NEW FROM COMPASS:

| *April 1999* | *August 1999* | *December 1999* | *April 2000* |

Vermont
$19.95 ($27.95 Can)
0-679-00183-2

Southern New England
$19.95 ($29.95 Can)
0-679-00184-0

Georgia
$19.95 ($29.95 Can)
0-679-00245-6

Pennsylvania
$19.95 ($29.95 Can)
0-679-00182-4

Compass American Guides are available in general and travel bookstores, or may be ordered directly by calling (800) 733-3000. Please provide title and ISBN when ordering.

Alaska (2nd edition)
$19.95 ($27.95 Can)
0-679-00230-8

Arizona (5th edition)
$19.95 ($29.95 Can)
0-679-00432-7

Boston (2nd edition)
$19.95 ($27.95 Can)
0-679-00284-7

Chicago (2nd edition)
$18.95 ($26.50 Can)
1-878-86780-6

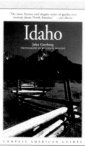

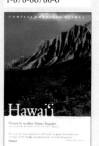

Coastal California
$19.95 ($27.95 Can)
0-679-03598-2

Colorado (4th edition)
$18.95 ($26.50 Can)
0-679-00027-5

Florida (1st edition)
$19.95 ($27.95 Can)
0-679-03392-0

Hawaii (4th edition)
$19.95 ($27.95 Can)
0-679-00226-X

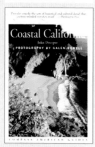

Idaho (1st edition)
$18.95 ($26.50 Can)
1-878-86778-4

Las Vegas (6th edition)
\$19.95 ($29.95 Can)
0-679-00370-3

Maine (2nd edition)
$18.95 ($26.50 Can)
1-878-86796-2

Manhattan (3rd ed)
$19.95 ($29.95 Can)
0-679-00228-6

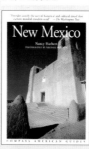

Minnesota (1st ed)
$18.95 ($26.50 Can)
1-878-86748-2

Montana (4th edition)
$19.95 ($29.95 Can)
0-679-00281-2

New Mexico (3rd ed)
$18.95 ($26.50 Can)
0-679-00031-3

New Orleans (3rd ed)
$18.95 ($26.50 Can)
0-679-03597-4

North Carolina (1st ed)
$18.95 ($26.50 Can)
0-679-03390-4

Oregon (3rd edition)
$19.95 ($27.95 Can)
0-679-00033-X

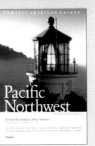

Pacific Northwest (2nd ed)
$19.95 ($27.95 Can)
0-679-00283-9

San Francisco (5th ed)
$19.95 ($29.95 Can)
0-679-00229-4

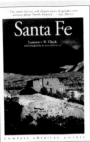

Santa Fe (2nd edition)
$18.95 ($26.50 Can)
0-679-03389-0

South Carolina (2nd ed)
$18.95 ($26.50 Can)
0-679-03599-0

South Dakota (2nd ed)
$18.95 ($26.50 Can)
1-878-86747-4

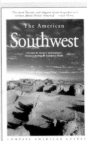

Southwest (2nd ed)
$18.95 ($26.50 Can)
0-679-00035-6

Texas (2nd edition)
$18.95 ($26.50 Can)
1-878-86798-9

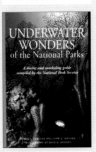

Underwater Wonders of the Nat'l Parks $19.95
0-679-03386-6

Utah (4th edition)
$18.95 ($26.50 Can)
0-679-00030-5

Virginia (3rd edition)
$19.95 ($29.95 Can)
0-679-00282-0

Washington (2nd ed)
$19.95 ($27.95 Can)
1-878-86799-7

Wine Country (2nd ed)
$19.95 ($27.95 Can)
0-679-00032-1

Wisconsin (2nd ed)
$18.95 ($26.50 Can)
1-878-86749-0

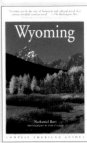

Wyoming (3rd edition)
$19.95 ($27.95 Can)
0-679-00034-8

KELLY DUANE

■ ABOUT THE AUTHOR

Born and raised in the San Francisco Bay Area, writer and editor Barry Parr brings to this guide a native's first-hand knowledge of the city and the perspective of a world traveler. Mr. Parr earned degrees in English literature from the University of California at Berkeley and from Cambridge University in England. He has lived for several years in England and Hong Kong, where he worked as a magazine editor and writer. He has contributed articles to *Travel & Leisure, Discover, Mandarin, Asiaweek,* and other publications, and is the author of *Hiking the Sierra Nevada,* published by Falcon Press. Currently he resides in the Bay Area with his wife and two children.

■ ABOUT THE PHOTOGRAPHERS

San Francisco-born photographer **Michael S. Yamashita** has been shooting pictures for National Geographic Society magazines and books since 1979. He is a frequent contributor to *Travel & Leisure* and *Portfolio,* and his many corporate clients include the Mexican Tourist Board, Singapore Airlines, and Nikon Cameras. Mr. Yamashita's work has been exhibited at the Smithsonian Institution's Museum of American History, the National Gallery in Washington, and Kodak's Professional Photographer's Showcase at EPCOT center in Florida.

Kerrick James grew up in the San Francisco Bay Area, and credits its cosmopolitan atmosphere and cultural variety in enriching his photography. His work often appears in *Arizona Highways, Alaska, Hemispheres,* and other travel and inflight magazines, as well as in other Compass titles including *Arizona, Las Vegas,* and *The American Southwest.* He lives in Arizona with his wife Theresa and sons, Shane and Royce.